PRIVATE LAW AND THE EMPLOYMENT CONTRACT

This book brings together leading scholars from private law and employment law to reflect upon private law doctrines as they relate to the employment contract.

Developing an interdisciplinary dialogue, these contributions explore the regulatory functions of private law doctrines at the cutting edge of modern employment law. Topics include the potential and limitations of private law damages; the role of injunctions and specific performance; the interactions between express and implied terms; vicarious liability; substantial performance and breach; and the common law right to work. The integration of scholarly perspectives from the realms of private law and employment law enriches and deepens our understanding of core private law doctrines.

Historically, employment law was defined in terms of its autonomy from general private law. This achievement of autonomy was highly prized, and considered necessary to facilitate industrial freedoms for trade unions and the protection of employees from exploitation. But the contractual basis of employment means that any such autonomy has always been partial and unstable. Furthermore, as trade unions have declined and governments have deregulated statutory employment rights, private law has assumed growing practical importance in strategic appellate litigation. In many common law jurisdictions, private law doctrines have become the new battleground between employers, workers and trade unions. The essays in this book examine specific doctrinal issues against this dynamic backdrop of changing social, economic and constitutional conditions. While focused mainly on English law, the essays also consider examples from other jurisdictions including Australia and Scotland.

As private law becomes the default regulation for most employment contracts in 21st-century labour markets across the world, this book is an essential resource for practitioners, judges, academics and students.

Private Law and the Employment Contract

Edited by

Alan Bogg

and

Paul S Davies

•HART•

OXFORD • LONDON • NEW YORK • NEW DELHI • SYDNEY

HART PUBLISHING

Bloomsbury Publishing Plc

Kemp House, Chawley Park, Cumnor Hill, Oxford, OX2 9PH, UK

1385 Broadway, New York, NY 10018, USA

Bloomsbury Publishing Ireland Limited, 29 Earlsfort Terrace, Dublin 2, D02 AY28, Ireland

HART PUBLISHING, the Hart/Stag logo, BLOOMSBURY and the Diana logo are trademarks of Bloomsbury Publishing Plc

First published in Great Britain 2025

A catalogue record for this book is available from the British Library.

A catalogue record for this book is available from the Library of Congress.

Library of Congress Control Number: 2025936844

ISBN: HB: 978-1-50998-158-8
ePDF: 978-1-50998-160-1
ePub: 978-1-50998-159-5

Typeset by Compuscript Ltd, Shannon

For product safety related questions contact productsafety@bloomsbury.com

To find out more about our authors and books visit www.hartpublishing.co.uk. Here you will find extracts, author information, details of forthcoming events and the option to sign up for our newsletters.

FOREWORD

As with many fields of human activity, the problems raised by employment law cannot be analysed or resolved within a single legal framework. Private law principles play a foundational role in the employment and trade union sphere, albeit that statutory protections may, and do in some cases, limit or override their application. While contract law establishes the work relationship, principles of tort govern employer liability for harm and worker protection, and have, by analogy, led to the development of the statutory torts of unlawful discrimination with compensatory remedies that mirror the approach to rights in tort. Recent decisions of the Supreme Court in the employment arena are testament to the fact that private law principles do provide trade unions and workers with winning legal arguments in the courts. This timely book explores many of those and other arguments, and in doing so, charts the 'rise' of the private law dimension in the employment field. It is a valuable and welcome contribution to an important and evolving discourse. By encouraging the adoption of fresh private law perspectives, long-standing debates in employment law are greatly enriched.

As the introductory chapter explains, the fundamental change in the relationship between employer and employee over the course of the last century, leading to the development of a statutory scheme for the protection of employee and worker rights, has meant that characterisation of the contract is a critical gateway to such protection. In turn, creative 'armies of lawyers' intent on presenting the contractual relationship in a way that avoids such protection have had to be met with purposive approaches to identifying the contract drafted in from private law and enabling a more realistic approach to determining employment status: *Autoclenz Ltd v Belcher* and *Uber BV v Aslam*. The use of terms implied by law into all contracts of employment has been a source of perhaps the most transformative development in employment law. Most recently, orthodox contract law principles were applied in *Tesco Stores v Union of Shop, Distributive and Allies Workers* to examine the interaction between the express contractual right to terminate on notice, the provision of 'permanent' pay benefits agreed through the mechanism of collective bargaining and terms implied in fact. The scholarly examination of these and other problems in this book identifies new ways for a private law perspective to assist in their resolution.

But this book does not confine itself to examining how contractual principles and perspectives can usefully be applied to employment law problems. Difficult questions arise in relation to the appropriate remedy for breach of the employment contract – damages are all too often low or inadequate, or in relation to some heads of loss, irrecoverable. Can a private law analysis provide a better framework for addressing some of these issues? Several chapters seek to answer these questions. Others focus on the possibility of greater use of the equitable remedy of specific performance and injunctions where damages are quite simply inadequate in a particular sort of case. Another chapter asks how principles of vicarious liability in tort can be used to broaden the existing employment status tests that qualify a person for statutory employment rights.

The book's mission as described by Alan Bogg and Paul S Davies is to examine afresh the intellectual value of private law perspectives in resolving discrete legal problems in the employment field. In my view, it delivers exactly that. Each chapter offers a thought-provoking analysis of the issues and provides practical and innovative answers to the difficult questions raised. By adopting a private law lens through which to view the particular problem of the chapter, each author draws on this wider perspective to push the boundaries and more fully exploit the potential of private law arguments. The book is proof that it is fruitful for employment lawyers and private lawyers to spend more time together. I am delighted to have been asked to write this foreword and confident that it will prove to be a valuable resource.

Ingrid Simler
March 2025

PREFACE

This book has its origins in a conference held at UCL in June 2024, supported by the UCL Private Law Group. Long before then, the editors realised that friendship could prosper across disciplinary boundaries. Now and again, they both learned the odd thing or two from listening to the other one. A workshop was mooted, then forgotten, and then we finally got round to organising it.

At the conference, each chapter was commented upon by a practitioner in a session chaired by a judge. We are very grateful to Lord Burrows, Dame Jennifer Eady, Lady Simler and Sir Nicholas Underhill for acting as chairs, and to Richard Calnan, Shantha David, Sarah Fraser-Butlin KC, Rachel Hunter, Adam Kramer KC, Nadia Motraghi KC, Daniel Oudkerk KC, Amy Rogers KC, Rebecca Tuck KC and Charles Wynn-Evans for being commentators. The conference was well-attended and the discussion lively. All the chapters were improved by feedback both at and after the event.

We have benefited from the excellent research assistance of Rivu Chowdhury, and the team at Hart Publishing have, as ever, been a pleasure to work with: particular thanks to Roberta Bassi, Linda Goss, Sinead Moloney, and Verity Stuart. Paul would also like to thank the Leverhulme Trust for their generous support through a Philip Leverhulme Prize.

LEVERHULME
TRUST

CONTENTS

LIST OF CONTRIBUTORS

Alysia Blackham is a Professor at Melbourne Law School, the University of Melbourne.

Alan Bogg is Professor of Labour Law at the University of Bristol, Barrister at Old Square Chambers, and an Emeritus Fellow of Hertford College.

Douglas Brodie is Professor of Employment Law at the University of Strathclyde.

David Cabrelli is Professor of Labour Law at the University of Edinburgh.

ACL Davies is Professor of Law and Public Policy at the University of Oxford, and a Fellow of Brasenose College.

Paul S Davies is Professor of Commercial Law at University College London and a Barrister at Essex Court Chambers.

Simon Deakin is Professor of Law and Director of the Centre for Business Research at the University of Cambridge.

Jordan English is an Associate Professor of Law at the University of Oxford and a Fellow of Magdalen College.

Gabrielle Golding is a Senior Lecturer in Law at the University of Adelaide.

Catharine MacMillan is Professor of Private Law at King's College London.

Robert Stevens is the Herbert Smith Freehills Professor of English Private Law at the University of Oxford.

TABLE OF CASES

TABLE OF LEGISLATION

1

Private Law Perspectives on the Employment Contract

ALAN BOGG AND PAUL S DAVIES

Forty years ago, a book exploring private law perspectives on the employment contract in the common law world would have provoked a mixture of horror, derision, bemusement, and fury. While derision and bemusement may well have dominated in the private law camp, horror and fury would certainly have been the reaction from labour lawyers. In the private law camp, the great cases of the English law of contract were usually not employment cases. While the employment contract was certainly a contract, the courts and common law were rarely troubled by it. There were some notable exceptions, of course. *Lumley v Gye*[1] and *Addis Gramophone Co. Ltd*[2] have endured as landmarks of the English common law. For the sceptical labour lawyer, this may be testament to their pivotal role in restricting strike action and wrongful dismissal remedies, respectively. For much of the twentieth century, the common law was a mere footnote to the social institutions of collective bargaining and strike action. The law of the employment contract was far more likely to be considered in a specialist treatise on the law of Master and Servant. In the labour law camp, private law was generally regarded as an instrument of repression wielded against workers and trade unions by unelected judges. The common law doctrines of private law, such as restraint of trade or the economic torts, were usually obstacles in the way of emancipation through trade union action. The worker-protective purposes of employment law depended upon the extirpation of private law. This polarisation may seem surprising to the enlightened modern lawyer. After all, employment law is still based fundamentally upon the employment contract. This foundational category is regulated by the law of contract. The law of contract, like the law of property and the law of torts, is properly regarded as a compartment of private law. Given the basic juridical category of employment law is a contract, how could we adopt anything other than a private law perspective? What other legal perspective could there be?

[1] *Lumley v Gye* (1853) 2 E & B 216.
[2] *Addis v Gramophone Co Ltd* [1909] AC 488.

The most canonical statement of this bifurcation of employment law perspectives and private law perspectives on the employment contract was set out in chapter one of Professor Sir Otto Kahn-Freund's Hamlyn Lectures, *Labour and the Law*.[3] According to Kahn-Freund, 'the law does and to some extent must conceal the realities of subordination behind the conceptual screen of contracts considered as concluded between equals. This may partly account for the propensity of lawyers to turn a blind eye to the realities of distribution of power in society'.[4] In concealing this asymmetry of power, through its assumption that the parties to the contract were free and equal, the private law perspective was regressive. It also obscured the collective realities of working life for many workers in post-war Britain. Collective bargaining between trade unions and employers ensured that workers could exercise a measure of influence over their terms and conditions. The individual employment contract was a mere conduit for the norms negotiated through collective agreements. In this way, inequality of bargaining power could be redressed through collective empowerment. These conflictual social processes were rather remote from the pristine world of contract doctrine and private law theory. By contrast, this sociological perspective was central to the scholarly values of British labour law in the hands of Kahn-Freund and Lord Wedderburn. This was often described as 'collective laissez-faire', which was quite different from the *individual* laissez-faire of classical English contract law.[5] Since labour lawyers were preoccupied with inequalities and abuse of power, there were much stronger taxonomical affinities with the doctrines and theory of public law.

Of course, Kahn-Freund's reservations about the private law perspective in *Labour and the Law* were not simply philosophical. Kahn-Freund was a scholar deeply immersed in the history of British labour law and its trade union movement. One of his pluralist contemporaries, Allan Flanders, famously described 'distrust of courts' as the leitmotif of British industrial relations.[6] For present purposes, this 'distrust' was focused more specifically on the experience of workers and trade unions in their encounters with English private law. Throughout the nineteenth century, private law doctrines such as restraint of trade and the economic torts were weaponised by employers and hostile governments to suppress trade unions and collective bargaining. Individual litigation against employees was usually focused on employers using the criminal law to stymie insubordination and to disrupt strike action in breach of the employment contract.[7] For the trade unions, salvation tended to come through legislation rather than the common law. The basic legal

[3] PL Davies and MR Freedland (eds), *Kahn-Freund's Labour and the Law*, 3rd edn (London, Stevens, 1983).

[4] ibid, 15.

[5] On collective laissez-faire in the post-war period, see A Bogg, 'The Hero's Journey: Lord Wedderburn and the "Political Constitution" of Labour Law' (2015) 44 *Industrial Law Journal* 299.

[6] A Flanders, 'The Tradition of Voluntarism' (1974) 12 *British Journal of Industrial Relations* 352, 354.

[7] D Simon, 'Master and Servant' in J Saville (ed), *Democracy and the Labour Movement: Essays in honour of Dona Torr* (London, Lawrence & Wishart, 1954) ch 6.

structure of the statutory 'immunity' is usually associated with the Trade Disputes Act 1906, though there were earlier examples in the nineteenth century.[8] This was described by Kahn-Freund as 'negative' law because its legal function was to exclude or 'negative' the common law; in the case of the 1906 Act, by the exclusion of certain liabilities for torts. This 'immunity' based approach created permissive legal space for the development of collective bargaining between trade unions and employers. This was the primary mechanism for setting terms and conditions of employment for much of the twentieth century. It occupied the same regulatory space taken up by labour codes guaranteeing individual employment rights in other jurisdictions.

It is tempting to regard this as democratically imposed exile for the private law approach to employment contracts, at least while collective laissez-faire was in its ascendancy. In some respects, this exile perspective captures some important features of legal development. Until the late decades of the twentieth century, there were relatively few reported contract cases in employment law. This reflected the great success of collective bargaining and workplace dispute procedures, which had reduced the need for individual litigation.[9] In Kahn-Freund's assessment, this had led to the legal 'atrophy' of contract because there was such a stunted jurisprudence of the employment contract.[10] Common law development depends upon judicial elaboration, which in turn requires litigation in the courts. For example, it was not until the late 1970s that the judicial elaboration of terms implied in law, such as mutual trust and confidence, started to occur. In this respect, then, the private law of contract was a marginal feature of British labour law until the latter part of the twentieth century.

The dominant regulatory role of collective bargaining could also be viewed as aligned with the values and techniques of public law. Auxiliary state support for collective bargaining depended upon administrative intervention by government departments, providing capacity-building and support for sectoral institutions. The legal form of this intervention was very much in the province of administrative and constitutional law, not private law.[11] The values of collective bargaining reflected this public law alignment. A concern to protect workers and citizens from abuse of power provided a basis for the unity of labour law and public law.[12] Historically, collective bargaining was justified in terms of economic democracy and industrial citizenship, not private rights and corrective justice. Even here, in the realm of collective labour relations, the private law perspective never disappeared fully. For example, the treatment of collective agreements as binding in

[8] According to Orth, the 1906 immunity was likely to have been modelled on the immunity from criminal conspiracy in the Conspiracy and Protection of Property Act 1875. See JV Orth, *Combination and Conspiracy: A Legal History of Trade Unionism 1721-1906* (Oxford, OUP, 1991) 151.

[9] Davies and Freedland (n 3) 34.

[10] O Kahn-Freund, 'Blackstone's Neglected Child: the Contract of Employment' (1977) 93 *Law Quarterly Review* 508, 524.

[11] KD Ewing, 'The State and Industrial Relations: "Collective Laissez-Faire" Revisited' (1998) 5 *Historical Studies in Industrial Relations* 1.

[12] J Laws, 'Public Law and Employment Law: Abuse of Power' [1997] *Public Law* 455.

honour only was rationalised through the general doctrine of intention to create legal relations.[13] This doctrine lies in the very heartlands of private law. More ominously, judicial creativity in the law of torts provided new opportunities for courts to impose limits on strike action, as with the controversial judgment in *Rookes v Barnard*.[14] In this way, private law supported the voluntary quality of collective bargaining while at the same time circumscribing the perimeter of legitimate collective action through the law of torts.

From the 1970s onwards, the legal and public policy environment shifted significantly. These shifts would have profound implications for the presence and character of private law in the employment law field. The effects are still being felt today. First, the coverage of collective bargaining declined steadily across this period, driven by structural changes in the labour market and a hostile political environment for trade unions from 1979 to 1997. Second, there was a growing recognition that all employees, regardless of collective bargaining coverage, should enjoy basic statutory protections, such as through unfair dismissal laws and anti-discrimination laws. The introduction of 'industrial tribunals' to provide an accessible form of justice for workers led to the growing 'juridification' of employment disputes, which were now more likely to be resolved by a judge declaring legal rights than a shop steward hammering out an industrial compromise with management. In short, there was more litigation and so more appellate caselaw. This prompted the introduction of specialist law reports such as the Industrial Cases Reports (introduced in 1972) and the Industrial Relations Law Reports (also 1972).

Did the increase in case law support or subvert the goals of worker protection? The first point is that many of the new statutory rights, such as the right not to be discriminated against because of race or sex, were analogous to employment torts. The basic correlative structure of a right-holder (the employee/worker), the duty-bearer (the employer), and recourse to compensatory remedies in a court reflected the basic architecture of a private law right.[15] More practically, though these new rights were statutory, the framework for assessing compensation (for example, the nature of aggravated damages and their relation to compensatory remedies) was influenced by the conceptualisation of damages in private law. This phenomenon of the 'tortification' of employment law can be seen in other jurisdictions, such as the US, where it has provided an alternative form of recourse as unionisation declined.[16] While much of the hostility to private law perspectives has centred on contract, the law of torts is also an important part of private law.

[13] *Ford Motor Co v AUEF* [1969] 2 QB 303. See B Hepple, 'Intention to Create Legal Relations' (1970) 28 *Cambridge Law Journal* 122.

[14] *Rookes v Barnard* [1964] AC 1129. For a thoughtful discussion of the case, see R Bagshaw, 'Rookes' Tale' in J Adams-Prassl and others (eds), *Landmark Cases in Labour Law* (Oxford, Hart Publishing, 2022) ch 5.

[15] E Weinrib, *Corrective Justice* (Oxford, OUP, 2016).

[16] See the discussion of 'tortification' and relevant literature in C Estlund, 'The Fall and Rise of the Private Law of Work' in H Dagan and others (eds), *Research Handbook on Private Law Theory* (Cheltenham, Edward Elgar, 2020) 422.

Since the enactment of (in Wedderburn's enduring language) the statutory 'floor of rights' in the UK in the 1970s, the law of torts has provided an important vehicle for worker-protective litigation. This is quite different from its historical role in stymieing strike action through the economic torts.

This statutory 'floor of rights' also stimulated the private law of contract. These statutory rights ordinarily depended upon a contract of employment or a worker contract. It meant that the characterisation of the contract was a critical gateway into the statutory protections. As those rights became more important, employers sought to avoid liability through contractual devices to present the relationship as a commercial contract with an independent business undertaking. In this way, the law of contract was deployed as a mechanism for shielding employers from statutory tort liabilities. This led to the development of a 'purposive and realistic' approach to identifying the contract.[17] Sometimes this was formulated in terms of enforcing the 'true agreement'.[18] While this quest was still recognisably contractual, the contractual tests were themselves being reshaped by the worker-protective statutory purpose. More specifically, the statutory unfair dismissal regime triggered the elaboration of terms implied in law, such as mutual trust and confidence. Initially, this was because 'constructive dismissal' depended upon the employee resigning in response to a repudiatory breach of contract by the employer. In due course, mutual trust and confidence would take on a life of its own as an independent source of regulation encompassing behavioural standards and a technique for judicial review of contractual powers. These developments pointed to an 'autonomous' common law of the employment contract, with rules and principles sensitive to the inequality of bargaining power.[19] Even as human rights have become more important in litigation strategies, this has occurred principally through techniques of statutory interpretation of existing 'private' rights, such as unfair dismissal. Employment law is a fertile site where private law is always open to being 'constitutionalised' through public law standards.

Even in the citadel of collective labour law, the 'binding in honour' collective agreement, there has been recent litigation at the highest appellate level. This has examined the role of privity of contract,[20] the availability of rectification,[21] and the interaction between collectively agreed 'permanent benefits' and terms implied in fact.[22] These cases all involved the application of core private law doctrines to that most collective of institutions, the collective agreement. In each case, private

[17] *Uber BV v Aslam* [2021] UKSC 5, [2021] 4 All ER 209.

[18] *Autoclenz Ltd v Belcher* [2011] UKSC 41, [2011] 4 All ER 745.

[19] D Brodie, 'The Autonomy of the Common Law of the Contract of Employment from the General Law of Contract' in M Freedland and others (eds), *The Contract of Employment* (Oxford, OUP, 2016) ch 6.

[20] *Secretary of State for the Department for Environment, Food and Rural Affairs v Public and Commercial Services Union* [2024] UKSC 41, [2024] 3 WLR 1059.

[21] *National Union of Rail, Maritime and Transport Workers & Anor v Tyne and Wear Passenger Transport Executive (t/a Nexus)* [2024] UKSC 37, [2024] 3 WLR 909.

[22] *Tesco Stores Ltd v Union of Shop, Distributive and Allied Workers* [2024] UKSC 28, [2025] ICR 107.

law fortified the collective agreement from erosion. In the heyday of collective laissez-faire, this kind of litigation would have been unthinkable to the general secretaries of most trade unions. Today, private law doctrines (and private lawyers) can provide trade unions and workers with some of the most powerful legal arguments to pursue strategic goals in the courts. These developments, which might be viewed as 'the rise of private law',[23] provide the context to this edited collection.

The opening chapter by Simon Deakin provides a panoramic comparative vision of the position of private law in regulating employment contracts. It does so by examining the 'principle of favourability' which in fact encompasses a range of sub-rules and principles. It is strongly represented in civilian systems and in South American labour law. It seems to be less well-established in common law systems. Specifically, it accords priority to public law standards over private law rights, and it holds that a lower-level source has priority over a higher-level source where the norm operates to the benefit of the weaker party. This is supported by an even more fundamental 'principle of protection' in labour law, such that the specific rules of employment law are geared towards protecting the worker given the structural inequalities in the labour market. These principles provide a basis for selecting norms in situations of conflict (choose the most favourable one) and applying norms in circumstances of ambiguity (adopt the interpretation that favours protection of the weaker party).

What is striking about British labour law are the enduring difficulties in entrenching these foundational principles, particularly in appellate decisions. While some judgments such as *Autoclenz*[24] and *Tesco*[25] have prevented the subversion of protective statutory norms and collective agreements, other cases, such as *Johnson v Unisys*,[26] appear to have inverted the 'principle of protection' and accorded priority to the interests of the employer. In certain respects, this may be endemic to the English common law, given the residual dominance of individual freedom of contract. Freedom of contract always favours the stronger party. This was an enduring theme in the critical work of Kahn-Freund and Wedderburn. We could interpret that work as identifying private law as the barbarian inside the protective gates of employment law, subverting it from within. Deakin does not leave us with mere deconstruction, however. His chapter sets out some specific changes, best codified in legislative reforms, that would entrench the 'principle of favourability' in British labour law. We might view this law reform project as imposing constitutional limits on private law so that it operates in accordance with the protective logic of labour law. By keeping private law in its constitutional place, freedom of contract then provides an opportunity for workers and trade unions to bargain upwards *from* the 'floor of rights'. Deakin's chapter thus represents a

[23] This phrase is from C Estlund, 'The Fall and Rise of the Private Law of Work' in H Dagan and others (eds), *Research Handbook on Private Law Theory* (Cheltenham, Edward Elgar, 2020) 422.
[24] Above n 18.
[25] Above n 22.
[26] *Johnson v Unisys* [2001] UKHL 13, [2003] 1 AC 518.

radical vision of the emancipatory potential of private law, supporting the public regulatory role of collective agreements.

In the following chapter, David Cabrelli explores the private law dimensions of variation and termination of employment contracts, focusing on the controversial topic of 'fire and rehire'. Employment contracts are often long-term and open-ended. The contractual basis of employment presents governance challenges for employers and employees. This is because businesses face an unpredictable economic landscape with unanticipated economic risks, whereas the classical vision of contract is the crystallisation of rights and obligations at a specific moment. How can long-term contracts accommodate flexibility and adaptability while protecting the security and legitimate expectations of employees? Cabrelli's chapter explores the full range of private law techniques for reconciling these competing goals of adaptability and security. While this might be achieved through an act of variation corresponding with an express consent to variation, this is cumbersome and often impractical. Contract doctrines provide for a wide range of alternative mechanisms, such as contractual powers to vary, as well as techniques of contract interpretation and implied terms.

Does the sheer breadth of these techniques threaten employees' interests in security and stability of expectations? Should the common law tighten up its approach and insist upon a stronger manifestation of express consent to direct variation? Cabrelli examines the difficult inter-relationship between variation and termination. If the law tightens up its approach to variation, employers have stronger incentives to 'fire and rehire'. This involves terminating contracts lawfully with notice and reissuing new contracts with the disadvantageous terms and conditions. The existing statutory restrictions on 'fire and rehire' are also relatively light, though there are currently proposals to strengthen the law of statutory unfair dismissal for 'fire and rehire'. Cabrelli concludes that any changes to the law on variation should be undertaken with circumspection. Beyond its forensic examination of the current jurisprudence on variation, Cabrelli's chapter also provides broader reflections on the nature of judging in the common law system. Judges developing common law doctrines in employment contracts must be alive to wider tendencies in private law more generally and the principles established in legislation. The law should be coherent, and legal developments must not be counterproductive. If a tightened common law of variation leads to extensive job losses, this provides a reason in favour of developing variation and termination in lockstep.

Chapter four, by Jordan English, reflects on the concept of substantial performance in English contract law, in the context of industrial action short of a full strike. The English common law adopts a notoriously draconian approach to deductions from pay where a striker is engaged in industrial action short of a full strike. This draconian approach arises out of the decision in *Wiluszynski v Tower Hamlets London Borough Council*.[27] According to English, the courts took a wrong

[27] *Wiluszynski v Tower Hamlets London Borough Council* [1989] ICR 493.

turn in employment contracts by excluding substantial performance from the analysis of industrial action short of a full strike. This has led to a *harsher* approach to employment contracts compared with commercial contracts. Properly understood, substantial performance concerns the proper construction of a contract and the condition for payment under that contract. There is nothing about employment contracts that justifies treating full performance as a default condition for payment. By restoring substantial performance to its rightful place in the context of employment contracts, this would mean that the employee should be entitled to payment where substantial performance had been rendered, subject to the employer being able to withhold a proportionate sum corresponding to the performance withheld. These are 'general damages' and represent what the employer bargained for but did not receive.

In many ways, English's chapter vindicates the project of this volume. There is a very extensive literature on the human right to strike and its implementation in legal systems. We might regard this as the *public law* of the right to strike. By contrast, the private law of the right to strike is underdeveloped. This aversion may reflect a pessimism about the common law method in relation to strikes, which has characteristically supported harsh legal treatment of strikers and strike organisers. However, English's chapter demonstrates the value of the doctrinal method in parsing the different meanings of 'entire contracts' and conditions for payment and salvaging the idea of substantial performance. It also demonstrates how employment contracts jurisprudence has adopted a harsher approach to these matters than commercial contracts jurisprudence, where substantial performance is a less controversial approach. This is a helpful reminder that the 'autonomy' of the common law of employment may not always benefit employees, where those distinctive rules operate in an oppressive way against the weaker party. In the context of strikes, perhaps we can still detect the clanking chains of Master and Servant in the basement of the common law.

Remedies is a notoriously tricky area. It often does not receive the attention it deserves. Partly this is the result of the way litigation often works: the parties need a court to determine liability but are then often able to negotiate a remedy without external assistance. Remedies in private law generally were once thought not to require much theoretical attention; the common sense of the judges could be trusted to award appropriate relief. But over the past 50 years, there has been an explosion of interest in difficult questions concerning remedies, both theoretical and doctrinal. And cases from the employment context have been instructive in private law more generally.

The chapters by Blackham and Golding both consider damages. Blackham analyses remedies for workplace discrimination claims and draws upon empirical work to highlight that the damages awarded are often very low. This can act as a significant disincentive to bringing a claim and therefore to the overall enforcement of discrimination law. Blackham sensibly considers whether lessons from tort law may help to strengthen the award of damages in employment discrimination cases in both Australia and the UK. Ultimately, there seem to be limits as to what can be expected of private law in this context. Private individuals are able to recover their loss, but if damages are low, that does little to deter future breaches or achieve systemic change. That perhaps highlights that private law will not have all the answers to difficult questions posed in the employment context: discrimination law, for instance, straddles the public and private spheres. Nevertheless, private law does provide a helpful springboard and framework to analyse some of these issues, but coherence with private law perhaps suggests that it will be some time before the level of damages awards increases substantially in this area, since the tariffs for damages in personal injury cases also remain low.

Golding focuses upon loss of chance damages for breach of the contract of employment. Loss of chance is a famously difficult area in contract and tort more generally, but the employment cases analysed by Golding illustrate many of the problems courts must face, and that general principles of contract can apply and be developed via cases on the contract of employment. One controversial area in contract damages presently concerns the minimum performance rule, which provides that a court should award damages on the basis that the defendant performed its contractual obligations in the least onerous way available. That is often supported by reference to the fact that where an employer has wrongfully dismissed an employee, damages will be awarded on the basis that the employer would have dismissed the employee at the earliest lawful opportunity. Golding highlights that the employment cases have shifted in a somewhat inconsistent way on this point, which reflects the cases in contract law more generally. It is to be expected that much will be gained from looking at employment cases as the law continues to develop. More particularly, Golding considers the possibility of damages for loss of a chance of maintaining an employment relationship, which, if accepted, could in turn influence other contracts that might come to be recognised as 'relational'.

Damages are the primary remedy awarded for breach of contract. But sometimes, in accordance with general principle, damages will be said to be 'inadequate' such that equitable remedies should be awarded. Damages may well be thought to be inadequate for breach of the employment contract in circumstances where, as discussed above, the award of damages tends to be very low for some wrongs, and valuing non-pecuniary loss or compensating for non-economic harms more generally is very difficult. There are legitimate reasons why courts are reluctant to grant specific relief; after all, it can have the practical effect of elevating the consequences of a breach of contract, since breach of an equitable order constitutes contempt of court. As Tony Weir pithily observed, it risks a judge 'exchanging his wig for a helmet' as he goes into battle with the defaulting party.[28]

There has long been a general reluctance to grant specific relief in the employment context, based on the idea that no party should be forced into a relationship of personal service. This still generally makes sense as regards an employee: forcing

[28] T Weir, 'Discrimination in Private Law' [1966] *CLJ* 165, 169.

them to work runs into fears of forced labour and slavery.[29] However, there is a plausible distinction between contracts where a particular individual is named as being bound to perform and contracts with corporate entities who promise to ensure a service is provided. This is increasingly recognised in contracts between commercial parties,[30] and it seems likely that both specific performance and injunctions will be granted more readily in the employment context following the decision in *Tesco Stores Ltd.*[31] In that case, the Supreme Court granted an injunction, amounting to indirect specific performance, to require an employer to continue employing employees. The judgments feature prominently in the chapters of MacMillan, on specific performance, and Davies, on injunctions.

MacMillan sheds light upon the development of the law concerning specific performance, explaining what factors have influenced courts when confronted with the issue of whether to enforce contractual obligations. These considerations have not often been expressly identified. The key issue is whether an employee can specifically enforce a contract of employment. Courts now appear less worried about ordering a business as to how to conduct its affairs, and the supposed 'bar' to specific performance on the basis of 'mutuality' has been substantially eroded: that specific performance would not be ordered against the employee is no reason not to grant specific performance against the employer. Ultimately, as MacMillan concludes, the key factor will be whether there remains a sufficient degree of trust and confidence between the parties for the court to decide that specific performance is the appropriate remedy.

However, MacMillan recognises that it should not be too readily accepted, upon an employer's assertion, that an employer no longer has trust and confidence in an employee. This is amplified by Davies, who argues that the legal barriers to injunctive relief have been substantially lowered. Davies further highlights that a worker's fundamental rights may be are infringed by an employer's breach, leading to losses that are important but hard to quantify, and injunctive relief better helps to protect workers' rights and deter employers' breaches. Such considerations suggest that injunctive relief should be more readily available at the interim stage, but this faces serious practical problems that are difficult to overcome – most importantly, perhaps, the expense of seeking such relief and the need to give the usual undertaking in damages. In addition, employment tribunals are unable to grant injunctions. Davies considers the possibility of developing a novel 'injunctive-lite' remedy, which could be awarded by tribunals to get the employer to comply with whatever obligation it is threatening to infringe. Such a remedy would be cheaper and easier to obtain. However, without the sanction of contempt of court for breach, it is doubtful whether any such remedy could replicate the effectiveness of the current injunction jurisdiction.

[29] *Francesco v Barnum* (1890) 45 ChD 430, 438.
[30] Eg, *LauritzenCool AB v Lady Navigation Inc* [2005] EWCA Civ 579, [2005] 1 WLR 3686.
[31] Above n 22.

Douglas Brodie's chapter considers the law on vicarious liability within the broader context of the role of torts in labour law. Brodie endorses the enterprise liability justification for vicarious liability. This is the idea that an enterprise that takes the benefit of activities of persons integrated into it should also take the burden of liabilities for harm wrongfully caused by those activities. This correlativity of benefits and burdens, coupled with the greater resources of the enterprise and its capacity for insuring against risks, reflects a notion of distributive fairness. This underlying theory has supported an expansion of the scope of vicarious liability, encompassing not only employees but also those acting in relationships that are akin to employment. It has been particularly important in securing redress for victims of institutional sexual abuse, though the High Court of Australia has recently reasserted the narrower requirement of an employer-employee relationship.[32] This judgment cuts against the expansionist approach favoured by Brodie in his chapter.

Brodie also explores the possibilities for tort law developments expanding vicarious liability as a basis for broadening the existing employment status tests for statutory employment rights. As Brodie acknowledges, it is not entirely clear what legal coherence would demand across different areas of the law. The policy questions in employment status are different from those in vicarious liability. Brodie also notes the stricter approach to the employer's tort liability in respect of harms sustained by employees at work, such as in occupational stress claims. Again, this may simply reflect the fact that the policy considerations in respect of employee and third-party injuries are distinct, and enterprise risk is a relatively malleable normative tool for fixing the liability rules in these different policy contexts.

The final chapter by Robert Stevens considers the nature of the 'right to work' as a common law right. While the right to work has attracted the sustained attention (and allegiance) of human rights lawyers, Stevens adopts a more sceptical approach. The 'right to work' often involves an elision of distinct juridical categories of liberties and rights, at least in its common law form. Rights are correlative to duties, whereas liberties are not. This is a vital distinction because duties restrict the freedom of the duty-bearer. For Stevens, this distinction should also be important to the availability of remedies such as injunctions. The recognition of a right (and a court-issued injunction) is a significant normative step, and it is important to maintain conceptual clarity so that we can be clear-sighted about those normative implications. Stevens provides a wide-ranging examination of the economic torts, the (overly?) expanding scope for injunctive remedies, and the regulation of the closed shop. For Stevens, the pantheon of common law rights (correlative to duties) in private law is and should be limited. This includes the 'right to work', which must depend upon statutory enactment for its concrete realisation as a right with correlative duties. In the modern era, the main statutory implementation of the 'right to work' has been through discrimination law and unfair dismissal law.

[32] *Bird v DP* [2024] HCA 41.

Stevens' policy minimalism is aligned with a venerable view of the role of the judiciary, fully developed in the theory of collective laissez-faire. The judges, and the common law, should operate within narrow confines in elaborating and enforcing rights. Labour rights are really the province of the legislature and employment protection statutes. For the judges and the common law, policy minimalism is the wise course in a parliamentary democracy. This closes the volume nicely, as it circles back to the constitutional dimension of private law elucidated in Deakin's opening chapter.

We hope that readers will agree that the initial aspirations for this volume have been achieved (and exceeded) through this rich collection of chapters. In their different ways, each of the chapters vindicates the intellectual value of private law perspectives in examining discrete legal problems. Does this volume reveal anything about the broader taxonomy of employment law? Certainly, we reject the 'hostile takeover' model of private law,[33] and we see no basis for regarding employment law as an exclusively private law discipline. We also agree with Professor Estlund's assessment, developed in the US context, that we have witnessed a similar 'fall and rise' of private law in other common law jurisdictions. We regard this 'rise', much of which has been charted in this volume, as intellectually productive. It has been beneficial for workers and trade unions in all sorts of ways. The private law dimension of work is inescapable, reflected in its contractual foundations, and we should regard employment law as a hybrid discipline of public and private law norms.[34] In methodological terms, this also supports the renaissance of doctrinal scholarship in employment law. Sometimes, private lawyers have paid insufficient attention to employment law as 'real' private law. And perhaps employment lawyers have sometimes given up too easily on doctrinal private law as a lost cause, taking refuge in critical social theory while leaving the official reports to gather dust on the shelf. Private lawyers and employment lawyers should spend more time together. This volume is testament to the fact that we have much more in common than we might think.

[33] This language is Mark Freedland's: see M Freedland, 'Employment Law Revisited' (2020) 43 *Dalhousie Law Journal* 515.

[34] On the hybridity (and complexity) of public law and private law perspectives in labour law, see A Bogg, '"Labour Law is a Subset of Employment Law" Revisited' (2020) 43 *Dalhousie Law Journal* 479.

2

Why There is Not Yet (But Could be Soon) a Principle of Favourability in British Labour Law

SIMON DEAKIN

I. Introduction

The principle of favourability is a foundational feature of labour law in civil law countries. In its simplest form, it holds that in the event of a conflict between two norms or sources of law, the norm most favourable to the employee or worker should be applied. No such principle exists, it seems, in English law, or at least, none has been explicitly formulated. This is not because issues arising from conflicts between norms or sources of labour law do not come up. They do arise all the time, although without always being recognised as such. When this occurs, the possibility of applying a version of the favourability principle has arisen, and, very occasionally, the courts have been alive to its potential. More often, the principle is overlooked. In addition to the doctrinal incoherence that results, there are seriously detrimental consequences for the practical operation of labour law rules.

To explore this theme, section II below introduces the principle of favourability as it applies to labour law in civil law systems. Section III explores the absence of the principle in some of the leading cases of British labour law of the last few decades and its nascent if unacknowledged presence in others, as well as academic writings on the question. Section IV takes a closer look at the possible application of the principle to resolve conflicts between statute and contract, and section V similarly dissects the relationship between contract and collective bargaining. Section VI widens the perspective to include the role of the principle in debates over the flexibilisation of labour standards. Section VII argues that an emergent version of the principle can be seen in recent UK developments, including the drafting of parts of the Employment Rights Bill 2025. Section VIII concludes.

II. The Principle of Favourability in the Civil Law

'Favourability' is one of a number of 'general principles' of labour law that civil law systems recognise.[1] 'Principles', in this sense, are used to inform interpretation and guide the courts in cases of doubt.[2] They can be ousted by specific rules,[3] so they have something in common with 'general clauses' such as reasonableness or good faith, or with concepts that in English law are subsumed under the heading of 'implied terms', such as the duty of mutual trust and confidence.[4]

There is no single definitive list of the principles of labour law, and various taxonomies have been proposed. It is nonetheless possible to identify a core set of principles that is common to more or less all the civilian systems.

Favourability is one of these. It is closely related to a number of other concepts or principles that are characteristic of civil law thinking. These include the principle of non-waivability (rights guaranteed by law cannot be waived by the worker)[5] and the principle of the primacy of reality (substance prevails over form).[6] In some senses, operating as a meta-principle informing all the others is the 'principle of protection', according to which the originating purpose of labour law rules, the reason they exist at all, is the protection of the worker against the consequences of the inequality inherent in the employment relationship.[7]

Not as such a general principle of labour law, but a core feature of civil law thinking, is the idea of the hierarchy of sources in labour law.[8] A given source has more or less weight according to its place within the hierarchy of norms. In the event of a conflict of sources, public and collective norms prevail over private and individual ones. According to the image of the pyramid of sources that can be invoked to explain this concept (see Figure 1), the constitution, as the apex of the national system (if potentially subject to some international law norms), prevails over primary legislation, which prevails over secondary legislation (orders, decrees, and regulations). Relatedly, all public (legal) sources prevail over conventional ones (collective agreements and contracts). Within the category of conventional sources, sectoral agreements prevail over company-level ones. Doctrine, in the sense of legal scholarship, is also a source in civil law systems. The source with the least weight is individual (employer-employee) agreement.

[1] A Plá Rodriguez, *Los Principios del Derecho del Trabajo*, 4th edn (H Barreto Ghione ed, Montevideo, Fundación de Cultura Universitaria, 2015).
[2] ibid 34.
[3] ibid 40.
[4] Z Adams, C Barnard, S Deakin, and S Fraser Butlin, *Deakin and Morris' Labour Law*, 7th edn (Oxford, Hart Publishing, 2021) (subsequently *Deakin and Morris*) [3.4].
[5] Plá Rodriguez (n 1) ch 5.
[6] ibid 271.
[7] ibid 91.
[8] L Mariucci, *Le fonti del diritto del lavoro* (Turin, Giappichelli, 1998).

Figure 2.1 The principle of favourability in civil law systems

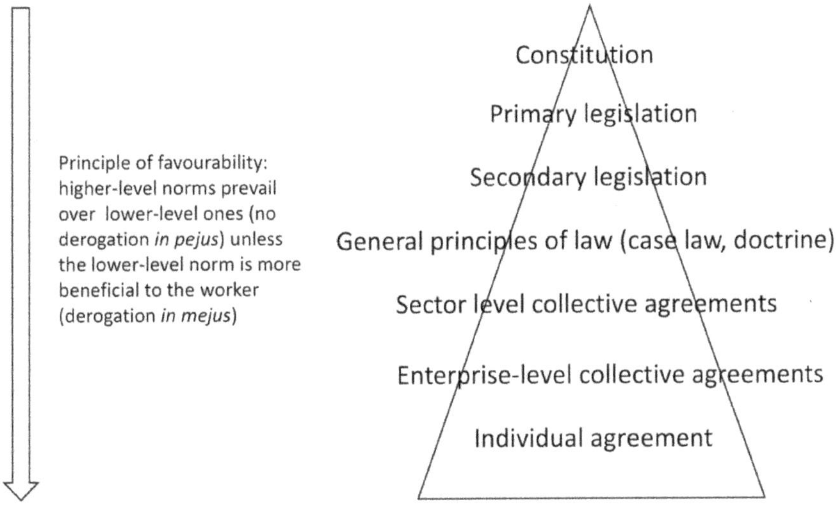

The concept of the hierarchy of sources implies a certain relationship between private law and public law. Essentially, private law norms, such as those associated with the law of contract in its general sense, cannot be allowed to take away, or derogate from, the protections set out in legislation, constitutions, and, in some contexts, international law: in other words, no derogation *in pejus*. The hierarchy of norms can be thought of as affirming the concept of worker-favourability in a broad sense: the more worker-protective norms, being public and/or collective in character, carry greater weight in the system as a whole.

The principle of favourability in its more narrow or specific sense holds that lower-level sources *can* prevail over higher ones, *but only* if they offer greater protection to the worker. In other words, derogation *in melius* is permitted. In some versions of the principle, this 'upwards' derogation is not just allowed, it is mandatory: the norm that is most favourable to the worker *must* be applied, whatever its position in the juridical hierarchy.[9]

This is the case in the Latin American systems. These systems share not just a common juridical root in French civil law, but a particular understanding of labour law as public in character and mandatory in its application.

An influential text across Latin America since its first appearance in the 1970s is *Los Principios del Derecho del Trabajo*, by the Uruguayan jurist Américo Plá Rodriguez. Plá Rodriguez understands the principle of favourability as one of three 'rules' that give effect to the wider 'principle of protection' (*principio protector*).[10]

[9] Plá Rodriguez (n 1) 104.
[10] ibid 91.

Favourability (*la regla de la norma más favorable*)[11] means that in a situation of contending standards, the standard most favourable to the worker must be applied, even if that standard is lower in the hierarchy of norms. Thus, a collective agreement must be given priority over a statutory norm if doing so benefits the worker.

The second rule identified by Plá Rodriguez is the rule of *in dubio pro operario*:[12] if there are contending interpretations of a norm, the interpretation most favourable to the worker must be applied. This rule is expressly recognised in the constitutions and civil codes of several Latin American states.[13]

The third rule is captured by the concept of 'the more beneficial condition' (*la regla de la condición más beneficiosa*):[14] a new standard cannot take away from the rights contained in a pre-existing one, even if the latter is lower in the hierarchy. Thus, the introduction of legislation implementing an international standard, such as an ILO Convention, must not be to the detriment of a national law that is more favourable to the worker. In international labour law, this principle is understood by the concept of the 'non-regression clause'. The original non-regression clause is Article 19.8 of the ILO Constitution, which dates back to the founding of the ILO in the Treaty of Versailles (1919).[15]

The bar on derogations *in pejus* (the hierarchy rule, or favourability in a broad sense) and the requirement of derogation *in melius* for the workers' benefit (the favourability rule in its narrow sense) do not at all rule out a role for norms of private law as a source of labour law. Rather, private law operates in a realm framed or demarcated by public, statutory law. The public-statutory rule is only a minimal or basic standard, to be improved on through bargaining, whether collective or individual. Thus, the statutory rule *presupposes* improvements through private ordering.

This point comes across especially clearly in French doctrine. As explained by Alain Supiot in *Critique du droit du travail* (first published in 1994), the concept of the mandatory effect of social law, *ordre public social*, far from foreclosing the possibility of the negotiation of terms and conditions of employment, 'opens up the field' for precisely this.[16] It is because of this complementarity between public and private sources of labour law that *ordre public social*, in Supiot's words, serves as the 'keystone' of the French system.[17]

Where does that leave the concept of contract? Far from being marginalised by the prevalence of statutory and collective standards, the individual contract of work or employment is a foundational concept of civilian labour law, just as it is in the systems of the English common law. It is nonetheless the case that, in the civil law, the concept of contract has undergone a mutation of a certain kind through its encounter with labour law.

[11] ibid 103.

[12] ibid 91.

[13] ibid 92–96.

[14] ibid 109.

[15] On Art 19.8 of the Constitution of the International Labour Organisation (ILO), see section VII.B, below.

[16] A Supiot, *Critique du droit du travail* (Paris, Quadrige, 2015) 139.

[17] ibid.

In the French understanding, the individual contract operates as an 'act-condition' that 'triggers the application of a systematic ensemble of norms, irrespective of the will of the parties'.[18] This formulation, suggested by Georges Scelle in the 1930s, was reaffirmed by the Plenary Chamber of the Court of Cassation in the 1980s when it wrote that 'the will of the parties cannot have the effect of taking away from workers the social status which necessarily follows from the conditions under which they must complete their accorded' task.[19]

While dependent on the will of the parties for its existence, the civil law contract of work[20] comes into being against a backdrop of mandatory norms that pre-exist its formation and that necessarily apply to it. The legal form is no less synallagmatic or consensual in nature for being regulated in this way. In the French tradition, the 'subordination' of the worker is understood as a juridical condition, itself a kind of status, which signifies, on the one hand, subjection to the employer's commands and, on the other, access to social rights, guaranteed by the public power of the law.[21] In the German tradition, subordination is understood as a 'personal' relation, in which the worker's 'duty of loyalty' is counterbalanced by the employer's 'duty of care'.[22] While the German definition of the work relation has been termed 'communitarian' in contrast to the 'exchange-based' or synallagmatic approach of French law, this distinction only extends to the contents of the relationship once it has been formed; in German, as in French and English law, the hiring process is understood to give rise to a contract between the individual worker and the employer.[23]

III. The Principle of Favourability in English Law

A. Absence of the Principle of Favourability

It is clear that the principle of favourability reflects the protective logic of labour law: the individual worker, faced with the employer's superior contractual power, is in need of the protection granted by legislation and collective bargaining. Britain has a mature, long-standing, and highly developed labour law system. Why, then,

[18] ibid 30.

[19] Cass. Ann. plén, 4 mars 1983, D. 1983, J. 381; Supiot (n 16) 30–31.

[20] *Contrat de travail* in French, with equivalent terms used in other mainland European languages. While the civil law concept of the 'contract of work' is roughly analogous to the English law 'contract of employment' as the foundational concept of individual employment law, the use of the term 'work' in place of 'employment' indicates not just the broader scope of the civilian form but a different genealogy to that of the common law, emphasising its universal coverage as well as its public-regulatory function: S Deakin, 'Anthropogenic Labour Law: The Coevolution of Law and Work' in G Davidov, B Langille and G Lester (eds), *Oxford Handbook of the Law of Work* (Oxford, OUP, 2024).

[21] Supiot (n 16) 114. In other words, the French law concept of *subordination juridique* does not purport to describe a social reality as such, but imputes a legal status to the wage earner. The power which the employer exercises is similarly juridical in nature, as it derives from the way in which the law also accords a particular form to the enterprise.

[22] ibid 29, discussing the concepts of *persönliche Abhängigkeit*, *Treuepflicht* and *Försorgepflicht*.

[23] ibid 33.

is there no principle of favourability in British labour law or in English private law more generally as it applies to the employment relationship?

Had there been a principle of favourability in English law, some of the leading labour law decisions of recent years would most likely have been decided differently. The following is a non-exhaustive list.

i. Johnson v Unisys Ltd *(2001, HL)*[24]

Statutory unfair dismissal law (currently set out in Part X of the Employment Rights Act 1996) constitutes a ceiling of rights in the matter of termination of employment, preventing the application of the implied term of mutual trust and fairness to create a private law duty on the part of the employer to act fairly when dismissing an employee. As contract law is prevented from improving on statute, the effect is to bar derogation *in melius*.

ii. Edwards v Chesterfield Royal Hospital Foundation NHS Trust *(2011, SC)*[25]

Statutory unfair dismissal law again constitutes a ceiling, this time preventing a claim for substantial damages for breach of contract arising from an express term governing the procedure to be followed when terminating the employee's contract for alleged misconduct. Here, individual agreement, and by extension, a collective agreement whose normative terms have been incorporated into the contract, are prevented from improving on the statute. The effect is the same as *Johnson*: no derogation *in melius*.

iii. McKenzie v Chancellor, Masters and Scholars of the University of Cambridge *(2019, CA)*[26]

The limited remedy provided by statutory unfair dismissal law (an order of reinstatement can be avoided by the employer paying a higher sum of money, the amount of which is capped by the statute[27]) is one factor preventing the court from issuing a quashing order to nullify an arguably ultra vires termination of employment. Here, the public law remedy for arguably irrational behaviour by the employer is prevented from improving on statute: no derogation *in melius*.

[24] *Johnson v Unisys Ltd* [2001] IRLR 270; *Deakin and Morris* (n 4) [4.43].

[25] *Edwards v Chesterfield Royal Hospital Foundation NHS Trust* [2012] IRLR 129; *Deakin and Morris* (n 4) [4.45].

[26] *McKenzie v Chancellor, Masters and Scholars of the University of Cambridge* [2020] IRLR 324; *Deakin and Morris* (n 4) [4.140].

[27] Employment Rights Act 1996 (ERA 1996), s 117.

iv. Independent Workers Union of Great Britain v (1) Central Arbitration Committee and (2) Roofoods Ltd (Trading as Deliveroo) *(2023, SC)*[28]

A 'substitution' clause in a gig worker's agreement with a platform has the effect of denying the worker protected status with respect to the law governing the recognition of a trade union for the purposes of collective bargaining. Since the contract term has the effect of defeating a wide range of statutory[29] and constitutional rights[30] intended for the worker's protection, this is an instance of *derogation in pejus*.

In short, in several of the most important labour law cases decided by the higher appellate courts since the turn of the millennium, the absence of the principle of favourability was critical to the decision for the employer.

B. Presence of the Principle of Favourability

The absence of the favourability principle in certain key decisions is by no means the whole story, however. There are instances of a version of the principle being applied, if not named as such. Some of these decisions have also been of the highest importance for the evolution of labour law.

i. Autoclenz Ltd v Belcher *(2011, SC)*[31]

Boilerplate introduced by the employer should be disregarded for the purpose of construing the parties' agreement and classifying it as a work or employment contract where the term relied on by the employer is a 'sham', a relevant test of a 'sham' being that the term did not correspond to the 'reality' of the way the work was performed and the parties' mutual understandings. The employer cannot, by its unilateral declaration or action, alter the contract terms so as to deprive the worker of statutory protections, so here, derogation *in pejus* is ruled out. This decision is close to the civil law concept of the 'primacy of reality', or substance over form.

[28] *Independent Workers Union of Great Britain v (1) Central Arbitration Committee and (2) Roofoods Ltd (trading as Deliveroo)* [2023] UKSC 43; Gwyneth Pitt, '"The Simple Things You See Are All Complicated": Thoughts On *Deliveroo*' (2024) 53 *Industrial Law Journal* 784.

[29] In this case, the panoply of collective labour law rights provided for by the Trade Union and Labour Relations (Consolidation) Act 1992 (TULRCA).

[30] The effect of the Supreme Court ruling in *Deliveroo* is to render inapplicable the rights that would otherwise be accorded to workers under Art 11 of the European Court of Human Rights, which, in English law, might be thought of as constitutional in character by virtue of its embedding in the Human Rights Act 1998, or, conceivably, as equivalent to the international law norms which have a quasi-constitutional status in domestic law; either way, they would prevail not just over contract terms but also over legislation according to the civil law concept of the hierarchy of sources.

[31] *Autoclenz Ltd v Belcher* [2011] IRLR 820; *Deakin and Morris* (n 4) [2.9].

ii. Uber BV v Aslam *(2021, SC)*[32]

Statutory anti-avoidance clauses[33] are one factor in limiting the scope employers can make of boilerplate to avoid employee or worker status: according to Lord Leggatt, section 49(1) of the National Minimum Wage Act 1998 renders void any contract term purporting 'to prevent a driver from claiming that he falls within the statutory definition of a "worker" so as to qualify for the rights conferred on workers' by that Act.[34] The effect is that the contract made by the parties cannot be used to undermine statutory rights: no derogation *in pejus*.

iii. Tesco Stores Ltd v USDAW *(2024, SC)*[35]

The employer cannot escape provisions of a collective agreement that purported to confer a 'permanent' or non-renegotiable benefit (a 'retained pay term') on an employee by the expedient of dismissing them with notice under the terms of their current contract and re-employing them on another containing inferior terms and conditions (a 'fire and rehire'). Upholding the judgment at first instance and reversing the Court of Appeal, the Supreme Court granted an injunction to prevent the dismissal. According to the leading judgment of Lord Burrows and Lady Simler, it was 'necessary, applying the business efficacy test, to imply a term in the contracts to qualify Tesco's right to dismiss on notice so that it cannot be exercised for the purpose of depriving the claimants of their right to permanent retained pay'.[36] This had the result of entrenching the collectively agreed term against a contractual derogation (so no derogation *in pejus*).

iv. Case Law on the Written Statement, Sections 1–4 ERA 1996

The three decisions just discussed are equivalent to applying the rule of the hierarchy of sources, that is, the principle of favourability in a broad sense. It is more difficult to find examples of English courts applying the principle of favourability in the narrow sense of requiring derogation *in melius*, but there is at least one significant instance.

In principle, the written statement issued by the employer under section 1 ERA 1996 is not a source of law; in other words, it does not have normative effect in its own right. It is only evidence of the contract, which does not have normative effect. However, a provision of a written statement is more likely to be regarded as evidence of a contract term when it operates in the employee's favour than when

[32] *Uber BV v Aslam* [2021] UKSC 5; *Deakin and Morris* (n 4) [2.9], [2.22], [2.54].

[33] Principally contained in ERA 1996, s 203(1); National Minimum Wage Act 1998 (NMWA 1998), s 49(1); Working Time Regulations 1998, reg 35(1); and TULRCA 1992, s 288. On ERA 1996, s 203, see further, below.

[34] [2021] UKSC 5, [82].

[35] *Tesco Stores Ltd v USDAW* [2024] UKSC 28.

[36] ibid [13].

it operates in favour of the employer, according to Browne-Wilkinson J. in *System Floors (UK) Ltd v Daniel*,[37] and Ackner LJ in *Robertson v British Gas Corp*.[38] This is an instance of derogation *in melius*: the unilateral statement of contract terms made by the employer cannot be used to derogate from rights the employee would otherwise have had through custom or collective bargaining but should be interpreted as benefiting the employee, so improving on those rights.

C. Academic Writings

In addition to these judicial applications of something approximating the principle of favourability, there is a small but nonetheless significant academic literature discussing the issue of sources of labour law and their interrelationship. A non-exhaustive list includes the following.

i. Kahn-Freund: Collective Agreement as Sources of Labour Law (1943)

Sir Otto Kahn-Freund's article 'Collective agreements under war legislation', published in 1943,[39] seems to have been the first to introduce into English law the civil law terminology that distinguishes between the 'contractual' or 'procedural' effect of the collective agreement and its 'normative' or rule-making effect. The article identified the absence of a general framework for giving collective agreements compulsory normative effect but noted that this option was far from unknown before the outbreak of World War Two, having been introduced in the short-lived Coal Mines Act 1931 and then in the longer-lived Cotton Manufacturing Industry (Temporary Provisions) Order 1934, before becoming of general application in wartime by virtue of Order 1305, the Conditions of Employment and National Arbitration Order.[40] Kahn-Freund acknowledged that British trade unions mostly did not need terms negotiated by collective agreement to be made legally binding, as they had the economic means to enforce them, including, if necessary, through industrial action, but noted that they had accepted the principle of legal intervention during times of economic crisis (the slump of the 1930s) and national emergency (wartime).

ii. Wedderburn: The Concepts of the 'Floor of Rights' and 'Inderogability' (1975, 1992)

Lord Wedderburn appears to have been the first to use the phrase 'floor of rights' to refer to the role employment protection laws were playing, from the 1970s

[37] *System Floors (UK) Ltd v Daniel* [1982] ICR 54, 58 (EAT); *Deakin and Morris* (n 4) [3.16].
[38] *Robertson v British Gas Corp* [1983] ICR 351, 355 (CA); *Deakin and Morris* (n 4) [3.16].
[39] O Kahn-Freund, 'Collective Agreements Under War Legislation' (1943) 6 *Modern Law Review* 112.
[40] 'Conditions of Employment and National Arbitration Order, SR & O 1940/1305'.

onwards, in providing a foundation of statutory rights for collective bargaining to build on.[41] His 1992 article, 'Inderogability, collective agreements, and Community law',[42] extended the idea of the floor of rights, adapting the Italian concept of *inderogabilitá* and exploring its application to English law. The article discusses the implications of the different forms of derogation *in pejus* and *in melius*.

iii. Freedland: ius cogens, ius dispositivum, *and the Personal Work Contract (2002)*

Building on Kahn-Freund's earlier (1967) discussion of 'status and contract' in labour law, which had introduced the civilian concepts of *ius cogens* and *ius dispositivum* (or mandatory and default rules) into British labour law discourse,[43] as well as Wedderburn's concept of 'inderogability',[44] Mark Freedland discusses several issues that anticipated later developments in the case law.[45] His analysis ranges over the fragility of the normative function of the collective agreement in the face of individual contract norms, the use of boilerplate to deflect employee and worker status, and the possibility that the contract could be used to undermine human rights standards.[46]

iv. Reynold and Hendy: Discussion of the Employer's Right to Reserve a Power to Make Unilateral Changes to Terms and Conditions (2012)

Writing academically, in a case note published in 2012,[47] Frederic Reynold KC and Lord John Hendy KC discuss the scope of express reservation and variation clauses, of the kind which purport to enable the employer to raise hours or cut pay at will. They suggest that, as a matter of construction, the court should be more reluctant to apply such a clause to vary terms and conditions which have been derived from a collective agreement. Their analysis can be read as an argument for introducing a version of the hierarchy of sources into English law.

[41] KW Wedderburn, 'The Employment Protection Act 1975. Collective aspects' (1976) 39 *Modern Law Review* 169.

[42] KW Wedderburn 'Inderogability, Collective Agreements, and Community Law' (1992) 21 *Industrial Law Journal* 245.

[43] O Kahn-Freund, 'A note on Contract and Status in British labour Law' (1967) 30 *Modern Law Review* 635.

[44] Wedderburn (n 42).

[45] M Freedland, 'Ius Cogens, Ius Dispositivum, and the Law of Personal Work Contracts' in P Birks and A Pretto (eds), *Themes in Comparative Law: In Honour of Bernard Rudden* (Oxford, OUP, 2002).

[46] See also M Freedland and N Kountouris, *The Legal Construction of Personal Work Relations* (Oxford, OUP, 2011) 186, discussing the operation of the principle of favourability in civilian systems.

[47] F Reynold and J Hendy, 'Reserving the Right to Changes Terms and Conditions: How Far Can the Employer Go?' (2012) 41 *Industrial Law Journal* 79.

v. Bogg: Default Norms in Labour Law (2024)

In the course of a recent paper, Alan Bogg argues that the English courts now have a better grasp of the distinction between *ius cogens* and *ius dispositivum* than they did when Freedland published his contribution to the debate in 2002.[48] According to Bogg, section 203 ERA, having previously been 'obscure', could be a new 'philosopher's stone',[49] capable of embedding labour rights as *ius cogens*. He argues for the priority of public law norms for worker protection over norms of private law, regardless of their precise origin in statute or contract. Elsewhere, he has argued for explicit recognition of a 'principle of favourability' in English law, according to which the courts should, wherever possible, favour 'the development of protective norms to protect the weaker party'.[50]

It can hardly be said, then, that discussion of the principle of favourability, or at least of the issues it raises, is absent from either judicial discourse or the work of legal scholars. On the other hand, the principle of favourability as such does not receive an extended analysis in any of the judicial decisions or scholarly works just cited.[51]

IV. Statute versus Contract: Common Law 'Culture' or Statutory Purpose?

Bogg considers some of the reasons for the underdevelopment of the concepts of *ius cogens* and *ius dispositivum* in English law. He cites Kahn-Freund on the familiarity of the distinction to 'every practising lawyer in any Continental legal system',[52] contrasting this to a corresponding 'conceptual gap',[53] in the common law, and Geoffrey Samuel[54] as authority for the 'relatively underdeveloped body of doctrinally focused taxonomy and systematisation in the English universities compared with their European counterparts'.[55] In *Negative Comparative Law*, Pierre Legrand cautions against transposing legal concepts out of their original context, arguing that law exists 'as a cultural intervention, as a modality of culture,

[48] A Bogg, 'Default Norms in Labour Law: From Private Right to Public Law', University of Bristol Law Working Papers Series, Paper #002/2024; also published in B Hacker and J Ungerer (eds), *Default Rules in Private Law* (Oxford, Hart Publishing, 2024).

[49] Bogg ibid 48.

[50] A Bogg, 'The Common Law Constitution at Work: *R (on the application of UNISON)* v *Lord Chancellor*' (2018) 81 *Modern Law Review* 509, 520.

[51] The only specific reference to the principle of favourability is by Bogg, ibid. He sees 'favourability' as a general clause which would enable courts to interpret extant legal rules in a way which favours the 'weaker party'. This is closer to the principle of *in dubio pro operario* than to the hierarchy rule or to the principle of the more favourable condition in the sense identified by civil law jurists (see above, section II).

[52] Kahn-Freund (n 43) 640.

[53] Bogg (n 48) 7. See also, Bogg (n 50) 518 ('The principle of favourability is often treated as alien to common law systems').

[54] G Samuel, 'Can Doctrinal Legal Scholarship Be Defended?' (2022) 4 *Amicus Curiae* 43.

[55] Bogg (n 48) 7.

as culture speaking legally'.[56] It could then be that the conceptual superstructure of the civil law is simply too distinct from common law modes of thought for any translation or cross-fertilisation to be possible.

There may, however, be more prosaic reasons for the, so far, limited reception of the principle of favourability in the English common law. The principle of favourability has a wider application than labour law, being mentioned in the texts of certain civil codes.[57] Its adaptation to the labour law context, where it is conditioned by the possibility of a lower level but more protective norm being applied in the worker's favour, is also explicitly set out in legal texts: in some countries, in constitutions;[58] in others, in codes and statutes;[59] in yet others, in the judgments of courts of cassation.[60] Thus, the idea is not simply the work of the taxonomical approach to legal doctrine, which is characteristic of civilian thinking.

If the principle of favourability has its roots in specific texts of the civil law, does the absence of such texts account for its marginality in English law? Let us first consider the constitutional context. The UK has an uncodified constitution, but a constitution nonetheless. One of its principles, perhaps the core one, is parliamentary sovereignty.[61] It is on this basis that, in English law, statutory norms prevail over those of the common law. Although there are multiple 'canons' of statutory interpretation, which, between them, do not necessarily contain much predictive value when it comes to ascertaining how exactly a court will construe a legislative text, there is nonetheless a general understanding that some combination of the form of words contained in a statute and that statute's purpose should inform its legal meaning, no less in the context of labour law than in other contexts.[62]

Let us now consider the interpretation given to the ERA 1996 by Lord Hoffmann in *Johnson v Unisys*. After outlining the provisions of the Act governing unfair dismissal and noting their limitations, Lord Hoffmann concludes: 'For the judiciary to construct a general common law remedy for unfair circumstances attending dismissal would be to go contrary to the evident intention of Parliament that there should be such a remedy but that it should be limited in application and extent.'[63] This is the basis on which the application of the implied term of mutual trust and confidence to the termination decision was rejected.

Lord Hoffmann makes no mention in his judgment of section 203. Headed 'restrictions on contracting out', this provision, reads:

> (1) Any provision in an agreement (whether a contract of employment or not) is void in so far as it purports – (a) to exclude or limit the operation of any provision of this Act.

[56] P Legrand, *Negative Comparative Law* (Cambridge, Cambridge University Press, 2022), 7.

[57] Plá Rodriguez (n 1) 91.

[58] Title I, Article 26 of the Constitution of Peru, for example, expressly refers to the principle of the non-waivability of fundamental labour rights and to the application of the principle of *in dubio pro operario* to labour cases.

[59] Plá Rodriguez (n 1) 91–94.

[60] Supiot (n 16) 30–31.

[61] On the relevance of the idea of a 'common law constitution' to labour law, see Bogg (n 50).

[62] On legislation as a source in British labour law, see *Deakin and Morris* (n 4) [1.39].

[63] *Johnson v Unisys* [2001] IRLR 270 [58].

Section 203(1)(a) explicitly rules out derogation *in pejus*; does it thereby create, if only implicitly, scope for derogation *in melius*? It is not hard to see that it could. In Wedderburn's formulation,[64] the Act was intended to function as a *floor* of rights. Prior to Lord Hoffmann's judgment in *Johnson*, there does not appear to have been any authority to suggest that it should act as a *ceiling*.[65]

In *Edwards v Chesterfield*, the Supreme Court passed up the chance to rectify *Johnson*, instead doubling down on the earlier decision. Now, an *express* contract term could not confer greater rights than the statute. Lord Dyson, extending dicta of Lord Hoffmann in *Johnson*, argued that a term whose inclusion in the contract could be traced to the Act's intended effect of stimulating the adoption of fairer and more effective disciplinary procedures must, *for that reason*, be accorded reduced normative weight: 'it must necessarily to be inferred from … [the] … statutory background that, unless they otherwise expressly agree, the parties to an employment contract do not intend that a failure to comply with contractually binding disciplinary procedures will give rise to a common law claim for damages'.[66] As a result, 'the unfair dismissal legislation occupies the unfair dismissal territory to the exclusion of the common law'.[67]

This is not so much to reject, or overlook, the principle of favourability, as to precisely invert it. It is as if the legislation creating the national *minimum* wage were interpreted as imposing a *maximum*.

In *Johnson* and *Edwards*, statute defeated contract, for the employer's benefit. In *Deliveroo*,[68] contract defeated statute, for the employer's benefit. The only common element across these three cases is that the employer prevailed. From the point of view of the hierarchy of sources, British labour law seems to have arrived at the distinct position of systematically favouring the *employer*.

Is this position sustainable? The worker-favouring civil law principle is founded in specific legal texts. What is remarkable about the current position in English law is that equivalent texts exist but have either been overlooked or considered and then given a meaning that inverts their ostensible purpose. Perhaps then there is, after all, some kind of inchoate common law 'culture' which dictates that, in cases of doubt or conflict, labour law norms should be interpreted and applied in the employer's favour.

Or maybe these are simply decisions that are ripe for reconsideration. If the existence of statutory texts is the issue, there is no good reason for English law not

[64] Wedderburn (n 41), (n 42).

[65] On the contrary, there are numerous earlier instances of courts extending the common law beyond protections provided by statute. The tort of breach of statutory duty, a common law action derived by implication from factory legislation designed for workers' protection (*Groves* v *Lord Wimborne* [1898] 2 QB 402), would not have been possible otherwise. The courts developed the common law concept of the employer's personal liability for negligence notwithstanding Parliament's expressed intention to make the statutory workmen's compensation claim the principal remedy for workplace injuries and disease: *Lochgelly Iron & Coal Co* v *M'Mullan* [1934] AC 1, circumventing s 29 of the Workmen's Compensation Act 1925.

[66] *Edwards v Chesterfield* [2012] IRLR 129 [39].

[67] ibid [52].

[68] [2023] UKSC 43; Pitt (n 28).

to recognise the principle of favourability in its true sense, of protecting the worker rather than the employer, and every reason for it to do so if this legislation is to be given an interpretation that is consistent with its purpose.[69]

V. Collective Bargaining versus Contract: On the Nature of a Labour Law 'Source'

It is not possible to rely on statutory texts for guidance on the relationship between collective bargaining and contracts. Since the repeal in 1980 of the successor to Order 1305, Schedule 11 of the Employment Protection Act 1975, there has been no possibility of extending a sector-level collective agreement by statutory means, nor any other legal mechanism to give compulsory effect to the normative terms of a collective agreement. The matter falls to be decided by reference to the common law.

It is generally understood that the theory of incorporation provides the best explanation for the inclusion of the normative terms in the individual contract of employment.[70] This means that the collective agreement can only acquire the status of a 'source' in the sense of giving rise to rights and obligations in so far as there is a contract term providing for incorporation. This 'bridge' term can be expressly agreed, but it is more likely to be implied from custom and practice or evidenced by the written statement.[71] The bridge, and hence the status of the collective agreement as a source, is precarious, since, as a contract term, it cannot easily be entrenched against the employer's superior bargaining power.

The civil law systems do not follow the theory of incorporation. Instead, the collective agreement is recognised as a normative source in its own right. The status of the collective agreement is generally set out in legislation and sometimes in the constitution. Supiot observes the resulting difference between the common law and civil law approaches. In the English common law, he suggests, the collective agreement is *res inter alios acta*, that is, an act of third parties external to the contract. Incorporation occurs by virtue of the willingness of the courts to align the juridical form of the contract with the practice, understood by both parties, of applying the normative terms on wages, hours, and other terms and conditions wherever there is a trade union recognised for the purposes of collective bargaining.[72]

In the civil law systems, by contrast, there is no need to talk of incorporation, since the collective agreement has the force of law behind it regardless of the

[69] G Davidov, *A Purposive Approach to Labour Law* (Oxford, Oxford University Press, 2016).

[70] A Sanders, 'The Content of Contracts of Employment: Terms Incorporated from Collective Agreements or from Other Sources' in M Freedland et al (eds) *The Contract of Employment* (Oxford, Oxford University Press, 2016).

[71] *Deakin and Morris* (n 4) [3.20].

[72] Supiot (n 16) 29.

contract terms. In systems influenced by French law, it is the public power (*puissance publique*) that guarantees this result. Writing of the Danish model, which, like the British one, emphasises the voluntary nature of collective bargaining, Supiot notes that it nonetheless recognises the principle of the hierarchy of norms, ensuring that the legal effect of the collective agreement does not depend on the exchange-based ('synallagmatic') logic of private law.[73]

Is the English common law capable of recognising a version of the principle of favourability with respect to the relationship between collective agreement and contract? As we have seen, Reynold and Hendy have argued that, purely as a matter of construction, very clear language should be needed in an express reservation clause to overcome a term derived from a collective agreement.[74] Why else would the parties have agreed (impliedly or otherwise) to a bridging term? In *USDAW*, the employer was held to have tied its hands by stating that the retained pay provision 'cannot be negotiated away by either Tesco, USDAW or USDAW shop stewards'.[75] In other words, the retained pay term was entrenched not just against any contractual variation but against any subsequent collective agreement. If an express commitment not to renegotiate is needed to entrench the collectively negotiated terms, however, *USDAW* will not get us very far. Without such an undertaking, the employer is likely to be able to fall back on the express contractual power to dismiss without cause simply by giving notice.

If the need to clothe the normative terms of collective agreement in contractual form is a weakness of the common law approach from the point of view of ensuring protection for the worker, the contractual foundation of the concept of a labour law 'source' also creates an opportunity for British labour law. The point here is that the employer's powers of direction and supervision also depend on the contract to take legal effect. In English law, the employer has no inherent right of direction of the kind which, in French law, is derived from the hierarchical organisation of the 'enterprise' as a form of production, and in German law from the notion of the enterprise as a 'community' in which labour and capital have a shared interest. Whatever their origins might have been in the master-servant law of the past, in English law the duties of obedience and cooperation are now expressed as implied terms of the contract of employment.[76]

Given the way that English law understands the normativity of a labour law source, two routes are available for protecting collective agreements against contractual derogations *in pejus*. The first is to counter one implied term with another: here, the duty of mutual trust and confidence can be invoked to limit the employer's prerogative power. As an implied term, it can be used to constrain the operation of the duties of cooperation and obedience, but it cannot formally override an express agreement, which is normally how the court interprets a unilateral

[73] ibid 31.
[74] Reynold and Hendy (n 47).
[75] [2024] UKSC 28 [41].
[76] *Deakin and Morris* (n 4) [3.3].

exercise of the employer's will, which the employee has no choice but to accept, either by carrying on working or by formally agreeing to new terms following a dismissal. However, Reynold and Hendy have shown[77] that the implied term of mutual trust can be invoked to allow the court to give a restrictive interpretation, in the manner of the *contra proferentem* rule, to express terms operating for the employer's benefit. Had the duty of mutual trust and confidence been extended, as the duty to act fairly, to the dismissal decision, a further constraint could have been imposed on the employer's power to fire and rehire. *Johnson* and *Edwards* stand in the way of this result, but they could be circumvented, in their turn, by the invocation of the so-called *Braganza* principle,[78] according to which the employer's decision to remove, for its own benefit, a right accorded by the contract to the employee has to be exercised in good faith, even where the employer is relying on an express term to do so.[79]

The second route is to deny that the employer's unilateral act has any binding force, by finding that it is not a valid variation of the contract terms. This was the route taken in *System Floors v Daniel*[80] and *Robertson v British Gas*,[81] but in these instances it required the background condition of the operation of the written statement law, with its purpose of protecting the interests of the employee in receiving clear and stable terms of employment.[82] By deciding that a purported variation contained in the section 1 statement was, in fact, only the employer's *view* of the contract, and that since this view was, in so far as it sought to depart from the previously agreed contract terms, an inaccurate and therefore legally defective one, the courts in these cases succeeded in fettering the employer's power to make contractual changes at will. These decisions are a reminder that, in the final analysis, it is for the courts, and not the employer, to decide what a legal source is. It is equally within the courts' power to determine the relationship between sources and thereby to align English law more closely to the civil law principles of hierarchy and favourability.

VI. Wider Challenges to the Principle of Favourability: Flexibilisation and Fragmentation of Labour Law Rules

If the principle of favourability has, at best, a marginal status in labour law in the common law world, it is under threat in the civil law one. The use of opening clauses in collective agreements, allowing plant-level agreements to depart from

[77] Reynold and Hendy (n 47).
[78] *Braganza* v *BP Shipping Ltd* [2015] UKSC 17.
[79] This was the view of Lord Leggatt in *USDAW* at [127]. The judgment of Lord Burrows and Lady Simler did not rely on *Braganza*.
[80] *Floors v Daniel* [1982] ICR 54.
[81] *Robertson v British Gas* [1983] ICR 351.
[82] See section II.B, above.

sectoral standards, is a widespread development in respect of working time standards since the 1980s and is one aspect of this. Allowing collective agreements to modify statutory standards also became possible in several countries from this period. The EU's Working Time Directive, while bringing much-needed protections to the UK after nearly two decades of a near complete absence of regulation of working hours, appeared as an instrument of flexibilisation in the civil law systems, thanks to its encouragement for the annualisation of hours and the related decentralisation of decision-making to the enterprise level (although hardly any other EU Member States followed the UK's lead in taking advantage of the individual opt-out).[83] In several countries affected by the fallout from the Eurozone financial crisis of 2008-09, 'structural reforms' that accompanied sovereign debt relief led to an expansion of the scope for company-level agreements to derogate from sectoral ones.[84] Even countries that had not sought debt relief adopted this approach, including France via its El Khomri Laws of 2016.[85] The fragmentation of sectoral floors to wages and working conditions is one of the causes of rising inequality across the EU in the past two decades.[86]

These challenges notwithstanding, it would seem that the principle of favourability has remained mostly intact. Insofar as the scope for derogation *in pejus* has been expanded, this process favours enterprise- or plant-level collective bargaining, or in some countries, works council accords, rather than recourse to unilateral employer decision-making, in the guise of individual agreements, which came to dominate in large parts of the British economy as a result of the decline in collective bargaining coverage that set in during the 1980s. Following the adoption of the Adequate Minimum Wages Directive (AMWD) in 2022,[87] the EU Member States are now committed to taking measures to increase the coverage of collective bargaining in any case where the national rate falls below 80 per cent. This is not the same as setting 80 per cent as a target rate, but it is likely to induce a significant strengthening of sectoral standards.[88]

The AMWD is not a direct source of British labour law, but it may, in time, come to have an indirect influence via the 'level playing field' clauses of the EU-UK

[83] B Burchell, S Deakin, J Rubery and D Spencer, 'The Future of Work and Working Time: Introduction to the Special Issue' (2024) 48 *Cambridge Journal of Economics* 1, 12.

[84] MCE Varniol, S Laulom, E Mazuyer and P Vielle (eds), *Quel droit social dans une Europe en crise?* (Paris, Larcier, 2012).

[85] On which, see P Petit, '"Our Elites Have Lost Consciousness of the French Social Model": An Interview with Alain Supiot' (*Verso Blog*, 12 December 2018 www.versobooks.com/en-gb/blogs/news/4172-our-elites-have-lost-consciousness-of-the-french-social-model-an-interview-with-alain-supiot?srsltid=AfmBOoooqVfOYWqCti4_qIxzFnnpV6eaMIa4bgklwP4zoJG6lN9g8DwM.

[86] S Spiegelaere, 'The Planned Obsolescence of Social Europe: How Weakening Collective Bargaining is Fuelling Inequality in Europe', *UNI Europa Snapshot Report* (2022-01) www.uni-europa.org/wp-content/uploads/sites/3/2022/02/CollBargaining_Inequality-1.pdf.

[87] Directive (EU) 2022/2041 of the European Parliament and of the Council of 19 October 2022 on Adequate Minimum Wages in the European Union, [2022] OJ L275/33.

[88] L Ratti, 'The Sword and the Shield: The Directive on Adequate Minimum Wages in the EU' (2023) 52 *Industrial Law Journal* 477.

Trade and Cooperation Agreement.[89] Moreover, elements of the same policy shift that informed the AMWD can be observed in the UK context. There appears to be a developing consensus to the effect that policies of deregulation and flexibilisation have reached their limit. These policies are seen as having bequeathed a combination of stalling productivity and rising inequality. As a result, the case for reinstating a floor of rights to terms and conditions is being taken more seriously than it has for several decades.[90] These are propitious circumstances for labour lawyers to begin thinking about how a common law version of the principle of favourability might be put into effect.

VII. An Emergent Principle of Favourability for British Labour Law

Bearing in mind that the civil law principle of favourability owes its existence not just to the synthesising work of legal scholars but to specific constitutional and statutory texts, making the principle a reality in the British context will require changes to legislation. Among the steps that could be taken are the following.

A. Clarification of the Role of Contract Terms in Determining Employee and Worker Status

The problem here is that it is currently too easy for employers to avoid employee and worker status through the use of substitution and similar clauses. *Deliveroo*[91] shows that the approach taken in the late 1990s, of using the 'contract for services' and related 'limb (b) worker' concept,[92] as the basis for the extension of labour rights to economically dependent workers, is no longer effective. The solution, it is suggested, lies not so much in eliminating 'contract' as the basis for employment status and more widely for employment rights as in reducing the scope for individual 'agreement' as a source of norms within the contract.

While it may seem counterintuitive to preserve 'contract' while limiting the influence of 'agreement', the point is that 'contract', in the labour law context, does not belong exclusively to the sphere of private law. Rather than being thought of as an agreement of the parties intended to have legal effect as in the context of the

[89] S Deakin and B Billa, 'The EU's Role in the Extra-territorial Enforcement of Labour Law' in Z Rasnaca, A Koukiadaki, N Bruun and K Lörcher (eds), *Effective Enforcement of EU Labour Law* (Oxford, Hart Publishing, 2022).

[90] UK Government, *Next Steps to Make Work Pay* (October 2024) www.assets.publishing.service.gov.uk/media/6707a5eb92bb81fcdbe7b62b/next_steps_to_make_work_pay.pdf.

[91] [2023] UKSC 43.

[92] *Deakin and Morris* (n 4) [2.18].

general law of contract,[93] 'contract' in the labour law context should be understood more broadly as a vehicle for expressing the effect on the parties' relationship of one or more of a number of sources.[94] Analogously to the civil law concept of the contract of work, common lawyers might be more willing than they have so far been to see the formation of the contract as the 'act-condition' that triggers the application of sources which predate the parties' agreement and whose normative force is independent of it.[95]

From this perspective, whenever work is carried out that objectively satisfies the conditions of dependence (in a manner akin to the 'principle of the primacy of reality'[96]), a contract of work should be regarded as coming into being, regardless of the presence of a substitution clause or equivalent status-deflecting term. Elements of this approach already exist, for example, in the definition of the term 'worker' used in the context of the whistleblowing jurisdiction in section 43K(1) ERA. Limb (a) of this definition refers to a worker as an individual 'who works or worked for a person' in circumstances where 'the terms on which he is or was engaged to do the work are or were in practice substantially determined not by him but by the person for whom he works or worked', there being no reference to contract at all. Limb (b) refers inter alia to situations in which a person 'contracts or contracted with a person, for the purposes of that person's business' where the work is done 'personally *or otherwise*' (emphasis added), the proviso targeting the intended effect of a substitution clause.

B. Achieving Compulsory Normative Effect for Collective Agreements and Addressing the 'Fire and Rehire' Problem

As Kahn-Freund demonstrated as long ago as 1943,[97] the principle of the compulsory normative effect of a collective agreement is far from unknown in British labour law. Between the adoption of Order 1305 and the repeal of Schedule 11 EPA in 1980, it was a central feature of the British system. Bringing back Schedule 11 faces the practical difficulty that sectoral-level bargaining is much reduced in scope by comparison to the late 1970s. In many sectors, there are no multi-employer agreements to be extended. Thus, restoring a sectoral floor to wages and conditions will initially be a work in progress. This does not mean that consideration

[93] cf GH Treitel, *The Law of Contract* (Oxford, OUP, 1965) 1 (and in subsequent editions): 'a contract is an agreement giving rise to obligations which are enforced or recognised by law'.

[94] 'The contract of employment is above all a mechanism through which one or more of a number of external sources of governance or regulation is given legal effect': *Deakin and Morris* (n 4) [3.1]. This definition is not incompatible with Treitel's, but might be thought to give a more specific, labour-law orientation to the meaning of 'contract'.

[95] Supiot (n 16) 30.

[96] Plá Rodriguez (n 1) ch 4.

[97] Kahn-Freund (n 39).

cannot be given to ways by which sector-wide terms and conditions could be made legally binding.

There are a number of options here. TULRCA section 179 could be amended to make legal enforceability the default (*ius dispositivum*), although, in itself, this reform would not address the need to distinguish between the contractual and normative effects of the agreement. If the aim is to achieve enforceability for the normative terms alone, the unilateral arbitration mechanism, which operated under Order 1305 and later the EPA 1975, offers one possible model, but this presupposes that a voluntary sectoral agreement is already in place and can be given the equivalent of an extension effect via the arbitral route.

In October 2024, the UK Government committed itself to introducing a 'Fair Pay Agreement process in the adult social care sector.'[98] Such agreements would 'empower workers, trade unions and employers to negotiate fair pay, terms and conditions, and training standards.'[99] Chapter 2 of Part 3 of the resulting Employment Rights Bill makes provision for the establishment of a Special Negotiating Body ('SNB') for the Social Care Sector. The Bill confers upon the Secretary of State the power to make regulations giving legal effect to agreements of the SNB at the level of individual contracts of workers in the sector.[100] The Bill also grants the Secretary of State the power to set wages and terms of employment by regulation directly if the SNB fails to reach an agreement.[101] Some 40 or so years after the repeal of Schedule 11, it seems that the compulsory normative effect of collective agreements is about to return to British labour law.[102]

Ensuring the normative effect of *all* sectoral and enterprise agreements according to the principle of favourability, as is currently the case in most mainland European systems and as envisaged for the EU as a whole by the Adequate Minimum Wages Directive, is still some way off for the UK.[103] Until that nettle is grasped for the whole of the economy and not just certain sectors, British employers will continue to try to escape the terms of collective agreements through contractual variations, with a dismissal and re-engagement the ultimate weapon at their disposal. The Employment Rights Bill addresses the 'fire and rehire'

[98] UK Government, *Next Steps to Make Work Pay* (2024) [19].

[99] ibid.

[100] Employment Rights Bill 2025, cl 43 (the version of the Bill as it stood at the end of March 2025 is the one cited here).

[101] ibid cl 45.

[102] Under cl 44 of the Bill, once the Secretary of State makes regulations to give effect to a fair pay agreement, in so far as the agreement refers to the remuneration of any worker, 'the worker's remuneration is to be determined and paid in accordance with the agreement' (cl 44(2)), while 'a provision of the agreement that relates to any other term or condition of a social care worker's employment has effect as term of the worker's contract' (cl 44(3)). Clause 44 also contains an anti-avoidance provision: 'A term of that contract has no effect to the extent that it makes provision that is prohibited by, or inconsistent with, the agreement'. Under cl 47, the enforcement provisions of NMWA 1998 are applied mutatis mutandis to the provisions of a fair pay agreement in so far as they apply to remuneration.

[103] In addition to the social care sector, the Employment Rights Bill makes provision for fair pay agreements for just one other group, school support staff (cl 35 and Sch 4).

issue by introducing a new category of automatically unfair dismissal in cases where an employer is seeking to bring about a contractual variation to which the employee does not agree or aiming to 'employ another person, or to re-engage the employee, under a varied contract of employment to carry out substantially the same duties as the employee carried out before being dismissed'.[104] This provision will not do much, in itself, to mitigate the risk of 'fire and rehire', not just because of the exception allowed to the employer in cases of 'financial difficulties',[105] but because, in the light of *McKenzie*,[106] the remedies available to an unfairly dismissed employee are confined to compensation. What is needed is, again, a mechanism akin to the civil law 'act-condition',[107] through which the collectively agreed terms, at sector or enterprise level, automatically flow back into any agreement made by the employer for the work in question, with the dismissed employee or their replacement, preventing derogation *in pejus* at the level of the individual contract.

C. Enlarging the Scope for Derogation *in melius*

Section 203 ERA 1996 explicitly rules out derogation *in pejus* but, as we have seen, is silent on the possibility of, let alone the necessity for, derogation *in melius*. In the light of *Johnson* and *Edwards*, it is essential, in any measure enacting new employment rights or strengthening existing ones, to make the scope for derogation *in melius* explicit. Models for doing this exist in the 'non-regression' and 'more favourable conditions' clauses found in international labour instruments. Thus, according to Article 19.8 of the ILO Constitution:

> In no case shall the adoption of any Convention or Recommendation by the Conference, or the ratification of any Convention by any Member, be deemed to affect any law, award, custom or agreement which ensures more favourable conditions to the workers concerned than those provided for in the Convention or Recommendation.

Article 16 of the AMWD, following earlier EU law precedents, reads:

> 1. This Directive shall not constitute valid grounds for reducing the general level of protection already provided to workers within Member States, in particular with regard to the lowering or abolition of minimum wages.
> 2. This Directive shall not affect Member States' prerogative to apply or to introduce laws, regulations or administrative provisions which are more favourable to workers or to encourage or permit the application of collective agreements which are more favourable to workers. It shall not be construed as preventing Member States from increasing statutory minimum wages.

[104] Employment Rights Bill 2024, cl 26, inserting new s 104I ERA 1996.
[105] This phrase is contained in the new s 104I(4) ERA 1996, as set out in cl 26 of the Bill.
[106] [2020] IRLR 324; above, section III.A.
[107] Section VII.A above.

Suitably adapted, these clauses should be used with a view to addressing the 'ceiling' approach in *Johnson* and *Edwards*. This would entail amending section 203 and equivalent anti-avoidance devices so that they also operate as 'more favourable conditions' clauses. Unless this step is taken, the risk of *Johnson*-type reasoning remains.

VIII. Conclusion

The civil law principle of favourability might seem a long way removed from English law. Some of the leading decisions in employment and labour law of the past 20 years, from *Johnson* and *Edwards* through to *McKenzie* and *Deliveroo*, are hard to justify when viewed through the favourability lens. However, the principle is not entirely absent from British labour law, as is evident from the written statement case law and the *Autoclenz*, *Uber*, and *USDAW* decisions. Explicit recognition of the principle would help bring interpretive coherence to issues which include the employment status of gig workers and the fire and rehire debate. The inclusion of non-regression and more favourable conditions clauses in future legislation, alongside existing anti-avoidance provisions such as ERA 1996 section 203, would help mitigate the effects of the wrong turning taken in *Johnson v Unisys* and reduce the risk of it being repeated.

3

The Variation of Commercial and Employment Contracts: Revisiting the Question of Explicit Worker Consent

DAVID CABRELLI

> When persons have bound themselves by a contract, not simply to do some one thing, but to continue doing something … for a prolonged period, without any power of revoking the engagement, which their perseverance in that course of conduct would otherwise raise in favour of its being advantageous to them, does not exist; and any … presumption which can be grounded on their having voluntarily entered into the contract … is commonly next to null.*

I. Introduction

In the above quote, Mill remarks that where contracting parties are deprived of the ability to change their mind and vary a contract, they cannot be treated as having consented to enter into or remain bound by it. Is Mill's characterisation of a contract that ties the hands of its protagonists without any escape hatch an accurate one from a legal perspective? Must a commercial contract – or a contract of employment for that matter – that possesses no machinery for its own ongoing adjustment be treated in such a way that any understanding of it being consensual is entirely illusory? This idea of tainted consent is challengeable for two reasons. First, by entering into a contract containing terms limiting one's future course of action, by definition, one has exercised one's consent to put oneself into that position for better or for worse: agreeing to be bound to act or not to act in a particular way restricts one's future freedom, but that situation is ultimately a product of the manifestation of one's consent and liberty.[1] And second, it is something of a mantra that all contracts, including employment contracts, can be varied with the

* JS Mill, *Principles of Political Economy* (Kitchener, Batoche Books, 2000) 1111.

[1] *cf* T Raphael, 'Tying Your Own Hands' (2022) 138 *Law Quarterly Review* 299.

mutual agreement of the contracting parties in any particular manner,[2] unless the parties have agreed in advance that their consent to modify their contract terms in the future must adhere to a particular form.[3] On this basis, the passage from Mill seems misconceived to the extent that it is suggested it is representative of contract law or employment law. However, one of the themes of this chapter is that it would be too hasty to be overly dismissive of Mill's basic point. As will become apparent, if the contracting party – with the superior bargaining power – or the employer A decides to adjust contractual or working practices and patterns without the explicit consent of the counterparty or employee B, there is the unvarnished reality that the law governing both commercial and employment contracts will act as nothing more than a minor irritant. Seen from that perspective, the notion that consent is in fact tainted and little but a fiction raises its head once again.

I cannot lay claim to any particular originality in addressing the role of the law of variation in shaping the normative content of commercial contracts or the contract of employment: others writing in the field of contract and labour law have done so before.[4] My objective in writing this chapter is to build upon this existing body of scholarship by adding something novel by way of insight(s) to the existing debate(s). Having first digested and analysed what is undoubtedly a complex morass of case-law material governing the law of variation (some of which appears to be conflicting in places), I will do this by focusing specifically on the implications of reforming the law governing the variation of commercial and employment contracts to tighten up the requirement for express counterparty or employee consent.

The structure of this chapter is as follows. Sections II and III set out how contract and employment law intercede between the core tension lying at the core of the orthodox static legal understanding of the commercial contract and contract of employment, and the reality of the dynamism of contractual and employment relationships. As part of that discussion, I will provide an account of the relevant legal rules, principally derived from the case law. These sections demonstrate how (and explain why) employment law imposes rules that act as little more than a nuisance on the ability of the employer to impose a variation without the employee's express consent and how this informs the question of whether the law governing variation ought to be adjusted. In particular, it

[2] *Robinson v Page* (1826) 3 Russ 114; *Wandsworth London BC v D'Silva* [1998] IRLR 193, 197 (Lord Wolff MR).

[3] *Rock Advertising Ltd v MWB Business Exchange Centres Ltd* [2018] UKSC 24, [2019] AC 119. Here, both of the contracting parties provided that any future variation of the terms of the contract would have to adhere to a particular form, in which case the issue was whether any subsequent non-compliant modification mutually agreed by them both was valid: it was held that the relevant provision was binding, and the non-compliant adjustment was of no effect.

[4] P Davies and M Freedland, *Labour Law: Text and Materials*, 2nd edn (London, Weidenfeld and Nicholson, 1984) 289–90; Freedland (n 1) 237–252; M Freedland and N Kountouris, *The Legal Construction of Personal Work Relations* (Oxford, Oxford University Press, 2011) 207–213; N Countouris and A Sanders, 'Variation and Suspension of the Contract of Employment and its Terms' in M Freedland et al. (eds), *The Contract of Employment* (Oxford, Oxford University Press, 2016) 492.

is shown how the part played by employee consent can effectively be elided by harnessing techniques and options made available by the common law. In section IV, the case for reforming the law of variation governing employment contracts to expand the requirement for the consent of the employee is described and critiqued. I make the point that it is open to question whether the legal position can be justified, particularly in light of the inequality of bargaining power and subordination present in the employment relationship. The principal insight offered by this chapter is that notwithstanding these concerns, reforming employment laws to diverge from contractual orthodoxy and restrain the ability of employers to vary contractual terms would be a mistake: it would have knock-on practical consequences on the behaviour and approach of employers towards the termination of the employment contract.[5] In effect, such changes to employment law would generate perverse incentives, insofar as by constraining the capacity of employers to change the terms of the employment contract, the more appealing firing (and rehiring or replacing) intransigent employees would become to them. And the so-called impending legislative 'ban' on 'fire and rehire' and 'fire and replace' in the Employment Rights Bill will at once fail to alter this reality and simply strengthen the force of this point. Finally, section V collates each of the separate strands considered in the preceding discussion and concludes.

II. The Nature of a Commercial Contract and the Relationship between Commercial Contractors

Imagine a written commercial contract where two parties establish a long-term relationship involving the mutual expectation of ongoing cooperation, but fail to include a provision clarifying its duration. As such, on its face, the contractual relationship is indefinite and envisages the ongoing exchange of mutual commitments; for want of a better phrase, we may call it a 'relational contract'.[6] After a period of time has elapsed, the question arises as to whether each of the contracting parties has the right, without limit of time, to continue to insist on the observance of the written terms of the original contract as struck at the formation of their relationship. In other words, is the written contract 'an initial treaty [whose provisions must at all times be honoured and] which remains in force until its termination'?[7] Alternatively, does contract law provide for a default rule

[5] M Freedland, *The Contract of Employment* (Oxford, Clarendon Press, 1976) 40.

[6] See *Yam Seng Pte Ltd v International Trade Corp Ltd* [2013] EWHC 111 (QB), [2013] 1 All ER (Comm) 1321; *Al Nehayan v Kent* [2018] EWHC 333 (Comm), [2018] 1 CLC 216; *Bates v Post Office Ltd (No 3: Common Issues)* [2019] EWHC 606 (QB).

[7] Freedland (n 1) 237. Historically, a variation of contract was treated as a termination of contract and subsequent re-engagement (*Morris v Baron & Co* [1918] AC 1), but that has not been the case for a long time now, see eg, *Kerry Foods Ltd v Lynch* [2005] IRLR 680 in the employment context.

that enables the contracting parties to amend the terms of the contract?[8] Well, the answer is clear. The orthodox rules of contract law stipulate that a contract, forged between two parties on the basis of agreement and an intention to be bound, can indeed be altered subsequently by their mutual consent: this is what we may call 'the general rule'.[9] This rule is the traditional legal response to the reality that when reduced to writing, a commercial contract is generally static and frozen in aspic at the point of formation.

Without any legal means of ongoing modification of the written contract, the position of the contracting parties would become wholly invidious. There are two overlapping and interdependent rationales for this claim. First, for the reason that commercial contracts that provide for an ongoing relationship – unlike a commercial sales contract, which envisages a short-term and predictable exchange – are characterised by incompleteness in the sense that there is a high degree of uncertainty about future performance of the parties' obligations.[10] At the inception of the contractual relationship, the parties are unable to be 'specific about the expected outcomes of their performance': but '[t]his indeterminacy is neither a failure of contractual draftsmanship, nor caused by an inability to foresee contingencies, but is rather a feature of a co-operative business venture in which methods and goals will be revised in light of experience.'[11] It is also more economical to recognise a law of variation rather than leave the contracting parties to incur the recurring upfront transaction costs that are involved in contemplating and drafting the commercial contract to cover every conceivable future contingency in advance.[12] To that extent, the branch of the law of contract that concerns variation is one of the gap-filling techniques supplied by contract law.[13] As a result, ongoing ex post adaptation of their working relationship is essential. The second justification for the claim that the parties' relationship would soon become unenviable in the absence of a legal rule permitting variation is that commercial relationships involve many interactions between people, goods, and services, which are constantly evolving and dynamic. As such, the contracting parties' performance of their obligations is subject to fluctuations and ongoing (technical and other) reorganisation as a matter of economic necessity. The fundamental point here is that room for the parties to manoeuvre is essential so that they can engage in recurring relational and cooperative exchanges.

How does the common law and statute mediate between the static nature of the legal understanding of contract and the evolutionary dynamism of the commercial

[8] I leave to the side the question whether termination of the contract is possible on the service of reasonable notice.

[9] *Robinson v Page* (1826) 3 Russ 114.

[10] H Collins, *Regulating Contracts* (Oxford, Oxford University Press, 1999) 160–172.

[11] H Collins, 'Employment as a Relational Contract' (2021) 137 *Law Quarterly Review* 426, 430.

[12] PS Davies and P Sales, 'Controlling Contract Discretions: *Wednesbury* Reasonableness, Good Faith and Proper Purposes' (2024) 140 *Law Quarterly Review* 106, 112–113.

[13] Alongside the law of implication of contractual terms (in fact or in law): H Collins, 'Legal Responses to the Standard Form Contract of Employment' (2007) 36 *Industrial Law Journal* 2, 7–10.

relationship? In other words, how does the law governing commercial contracts provide that necessary room for manoeuvre to both facilitate and restrain adjustments proposed by one of the contracting parties to the contract terms? Well, first, obviously, there is the general rule. However, this will only operate where both parties provide their explicit assent, and the question that raises its head concerns what the law says in the absence of mutual agreement, ie, where the counterparty is either silent, disagrees that its actions are indicative of consent, or expressly rejects the variation. What is particularly clear is that in such circumstances, the space occupied by future consent is malleable, inasmuch as the law recognises that the need for mutual future consent can become either attenuated or fall away altogether. For example, where A confers upon themselves a unilateral power in the written contract (in unambiguous terms) to vary the contract without the consent of B, such a contractual provision fully removing the future autonomy of B (to stick with the original term or to change its mind) is perfectly lawful, as is any subsequent variation (on the strength of that clause) imposed by A.[14] Likewise, if A has reserved no such power to vary a provision of the written contract, and A makes it clear to B that A intends to modify a term of the contract but B is silent in response, assent on the part of B may or may not be implied. For example, if A simply gives B unilateral notification of the proposed alteration, then in the absence of B's express consent, the variation will be ineffective.[15] However, if the conduct of B is such that, when viewed objectively, B has manifested their agreement to vary and consideration is present, then consent will be implied.[16] A classic manifestation of such agreement on the part of B is where B continues to perform their obligations under the contract without any demur or protest. Finally, there is the situation where A presents a proposal to B to adjust a term of the contract and B makes it abundantly clear that they are rejecting the change. In such a case, A will have the 'nuclear' option available, namely the termination of the commercial contract on the service of reasonable notice on B and the immediate service of an offer on B to enter into a fresh commercial contract which is identical, with the exception of the addition of the rejected adjusted term.[17] The reason that I have categorised this option as 'nuclear' is that there is no compulsion on the part of B to agree to continue contractual relations with A. To that extent, B may decide to refuse to accept A's offer of the new commercial contract and instead, search the commercial market to find a new contractor. In that way, this option is a route that is open to A, but it is fraught with uncertainty and risk from a practical commercial perspective.

[14] H Beale (ed), *Chitty on Contracts*, 35th edn, (London, Sweet & Maxwell, 2023) para 26-041 and *May and Butcher Ltd v R* [1934] 2 KB 17, 21 (Viscount Dunedin).

[15] *Cowey v Liberian Operations Ltd* [1966] 2 Lloyd's Rep 45.

[16] *Minevco Ltd v Barratt Southern Ltd* 2000 SLT 790; *Crimond Estates Ltd v Mile End Developments Ltd* 2021 GWD 11-141.

[17] As noted above, this is what a variation of contract was historically considered to be: *Morris v Baron & Co* [1918] AC 1.

Where a party A has the benefit of a clause in a written commercial contract, which empowers it to unilaterally vary the terms without the consent of the counterparty B, as we have seen, any modification by A without B's agreement will be valid, and the clause will be respected. However, the law provides a measure of protection for B. It does so via the mechanism of a distinctive contractual technique or criterion, albeit that its juridical nature and scope is hitherto somewhat undertheorised.[18] In short, I will refer to this construct as the '*Braganza* criterion'.[19] The small print of this rule of contract law is that any decision taken by A pursuant to the discretion conferred in favour of A (as an express term of the contract) must be exercised honestly, rationally, and in good faith as a means of upholding the reasonable expectations of the contracting parties.[20] In addition, the test of honesty, rationality and good faith also applies to the process adopted by A leading up to the decision to use the unilateral contractual power to vary. As such, by focusing on both process and outcome, the test is similar to *Wednesbury* unreasonableness,[21] and the academic literature has charted how it has come to pass that this standard of review has been transposed from public law to contract law.[22]

My justification for describing the *Braganza* criterion as 'undertheorised' is that neither its juridical nature nor its doctrinal position in contract law has been

[18] See *Socimer International Bank Ltd v Standard Bank London Ltd* [2008] EWCA Civ 116, [2008] 1 Lloyd's Rep 558 and *Braganza v BP Shipping Ltd* [2015] UKSC 17, [2015] 1 WLR 1661.

[19] Named after the UK Supreme Court case of *Braganza v BP Shipping Ltd* [2015] UKSC 17, [2015] 1 WLR 1661.

[20] There is a separate, significant, question and that is whether the unilateral variation clause in favour of A confers a discretion/power in favour of A, or an absolute contractual right. The Court of Appeal has ruled that where the clause confers an absolute contractual right, the restraints and controls exerted by the *Braganza* criterion will not apply: *Mid Essex Hospital Services NHS Trust v Compass Group UK and Ireland Ltd (t/a/ Medirest)* [2013] EWCA Civ 200, [2013] BLR 265. For example, the High Court has held that the right of a contracting party to terminate the contract in terms of an express termination clause, or in response to a repudiatory breach is an absolute contracting right, rather than a discretion: *Monde Petroleum SA v WesternZagros Ltd* [2016] EWHC 1472 (Comm), [2017] 1 All ER (Comm) 1009; *TAQA Britani Ltd v Rockrose UKCS8 LLC* [2020] EWHC 58 (Comm), [2020] 2 Lloyd's Rep 64; *Lombard North Central plc v European Skyjets Ltd* [2022] EWHC 728 (QB) [152] (Foxton J). However, in *Tesco v USDAW* [2024] UKSC 28, [2025] ICR 107, 143D–144A and 144G–145A [116]–[117] and [120], in obiter dicta, Lord Leggatt rejected the distinction between a contractual discretion/power and absolute contractual right forged by the Court of Appeal in *Mid Essex Hospital Services NHS Trust* and the application of that jurisprudence in *Monde Petroleum* and *TAQA Britani* to a contracting party's right to terminate.

[21] *Associated Provincial Picture Houses Ltd v Wednesbury Corporation* [1948] 1 KB 223.

[22] See D Oliver, *Common Values and the Public-Private Divide* (London, Butterworths, 1999) ch 8; T Daintith, 'Contractual Discretion and Administrative Discretion: A Unified Analysis' (2005) 68 *Modern Law Review* 554; J Morgan, 'Resisting Judicial Review of Discretionary Contractual Powers' [2015] *Lloyd's Maritime and Commercial Law Quarterly* 483; C Himsworth, 'Transplanting Irrationality from Public to Private Law: *Braganza v BP Shipping Ltd*' (2019) 23 *Edinburgh Law Review* 1; E Lim & C Chan, 'Problems with *Wednesbury* Unreasonableness in Contract Law; Lessons from Public Law' (2019) 135 *Law Quarterly Review* 88; M Bridge, 'The Exercise of Contractual Discretion' (2019) 135 *Law Quarterly Review* 227; A Bogg and M Freedland, 'Pensions Law, *IBM v Dalgleish* and the Public/Private Divide' in S Agnew, PS Davies and C Mitchell (eds), *Pensions: Law, Policy, and Practice* (Oxford, Hart Publishing, 2020) 223, 229–236; Davies and Sales (n 12).

sufficiently clarified. In many respects, it resembles an implied term in law, ie, a contractual term that is a necessary incident of a particular class of contract and implied into every contract of that type in question, based on 'wider' or 'general' policy considerations.[23] For example, Bogg and Freedland have argued that the *Braganza* criterion is an implied term in law.[24] Their position is predicated on its functional equivalence to the term of mutual trust and confidence that is implied as a matter of law into all contracts of employment. There is some force in this contention, since in *Braganza v BP Shipping Ltd*, both Lord Hodge and Baroness Hale seemed to equate or locate the *Braganza* criterion with, or within, the implied term of mutual trust and confidence.[25] While persuasive, the difficulty I have with the claim that the *Braganza* criterion is either a free-standing implied term in law or one that falls within the rubric of the implied term of mutual trust and confidence is that it is an axiomatic principle of contract law that an implied term in law can only be implied into an identifiable class of contract. And what is particularly hazy is the specific kind of contract in respect of which a '*Braganza* implied term' in law might arise. After all, the *Braganza* criterion has been applied to police contractual discretionary powers in many different kinds of commercial and non-commercial contracts, as well as employment contracts. One solution to this conundrum might be to evoke the concept of a 'relational contract' as the hook onto which a '*Braganza* implied term' in law would hang. But, whilst superficially appealing, this would raise as many questions as it answers. First, owing to the fact that the definition, content, meaning, and scope of a 'relational contract' are inherently vague: Davies and Sales have critiqued the concept on the grounds of its lack of stability and slipperiness.[26] And second, this would result in considerable overlap with the *Yam Seng* implied term in fact of good faith, which could lead to doctrinal incoherence.[27] In light of these reservations, in my view, the *Braganza* criterion is best thought of as a rule of contract law that operates as an aid to the interpretation of a particular sort of express term in a contract, ie, a clause conferring a contractual discretion. In that way, rather than conceptualising it as something that inserts implied terms in law into contracts, I would argue that it forms part of the law of contractual interpretation. And the *Braganza* criterion can be thought of as an interpretative technique that enables the courts to attribute meaning to clauses conferring discretion or power in favour of a contracting party by both supplying a particular context for the interpretative exercise and

[23] *Lister v Romford Ice and Cold Storage Co Ltd* [1957] AC 555, 576 (Viscount Simonds); *Liverpool City Council v Irwin* [1977] AC 239, 254F–255C (Lord Wilberforce); *Malik v BCCI* [1998] AC 20, 45–46 (Lord Steyn); and *Scally v Southern Health and Social Services Board* [1992] 1 AC 294, 306G–307F [12] (Lord Bridge). See also G Golding, *Shaping Contracts for Work* (Oxford, Oxford University Press, 2023) 159.

[24] Bogg and Freedland (n 22).

[25] [2015] 1 WLR 1661, 1673B-D, 1674D-G and 1677F-H and 1679C-H (Baroness Hale and Lord Hodge). However, Lord Neuberger was somewhat dismissive of this conflation, 1688D-H.

[26] Davies and Sales (n 12) 107 and 119–125.

[27] On this point, see the discussion below and Davies and Sales (n 12) 119.

establishing a set of reasonable presumptions regarding the probable content of such contractual provisions.

Pursuant to the standard prescribed by the *Braganza* criterion, the contracting party B, seeking to challenge the variation by A in terms of A's unilateral contractual power, must persuade the court that no rational or honest commercial contractor in the same or broadly similar position to A would have exercised that clause in the same manner that A had done in the case in question, either in terms of process or outcome. For example, famously, in *Paragon Finance plc v Nash*, a mortgage provider A reserved a contractual power enabling it to vary the interest rate it charged B under a consumer credit contract.[28] The interest charges that A had fixed bore no relationship to those offered by competing lenders in the same marketplace. When A unilaterally altered the interest rate and it was challenged by B as too high, the court found in favour of A on the ground that recent problems with its finances meant that it had to pass on an increasing number of its costs to its customers. In that way, although A's approach in charging the varied rate was unusual in the lending market, it could not be said to be irrational, arbitrary, dishonest, or in bad faith.

A pressing, but closely related, issue that is underdeveloped is the relationship between the *Braganza* criterion and the nascent implied term in fact of good faith – recognised in the *Yam Seng*, *Al Nehayan v Kent*, and *Bates v Post Office* line of cases ('*Yam Seng* implied term').[29] The English courts have held that the latter implied term functions to control the behaviour of commercial parties in the case of relational contracts, which naturally betrays a considerable amount of overlap with the *Braganza* criterion. By way of explanation, pursuant to the *Yam Seng* implied term, the contracting parties are obliged to act reasonably, honestly and with fidelity to the bargain or the substance of the contractual benefit bargained for, having regard to the interests of the parties and the provisions, aims, and purposes of the contract, objectively ascertained.[30] Seen from this perspective, by occupying similar regulatory and functional territory – and bearing in mind the similarity in the small print of the *Yam Seng* implied term and the *Braganza* criterion and their mutual open-textured nature – the question must be asked whether they are somehow the same thing or whether a convincing distinction can be crafted between each of them and their respective roles? In my view, there are at least four differences (and perhaps more). First, on its face, the *Yam Seng* implied term does much more than simply restrain the exercise of discretion or power conferred by an express contractual term. Its purpose is much broader, applying to all sorts of conduct and behaviour of the contracting parties, provided, of course, that it is a relational contract. Second, being characterised as a criterion applicable in the law of contractual interpretation (rather than implication), the *Braganza* criterion is not limited in its application to relational contracts. Instead, it imposes constraints

[28] *Paragon Finance plc v Nash* [2013] EWCA Civ 200, [2013] BLR 265.
[29] (n 6).
[30] *Al Nehayan v Kent* [2018] EWHC 333 (Comm), [2018] 1 CLC 216, 272F-G (Leggatt LJ).

on parties to all sorts or classes of contract, since the crucial factor is whether there is an express reservation of a contractual discretion. Third, unlike the *Braganza* criterion – which is one-dimensional in its restrictive capacity inasmuch as it holds the party with an express contractual discretion to account – the *Yam Seng* implied term can conceivably restrain the conduct of either of the contracting parties. Finally, there is an obvious difference between the *Braganza* criterion and the *Yam Seng* implied term to the effect that the latter is an implied term *in fact*, whereas, in my view, the former operates more in the manner of an aid to, or canon of, interpretation.[31] In that way, the precise juridical basis and justification for their legal recognition differ: in the case of the *Braganza* criterion, it is a tool that forms part of the court's general interpretative armoury, whereas the *Yam Seng* implied term is predicated on it being necessary, because, 'without [it], the [relational] contract would lack commercial or practical coherence'.[32]

Another key issue for consideration stems from the aforementioned point that the *Yam Seng* implied term is two-dimensional in nature, with the capacity to impose obligations on both contracting parties. For example, imagine circumstances in which contracting party A attempts to vary a relational commercial contract to increase various charges levied on B and B expressly withholds its consent. The question here is whether the courts would be persuaded to recognise the existence of the *Yam Seng* implied term to hold B to account in failing to consent on the basis that B's conduct constitutes a breach of the implied obligation to act in good faith. While seemingly far-fetched, one could conceivably see it as a relevant legal consideration where party A has sound commercial reasons for imposing the variation, eg, where A has sustained a sudden spike in utility or fuel costs or inflation and aims to pass on some or all of those costs onto B by way of additional charges. One might conjecture that the courts should make contracting parties such as B subject to the *Yam Seng* implied term so that their behaviour can be policed to ensure the continuation of fair dealing in a commercial relationship. On the other hand, the counterargument is that for the courts to deploy the *Yam Seng* implied term in this way smacks of illegitimacy insofar as it would appear to result in them rewriting the contract to save party A from a bad bargain.

[31] However, it should be highlighted that Lord Leggatt has remarked that the *Yam Seng* implied term could just as easily be an implied term in law 'on the basis that the nature of the contract as a relational contract implicitly requires (in the absence of a contrary indication) treating it as involving an obligation of good faith': *Al Nehayan v Kent* [2018] EWHC 333 (Comm), [2018] 1 CLC 216, 272C-D. I am sceptical about the accuracy of this claim for the same reasons given above regarding the inherent uncertainty in the meaning of a 'relational contract'. It should also be stressed that it would not be the first time that the courts have perhaps become a little confused over the nature of an implied term they have recognised and whether it is in law or in fact, eg, in the employment context, see H Collins, 'Implied Terms: The Foundation in Good Faith and Fair Dealing' (2014) 67 *Current Legal Problems* 297, 304–309 and H Collins, 'Implied Terms in the Contract of Employment' in M Freedland et al. (eds), *The Contract of Employment* (Oxford, Oxford University Press, 2016) 471, 480.

[32] *Marks & Spencer Plc v BNP Paribas Securities Services Trust Company (Jersey) Ltd* [2015] UKSC 72, [2015] 3 WLR 1843, 1851D (Lord Neuberger). See also *Secretary of State for the Department for Environment, Food and Rural Affairs v PCSU* [2024] UKSC 41, [2024] 3 WLR 1059, 1084D-1086F (Lord Sales and Lady Simler) and 1098G-1100B (Lord Burrows).

Indeed, the courts have said that they are generally only willing to imply a good faith obligation in respect of the parties' performance of their obligations under the contract, rather than in respect of their actions or omissions during the process of the formation of the contract. And it seems to me that for similar reasons, the courts would be unlikely to imply a good faith obligation to compel a contracting party to accept a variation against their will. What's more, on one view, the *Yam Seng* implied term would be inconsistent with the existing express term conferring the discretionary power in favour of A.

III. The Nature of the Contract of Employment and the Employment Relationship

The contract of employment and employment relationship share some of the aforementioned features with their commercial counterpart. For example, the contract of employment is bedevilled by the same 'static' versus 'dynamic' question,[33] and like the relational commercial contract, it is also characterised by incompleteness, is relational in nature, and demands ongoing cooperation and commitment between the parties.[34] Furthermore, the background environment against which the employer and employee originally contracted also evolves over time, eg, owing to 'regulatory changes, technological development, changing market conditions … business restructuring, the emergence of new working and human resource management practices … [and] the accumulation of skills and knowledge on the part of the workers within the enterprise'.[35] There is an underlying tension here between the employer's interests in effecting continuous changes and the employee's competing interest in sustained stability in working practices, patterns, and methods. As such, in what way do the common law and statute intercede between the static nature of the employment contract and the employee's interests in the maintenance of contractual stability on the one hand, and on the other, the dynamism of the employment relationship to provide the employer with the room they need to adjust themselves to oscillations in underlying market conditions?

The starting point for the discussion is that neither the employer nor the employee has the benefit of any implied contractual right to vary unilaterally the terms of the contract.[36] As such, variation must be by mutual consent, ie, the

[33] For a well-known example, see Case 426/11 *Alemo-Herron v Parkwood Leisure Ltd* ECLI:EU:C:2013:521, [2013] ICR 1116.

[34] W Brown and D Rea, 'The Changing Nature of the Employment Contract' (1995) 42 *Scottish Journal of Political Economy* 363, 363–4; *Johnson v Unisys Ltd* [2003] 1 AC 518, 532F–539C (Lords Steyn and Hoffmann); *Autoclenz Ltd v Belcher* [2011] ICR 1157, 1168E–G (Lord Clarke); *Uber BV v Aslam* [2015] UKSC 17, [2015] 1 WLR 1661, 1679E (Lord Hodge).

[35] Countouris and Sanders (n 4) 493.

[36] *Securities and Facilities Division v Hayes* [2001] IRLR 81, 85 (Peter Gibson LJ).

general rule applies.[37] However, it is peppered with a morass of exceptions – which comprise a 'permissive regime'[38] – whereby there is ample scope for a variation to be valid and enforceable in the absence of the explicit consent of the employee.[39] The means employed to effect a variation without employee consent can be usefully corralled into two distinctive groups. First, there are those that involve direct forms of variation of the terms of the contract of employment, which can be compared with the alternative, constituting much more indirect means of effecting change. I turn initially to the direct forms of modification, and there are three in particular. These are variations effected via the exercise of a flexibility clause or unilateral variation clause and finally where there is no written contractual provision, but the employer puts into effect a variation with the implied – rather than express/explicit – assent of the employee.

A. Direct Variation

The point of departure for my analysis of direct variation is the flexibility clause. This is a reference to a provision of a written contract of employment that empowers the employer to modify the employee's job responsibilities and tasks. An example would be a clause that provides that the employee is hired as an accountant, subject to any additional or other work required by the employer as may be necessary to meet the needs of the employer's business from time to time. If the employer were to alter the employee's position to remove some of the duties of the accountant, this would be effective in terms of the flexibility clause. However, there are measures recognised by the law to control this sort of variation. In *Land Securities Trillium Ltd v Thornley*,[40] an in-house architect's responsibilities were changed from a leadership and hands-on architect role in respect of large projects from inception to completion to one that was principally managerial in nature, entailing oversight of externally instructed firms of architects. The change pursuant to the flexibility clause involved a change in job title and also the omission of the key leadership element. The employee claimed that this effectively deskilled her, as it would make it more difficult for her to secure alternative employment as a practicing architect. The Employment Appeal Tribunal (EAT) agreed and ruled that the employer's exercise of the flexibility clause imposed a completely new job

[37] *Wandsworth London BC v D'Silva* [1998] IRLR 193, 197 (Lord Wolff MR).

[38] Freedland and Kountouris (n 4) 207.

[39] Which is odd in light of the 'elective' theory adopted by other areas of contract law, eg, see *White and Carter (Councils) Ltd v McGregor* [1962] AC 413 and *Société Générale (London Branch) v Geys* [2012] UKSC 63, [2013] 1 AC 523.

[40] *Land Securities Trillium Ltd v Thornley* [2005] IRLR 765. For a very similar, more recent, case, see *McCormack v Medivet Group Ltd* [2024] EWHC 1000 (Comm), albeit that the employee also argued that the employer's exercise of the flexibility clause amounted to a breach of the *Braganza* criterion. The employee was successful in this argument, ie, that the employer had not acted rationally, honestly or in good faith in applying the flexibility clause.

description and role on the employee, constituting a fundamental breach of the contract of employment. As such, she had been constructively dismissed.[41] In the final analysis, flexibility clauses are no panacea for employers who are seeking to vary the terms of an employee's contract, to the extent that the degree of change must fall within the existing scope of the job rather than amount to a significant change in the content of the duties contractually owed.

The unilateral variation clause is a play on the flexibility clause. Both clauses incorporate a reservation by the employer of the right to change the terms of the contract of employment without the employee's consent. On their face, they are legally valid,[42] and that is irrespective of whether they feature in the written contract of employment or a staff handbook.[43] However, that is only to the extent that they are clear and unambiguous and the courts are assiduous in policing matters here.[44] One might conjecture that the rationale for such a strict intensity of review can be laid at the door of the absence of express employee consent. For example, in *Norman v Audit Office*,[45] the EAT refused to recognise a unilateral variation clause where it provided that:

> The following … summarise[s] the main current terms and conditions of your employment … Detailed particulars of conditions of service are to be found in the relevant sections of the HR Manual … They are subject to amendment; any significant changes affecting staff in general will be notified by … Policy Circulars … while changes affecting your particular terms and conditions will be notified separately to you.[46]

In the view of the EAT, this wording came:

> nowhere near being clear and unambiguous … it does not seem to us that [the] clause … is in its language clearly reserving the right to amend unilaterally … we take the view that the words '[t]hey are subject to amendment' and the words that follow … establish nothing more than the fact of amendment and the need for notification. They do not in any way establish what the mechanism of amendment might be'.[47]

On that basis, the EAT issued a declaration to the effect that the employee's contractual terms remained unchanged.

The 'clear and unambiguous' test is not the only technique that the law adopts to control unilateral variation clauses. A further restraint on their exercise is presented by the implied term in law enjoining both parties to maintain

[41] A repudiatory breach of contract amounts to a constructive dismissal at common law and under the statutory unfair dismissal regime: *Western Excavating (ECC) Ltd v Sharp* [1978] QB 761.

[42] *Wandsworth London BC v D'Silva* [1998] IRLR 193.

[43] *Bateman v Asda Stores Ltd* [2010] IRLR 370; *Sparks v Department for Transport* [2016] IRLR 519. See F Reynold and J Hendy, 'Reserving the Right to Change Terms and Conditions: How Far Can the Employer Go?' (2012) 41 *Industrial Law Journal* 79.

[44] *Wandsworth London BC v D'Silva* [1998] IRLR 193, 197 (Lord Wolff MR).

[45] *Norman v Audit Office* [2015] IRLR 634. See also *Hart v St Mary's School (Colchester) Ltd* (UKEAT/0305/14, 8 January 2015); *Daniels v Lloyds Bank plc* [2018] IRLR 813 for similar cases.

[46] ibid 635 (Judge Hand QC).

[47] ibid 640 (Judge Hand QC).

mutual trust and confidence in the employment relationship.[48] Somewhat analogously to a flexibility clause,[49] the employer's exercise of the unilateral variation clause must be consistent with the obligations imposed by the implied term of mutual trust and confidence.[50] Stripped to its core, the implied term of mutual trust and confidence imposes obligations on both the employer and employee to perform their obligations and act generally in good faith by taking into account (as opposed to subordinating their own personal and financial interests to) the interests of the other party to the contract.[51] For example, in *Dresdner Kleinwort Ltd and Commerzbank AG v Attrill*,[52] a clause in a staff handbook contractually incorporated into the employee's employment contract conferred a unilateral power in favour of the employer to vary the terms of the handbook or the contract of employment in writing. The employer then introduced a material adverse change (MAC) clause pursuant to the unilateral variation provision that enabled it to modify the basis for the calculation of a discretionary bonus payable to the employee. When the employee claimed that the bonus payment was too low, it challenged the MAC clause on the basis that it represented the exercise of the contractual power of unilateral variation in a manner that was in breach of the implied term of mutual trust and confidence. The Court of Appeal agreed, ruling that the exercise of the unilateral variation clause via the MAC clause amounted to a 'volte face by the [employer]' relative to previous promises it had made not to change the measures involved in calculating bonuses.[53] For that reason, trust and confidence had been severely undermined and the implied term breached, thus invalidating the purported variation. This underscores the point that control of express or implied powers of variation by the implied term of mutual trust and confidence is not restricted to provision of reasonable notice as in *United Bank v Akhtar*.[54] Instead, the function of the implied term is wider and bears the capacity

[48] Famously recognised by the House of Lords in *Malik v BCCI* [1998] AC 20.

[49] The implied term of mutual trust and confidence was not invoked in *Land Securities Trillium Ltd* [2005] IRLR 765 to control the flexibility clause, since the question was whether the exercise of the clause amounted to a fundamental breach of the employment contract, which is a related, but different, question.

[50] Brodie has argued that if the employee in *Bateman v Asda Stores Ltd* [2010] IRLR 370 had claimed that the exercise of the clause was subject to the implied term of mutual trust and confidence, this may have resulted in the recognition of an attendant obligation on the part of the employer to provide the employee with reasonable notice of the variation: see D Brodie, '*Malik v BCCI*: The Impact of Good Faith' in J Adams-Prassl, A Bogg and ACL. Davies (eds), *Landmark Cases in Labour Law* (Oxford, Hart Publishing, 2022) 245, 264–265.

[51] *Eastwood v Magnox Electric plc* [2005] 1 AC 503, 523G (Lord Nicholls); *Imperial Group Pension Trust Ltd v Imperial Tobacco Ltd* [1991] ICR 524, 533 (Sir Browne-Wilkinson VC); *Johnson v Unisys Ltd* [2003] 1 AC 518, 536D (Lord Steyn); *Nottingham University v Fishel* [2000] ICR 1462, 1493C (Elias J). For discussion, see Lord Steyn, 'Contract Law: Fulfilling the Reasonable Expectations of Honest Men' (1997) 113 *Law Quarterly Review* 433, 442; D Brodie, 'Beyond Exchange: The New Contract of Employment' (1998) 27 *Industrial Law Journal* 79, 96–7; and D Brodie, 'Mutual Trust and the Values of the Employment Contract' (2001) 30 *Industrial Law Journal* 84, 94–96.

[52] *Dresdner Kleinwort Ltd and Commerzbank AG v Attrill* [2013] EWCA Civ 394, [2013] IRLR 548.

[53] ibid 562 (Elias LJ).

[54] *United Bank v Akhtar* [1989] IRLR 507.

to protect existing legal rights and quasi-equitable legitimate expectations,[55] eg, where the employer provides express or implied assurances that it will not withdraw some benefits which are (as in a case similar to the facts in *Tesco Stores Ltd v USDAW*),[56] or are not legally binding – but then applies a unilateral variation clause to ostensibly remove them.

A related issue I raise at this juncture represents a play on the question posed in section II above and the immediately preceding discussion, namely whether – in the absence of a flexibility or unilateral variation clause – an employer could evoke a legal technique of some sort to enable it to modify an express term notwithstanding the refusal of the employee's consent. To put the matter more directly, would it be legally possible for an employer to marshal the implied term of mutual trust and confidence to compel a non-consenting employee to accept the variation, lest the employee be held in breach of the attendant obligation to act in good faith imposed by the trust and confidence implied term? As far as I am aware, this is a hypothetical legal point that has never come before the courts or tribunals. In seeking to answer this question, it should first be pointed out that the implied term is by definition mutual. In that way, it imposes obligations on employees, and in some of the case law, it has been held that the employees were in breach.[57] Furthermore, if the employer's justifications for the change are commercially sensible, the tribunals and courts may be tempted to contemplate the deployment of the implied term to second-guess the employee's motives for withholding consent. Of course, the question is whether the courts would and should ride to the rescue of the employer in this way. On balance, although it would be theoretically possible for a court to rule that an employee's resistance was in breach of the implied term of mutual trust and confidence, the legal outcome will depend on the content of the contract of employment, the facts and circumstances of the case, including the behaviour of the employer in relying on the unilateral variation clause, and the employee's justifications for refusing consent.

Finally, I come to the most fraught technique available to an employer to effect a direct variation of an express term of a contract of employment without the express consent of the employee. The reason I say 'fraught' is that the courts are reluctant

[55] A Bogg, 'Good Faith in the Contract of Employment: A Case of the English Reserve?' (2011) 32 *Comparative Labor Law & Policy Journal* 729, 759–60; A Bogg, '*Bournemouth University Higher Education Corporation v Buckland*: Re-establishing Orthodoxy at the Expense of Coherence?' (2010) 39 *Industrial Law Journal* 408.

[56] *Tesco Stores Ltd v USDAW* [2024] UKSC 28, [2025] ICR 107. Having said that, in *Tesco Stores Ltd v USDAW*, rather than adopt a unilateral variation clause to reduce their employees' remuneration packages that they had provided past express assurances about, the employer fired and rehired the employees when the trade union and employees refused to accept the proposed variation. The Supreme Court implied a term in fact and provided the remedy of an injunction to the employees to prevent the employer from firing and rehiring. For commentary on the Court of Appeal's decision, see A Bogg and D Brodie, 'Every Little Helps: Permanent Benefits, Contract Interpretation and 'Fire and Rehire' (2023) 52 *Industrial Law Journal* 246, 262–263.

[57] *Briscoe v Lubrizol Ltd* [2002] IRLR 607; *RDF Media Group v Clements* [2008] IRLR 207; *Tubbenden Primary School v Sylvester* [2012] ICR D29; *Thomson Ecology Ltd v APEM Ltd* [2014] IRLR 184; *Omooba v Michael Garrett Associates Ltd* [2024] EAT 30, [2024] IRLR 440.

to accept implied forms of variation, ie, on the ground that the employee has given their implied assent by their conduct. In this sort of case, the employer announces a variation of the contractual terms of the employee with prior consultation with the workforce. In response, the employee may exercise one of four options. First, the employee may continue to work and fail to express their refusal of consent or voice any protest. If the variation by the employer is to the employee's benefit, then an inference may be drawn that the variation is legally binding without any articulation of approbation by the employee: this is effectively a case of implied assent by the employee.[58] However, this can be distinguished from circumstances where the variation is clearly adverse to the employee and there is no express communication of consent or unequivocal conduct on the part of the employee to show acceptance of the purported variation. Here, the courts divide cases into two groups: those where the variation is of immediate effect or impinges on the employee immediately and those where it is not or does not.[59] In general, if the variation applies immediately, eg, alterations to an employee's working hours or the introduction of a random drug policy, then the courts are more likely to accept that the variation is effective if the employee keeps working without demur.[60] I say generally, because this is not a hard-and-fast rule, since where the change is an immediate pay cut, or the trade unions have articulated a formal protest against the variation, the courts will be more searching in their enquiry and less prompt to treat the modification as legally binding.[61] However, where the change impinges on the employee at a later date, the failure of the employee to respond without protest and their continuation of the provision of their services cannot necessarily be equated with implied assent.[62] Here, implied assent can only be established by the passage of a sufficient period of time, albeit that there is no uniform period applicable in all cases since much will depend on the circumstances. In the past, the courts tended to be moderately conservative in setting the appropriate period. However, in *Secretary of State for the Home Department v Cox*, Lord Justice Lewis suggested that five years in such a case 'might be' sufficient, which represents a material prolongation of the boundaries and loosening of the period of time that must have elapsed from the point the variation was imposed by the employer.[63] In that regard, this represents

[58] *Hershaw v Sheffield City Council* [2014] ICR 1120.

[59] *Solectron Scotland Ltd v Roper* [2004] IRLR 4, 7 (Elias J).

[60] *Daley v Strathclyde* [1977] IRLR 414; *O'Flynn v Airlinks The Airport Coach Co Ltd* [2002] Emp LR 1217.

[61] *Abrahall v Nottingham City Council* [2018] ICR 1425, 1452A-G (Underhill LJ); *Secretary of State for the Department for Environment, Food and Rural Affairs v PCSU* [2024] UKSC 41, [2024] 3 WLR 1059, 1077E-H, 1080A-D, 1082F and 1092B-F (Lord Sales and Lady Simler). For discussion of the Court of Appeal decision, see P Lorber, 'Check-off, Variation of Contract and Collective Voice' (2023) 53 *Industrial Law Journal* 944, 948–950. cf *Cartwright v Tetrad Ltd* (UKEAT/0262/14/JOJ, 15 January 2015).

[62] See *Solectron Scotland Ltd v Roper* [2004] IRLR 4; *Wess v Science Museum Group* (UKEAT/0120/14/DM, 6 October 2014); *Re Carluccio's Ltd* [2020] IRLR 510.

[63] *Secretary of State for the Home Department v Cox* [2023] ICR 914, 936. Permission to appeal was granted by the UK Supreme Court from this decision of the Court of Appeal, but not on the legal point

a radical departure from general principles of contract law inasmuch as it is much less demanding of the non-varying party when it comes to making their intentions known or felt.

The second possibility is that the employee resigns in response to the employer's insistence on the variation and claims constructive (wrongful) dismissal at common law or unfair constructive dismissal under the statutory unfair dismissal regime in Part X of the Employment Rights Act 1996 ('ERA'). At common law, the imposition of the variation without the employee's consent will be a repudiatory breach of contract entitling the employee to damages, albeit that the damages award will be limited to net pay for the notice period (generally).[64] In the case of a statutory complaint of unfair dismissal, if the employer has a 'good, sound [business] reason' for the proposed change, the employee's dismissal (on the back of the employee's rejection of the proposed variation) will be treated as for 'some other substantial reason' in terms of section 98(1)(b) of the ERA.[65] And the effect of the decision of the EAT in *Catamaran Cruisers Ltd v Williams* is that it will be unlikely that a tribunal or court will treat the imposed variation as an *unfair* dismissal unless the employer has no pressing business case for the proposed variation and/or its motive(s) for the variation is arbitrary and it is unlikely to confer any benefit on the employer.[66] There is no requirement for the employer to establish that the variation is a necessity to avoid financial ruin or avert insolvency and it is perfectly (substantively) reasonable for an employer to (constructively or outright) dismiss an employee for rejecting the proposed variation, even where the employee's failure to accept was reasonable itself.[67]

A variation on this second possibility is the situation that arose in *Hogg v Dover College*.[68] Faced with a proposed variation, the employee may 'stand and sue', ie, remain in post but raise a legal claim that they have been unfairly dismissed. If the employer's proposed variation represents a substantial departure from the employee's original contract of employment,[69] this will constitute a 'dismissal' for the purposes of section 95(1)(a) of the ERA.[70] However, the employer will often

relating to the law of variation: see *Secretary of State for the Department for Environment, Food and Rural Affairs v PCSU* [2024] UKSC 41, [2024] 3 WLR 1059.

[64] However, merely proposing (rather than imposing) changes to the employee's contractual terms will not amount to a repudiatory breach of contract by the employer: *Kerry Foods Ltd v Lynch* [2005] IRLR 680.

[65] *Kerry Foods Ltd v Lynch* [2005] IRLR 680, 681 (P Clark); *Masiero v Barchester Healthcare plc* [2024] IRLR 774.

[66] *Catamaran Cruisers Ltd v Williams* [1994] IRLR 386. Having said that, the courts will tend to avoid scrutiny of the validity of the commercial reasons behind the proposed variations.

[67] *Garside and Laycock v Booth* [2011] IRLR 735; *Masiero v Barchester Healthcare plc* [2024] IRLR 774, 781–782 (Stout, D Smith and A Morris).

[68] *Hogg v Dover College* [1990] ICR 39.

[69] *Alcan Extrusions v Yates* [1996] IRLR 327, 329–330 (C Smith QC); *Jackson v University Hospitals of North Midlands NHS Trust* [2023] IRLR 796, 801 (Barry Clarke); *Humby v Barts Health NHS Trust* [2024] EAT 17.

[70] In other words, it will not be a 'constructive dismissal' in terms of section 95(1)(c) of the ERA.

be able to successfully defend any unfair dismissal complaint of this sort if it has a genuine commercial motive for the proposed alteration, once again, on the basis that the dismissal is 'for some other substantial reason' and not unfair in terms of the jurisprudence in *Catamaran Cruisers Ltd v Williams*.[71]

Turning to the third option available to the employee, this involves two stages. Initially, the employee affirms the employment contract (in response to the employer's repudiatory breach in imposing the variation without consent) by working under the new terms under protest. The employee will then go on to raise legal proceedings against the employer in court for damages in respect of the employer's repudiatory breach of contract or, alternatively, present a complaint to a tribunal of an unlawful deduction from wages under Part II of the ERA. In this case, the damages claim would relate to the difference in the monetary value of the contract of employment after and before the variation and likewise in the case of the statutory unlawful deduction from wages claim.

Finally, the fourth possibility open to the employee involves the explicit refusal to continue to provide work on the basis of the new terms. Where the employee explicitly declines consent in this way, the employee is effectively working on the basis of the old contractual terms, and there is no suggestion of any implied assent to the new terms or acceptance of the employer's repudiation of the original contract (in attempting to foist those terms on them).[72] The employer is then faced with a choice: either they cave in and accept that the new terms have been rejected, or they take the radical decision to either dismiss (and replace) the employee or dismiss and immediately offer to rehire the employee on the basis of a fresh contract of employment incorporating the rejected (and often, downgraded) terms.[73] It is in the latter case that termination and reengagement – or 'fire and rehire' – enters the fray. And of itself, 'fire and rehire' does not amount to a repudiatory breach of contract by the employer or an automatically unfair dismissal of the employee, since it simply constitutes the provision of lawful notice, with an offer of continuous employment on different contractual terms.[74] Once again, in this case, express consent performs no particular function, since the employer can apply considerable pressure on the employee to accept the rejected contractual change.[75]

[71] *Catamaran Cruisers* (n 66).

[72] *Rigby v Ferodo Ltd* [1988] ICR 29, 35E-G (Lord Oliver).

[73] *Adamas Ltd v Cheung* [2011] UKPC 32, [2011] IRLR 1014.

[74] *Kerry Foods Ltd v Lynch* [2005] IRLR 680, 683 (Peter Clark). Of course, if enacted, section 104I of the ERA (inserted by clause 26 of the Employment Rights Bill) would change the legal position by converting any 'fire and rehire' into an automatically unfair dismissal, subject to the exception in clause 26(4).

[75] For the employer to avoid a finding of unfair dismissal, there is no legal requirement for the contractual terms of the rehire offer to reach a threshold of reasonableness: *St. John of God (Care Services) Ltd v Brooks* [1992] ICR 715.

B. Indirect Variation

Each of the aforementioned direct means of modifying the express terms of the contract of employment without employee approval can be contrasted with the distinct analytical technique of putting them into effect indirectly. In each of these cases of indirect modification, once again, the employee has failed to explicitly consent, but the employer-initiated change is legally valid. This is predicated on the law treating the adjustments of the working practices and patterns as ones that technically do not formally involve the amendment of any express or implied term of the employment contract. For example, where the job responsibilities, duties, or tasks of the employee are altered by the employer, a distinction must be drawn between those entailing the amendment of the: (i) contractual terms setting out the employee's job description, duties, and tasks, and (ii) the working conditions, processes, and means of performing the prescribed job description, duties, and tasks. In the former case, the change will amount to a direct variation of the contract of employment,[76] whereas it will not in the case of the latter. As such, adjusting the means and processes relating to the discharge of the formal responsibilities and duties will have no impact on the existing contractual terms or obligations of the employee, and the question of consent is bypassed.[77] Instead, the employer will be able to rely on its inherent power of command pursuant to the managerial prerogative to effect the change, which will be supported by the implied terms in law of the employment contract recognised by the common law. In particular, the implied duty of the employee to adapt to new working practices will help ensure that the alteration to working practices is lawful,[78] as will the implied duty of the employee to obey reasonable instructions and orders[79] and the implied duty enjoining employees not to disrupt their employer's business (even if the interference is in conformance with the express terms of the contract).[80]

Another simple way for the employer to put into effect a change to working obligations on an indirect basis without employee approval is to modify the provisions of a staff handbook, works rulebook, or works manual. If these collateral documents have not been expressly or impliedly incorporated by reference into the contract of employment, there is no suggestion of the adjustment constituting an alteration of the contract's terms or the obligations that the employee had agreed

[76] For example, see *Bull v Nottinghamshire and City of Nottingham Fire and Rescue Authority* [2007] ICR 1631 where the changes to the duties to the firefighter employees were treated as work that they had not originally agreed to perform. In that way, their consent was essential.

[77] See *Wetherill v Birmingham City Council* [2007] EWCA Civ 599, [2007] IRLR 781.

[78] *Cresswell v Board of Inland Revenue* [1984] ICR 508, [1984] IRLR 190.

[79] *Turner v Mason* (1845) 14 M & W 112; *Pepper v Webb* [1969] 2 All ER 216, [1969] 1 WLR 514. See Freedland and Kountouris (n 4) 188. An order from the employer to the employee is not a term of the contract, since it is derived from the employer's power of command, ie, the managerial prerogative, and as such, there is no suggestion of any variation of a term in this context: P Elias, B Napier, and P Wallington, *Labour Law: Cases and Materials* (London, Butterworths, 1980) 442–3.

[80] *Secretary of State for Employment v ASLEF (No 2)* [1972] 2 QB 455.

to discharge.[81] In each of these cases of indirect variation, the issue of consent only enters into consideration where the proposed modification is so extreme/severe that the most appropriate interpretation is that the new responsibilities amount to work and obligations that the employee had never undertaken to perform.

Finally, there is the indirect approach of making changes via 'custom and practice'. In this case, the failure of the employee to expressly consent to the employer's proposed variation of an express term can be trumped by the evolutionary nature of the custom and practice of the employer's workplace. On one view, this is a heresy, for how can it ever be possible for informal conventions, ways and patterns of working (albeit not formally recognised as a contractual term) to disapply an express term of the employment contract? In *Solectron*, Mr Justice Elias ruled that whether the express term has been superseded by the custom depends on whether the tribunals and courts are 'able to infer from regular application of the practice that the parties must be taken to have accepted that the practice has crystallised into [a] contractual right'.[82] In this way, a sophisticated body of jurisprudence has been developed by the Court of Appeal to enable tribunals and lower courts to understand when the custom takes legal effect.[83]

IV. The Attenuated Role for Explicit Consent and the Case for and against Reforming the Law Governing the Variation of the Employment Contract

In sections II and III, I illustrated how private law speaks as one as regards the general rule applicable to contractual variation in respect of both commercial and employment contracts: that is to say that it is necessary for there to be mutual consent. Nevertheless, as I have made plain in the discussion, there are numerous exceptions recognised where contract and employment law both fail to insist on formal employee or counterparty consent. And both branches of the law generally track each other as regards the content and scope of these exceptions, save for one or two divergences.[84] In the final analysis, from the employer's perspective, the role of express consent – although afforded a heightened degree of prominence – performs a truncated role in the variation of employment relations, since the need to recognise the latter's inherent dynamism and the notion of formal freedom of contract are elevated to a superior and priority status. Perhaps one way of

[81] For the express and implied incorporation of staff handbooks, see *Keeley v Fosroc International* [2006] EWCA Civ 1277, [2006] IRLR 961; *Harlow v Artemis International Corp. Ltd* [2008] IRLR 629; *Briscoe v Lubrizol* [2002] EWCA Civ 508, [2002] IRLR 607; and *Sparks v Department for Transport* [2016] IRLR 519.

[82] *Solectron Scotland Ltd v Roper* [2004] IRLR 4, 6 (Elias J).

[83] *Albion Automotive Ltd v Walker* [2002] EWCA Civ 946; *Park Cakes Ltd v Shumba* [2013] IRLR 800.

[84] For example, in the employment context, the period of time for implied assent is more generous to the non-varying party where the imposed variation is not of immediate effect.

understanding this paradox would be to consider the law's role as a facilitator in enabling employers to elide the need for definitive employee consent as a necessary one in light of the evolutionary character of the law regulating the contract of employment and the latter itself. For example, Freedland has noted how the principles underpinning the law governing the contract of employment are both avowedly evolutionary and variable.[85] The variability can be seen in the way that the law divides variations into various forms and options and applies different legal rules to each. And the various twists and turns in the case law speak to the evolutionary nature of the law itself. As such, the space occupied by the 'express/explicit consent' of the worker oscillates as a result of the law governing the contract of employment relating to variation. But what can we make of this ebb and flow and is it justifiable in light of the nature of the working relationship?

What the malleability of the role of express consent in the case of employment suggests is that there may be a case for divergence between the laws regulating the variation of contracts of employment and the commercial contract in order to suppress the capacity of employers to vary without express employee consent through the direct or indirect means discussed earlier in this chapter. The basic argument is that, despite the similarities identified at the beginning of section III, the employment and commercial relationships differ to a sufficiently material degree to justify a break between the two.[86] The argument in favour of deviating from traditional contractual principles is twofold. First, it is based on the traditional inequality of bargaining power justification,[87] combined with the special context and nature of employment relationships, which incorporate the immensely significant collective dimension. For in the case of the contract of employment, the capacity of the employee to exercise their freedom to and of contract is arguably compromised. As Kahn-Freund famously remarked, although the contract of employment is consensual in nature, the autonomy of the employee is, in fact, an 'indispensable figment of the legal mind', representing a penetrable gloss, that only sparingly hides the subordination lurking beneath.[88] This can be ascribed to the distinction between the formal freedom (to and of contract) of the employee and the reality of the imbalance in the bargaining power in favour of the employer: in comparison, in the case of two contracting parties privy to

[85] M Freedland, 'The Legal Structure of the Contract of Employment' in M Freedland et al. (eds), *The Contract of Employment* (Oxford, Oxford University Press, 2016) 45–51.

[86] For a discussion of the circumstances in which divergence may be appropriate, see H Collins, 'Contractual Autonomy' in A Bogg et al. (eds), *The Autonomy of Labour Law* (Oxford, Hart Publishing, 2015) 45; D Brodie, 'The Autonomy of the Common Law of the Contract of Employment from the General Law of Contract' in M Freedland et al. (eds), *The Contract of Employment* (Oxford, Oxford University Press, 2016) 124; H Collins, 'The Contract of Employment in 3D' in D Campbell, L Mulcahy, and S Wheeler (eds), *Changing Concepts of Contract* (Basingstoke, Palgrave MacMillan, 2013) 65.

[87] For discussion, see D Cabrelli, 'Traditional Justifications of Labour Law' in G Davidov, B Langille and G Lester, *Oxford Handbook of the Law of Work* (Oxford, Oxford University Press, 2024) 104.

[88] P Davies and M Freedland, *Kahn-Freund's Labour and the Law* (London, Stevens & Sons, 1983) 18. It is an act of submission to enter into employment, with the result that the employee is subordinate in a positional sense to the employer.

a commercial contract, any power disparity generally will not be of an equivalent magnitude or strength. Under such conditions, it is meaningless to talk of employee 'autonomy', particularly where the terms of the contract of employment are presented on a 'take-it-or-leave-it' basis by the employer to the employee at the inception of the working relationship on the basis of a standard form contract drafted by the employer. And taken alongside such inequality of bargaining power, the fact that the legal rules governing the variation of the employment contract constitute a 'permissive regime' represents a superadded justification for the law to strike out in a direction that is both worker-protective and independent of the orthodox rules of contract law.

As for the collective angle and how it introduces complications into the equation, we can look no further than the decision of the Court of Appeal in *Secretary of State for the Home Department v Cox*.[89] Here, there was no suggestion of any individual employee protest to employer-driven variations consisting of the removal of check-off facilities. Under existing doctrine, the absence of explicit employee consent would be irrelevant, and their endorsement could be implied on the basis of the lack of individual protest and their continued personal performance. However, since objections to the proposed variations had been raised collectively by recognised trade unions, and collective grievances lodged and litigation proceedings raised after the implementation of the variation, this was sufficient to demonstrate the absence of assent on the part of the employees.[90] In such a case, the collective protest amounted to an indirect, albeit effective, means of ensuring that the continuation of performance could not be understood as employee acceptance of the variation. This kind of case is very much employment-specific, since there is no equivalent parallel to the collective angle in the commercial context.

If Kahn-Freund is right that the notions of 'agreement', 'consent', 'contract', 'liberty' and 'autonomy' are nothing but an inspired fiction in the case of the 'contract' of employment, then how can it ever be justifiable to accept the current law on the validity of contractual variation? In essence, the claim is that lending legal validity to employer-initiated variations without employee consent is wholly misconceived, overlooking the imbalance in bargaining power and subordination inherent in the employment relationship. On this basis, it would be more equitable to reform the law governing the employment contract to depart from the orthodox rules of contract law and either outlaw all variations of contractual terms that proceed without formal employee consent or, at least, circumscribe the operation of the rules regulating variation to confer greater protection in favour of employers. And so, reform is required, eg, invalidation of unilateral variation clauses, flexibility clauses, and other informal means of effecting employer-initiated

[89] *Secretary of State for the Home Department v Cox* [2023] ICR 914. Approved by the UK Supreme Court in *Secretary of State for the Department for Environment, Food and Rural Affairs v PCSU* [2024] UKSC 41, [2024] 3 WLR 1059.

[90] ibid 935–938 (Lewis LJ); P Lorber, 'Check-off, Variation of Contract and Collective Voice' (2023) 53 *Industrial Law Journal* 944, 948–950.

modifications in the absence of staff approval. On this view, reforming the law to expand the role played by mutual consent is part of the answer to the problem of the lack of worker freedom and autonomy.

While appealing, I am sceptical of the merits of any departure of this sort from general contract law. My rejection is rooted in an observation and two doctrinal considerations, which – specifically in the case of unilateral variation and flexibility clauses – make it both unnecessary and, in more general terms, counter-productive. First, the claim that the imbalance in power between employers and employees justifies divergence between the orthodox standards of contract law and employment law governing variations is arguably truncated to the extent that the latter provides some effective support to the bargaining power of the employees in comparison with a counterparty to an ordinary commercial contract or a non-employee seeking work. For example, any bargaining between the employer and employee regarding whether the latter should agree to or refuse the employer's proposed variation will take place in the shadow of statutory protections available to employees, such as unfair dismissal, redundancy, protections on the transfer of the employer's business, etc. Seen from that perspective, some of the edge is taken off of the power imbalance to the extent that the employer is aware that any wrong steps in the process leading up to the imposition of any proposed variation could enable the employee to avail him/herself of these statutory rights.

Second, any divergence from contract law is unnecessary in light of the existing legal doctrines that place a degree of constraint on the ability of employers to rely on and exercise unilateral variation and flexibility clauses to circumvent the application of the general rule. To recap, the courts will police such clauses to declare that they are not binding on the employee for either a want of clear wording (eg, *Norman v National Audit Office*),[91] or for the fact that their exercise breached the implied term of mutual trust and confidence (*Dresdner Kleinwort Ltd and Commerzbank AG v Attrill*).[92] And all things being equal, there are also the general contract law mechanisms, such as those supplied by the '*Braganza* criterion', whereby the employer must exercise a unilateral variation clause in good faith and not arbitrarily or capriciously and consistent with the contractual purpose of the unilateral power of variation.[93] A recent illustration of this point is the decision of the High Court in *McCormack v Medivet Group Ltd*.[94] In this case, the employer varied the duties and responsibilities of the employee pursuant to a unilateral variation clause, but it was held that this was not exercised rationally, honestly or in good faith. Finally, in terms of contract law, the employee benefits from additional machinery comprising the use of the *Yam Seng* implied term in fact of good faith.[95]

[91] *Norman v National Audit Office* [2015] IRLR 634.

[92] *Dresdner Kleinwort Ltd and Commerzbank AG v Attrill* [2013] EWCA Civ 394, [2013] IRLR 548.

[93] *Braganza v BP Shipping Ltd* [2015] UKSC 17, [2015] 1 WLR 1661. See also *BT Plc v Telefonica O2 UK Ltd* [2014] UKSC 42, [2014] 4 All ER 907, 923 (Lord Neuberger).

[94] *McCormack v Medivet* [2024] EWHC 1000 (Comm).

[95] Having said that, I am not aware of any employment case where the *Yam Seng* implied term has been invoked to control employer behaviour in general, and what the *Yam Seng* implied term

And since the decision of the UK Supreme Court in *Tesco v USDAW*, another implied term, albeit one in fact, has entered the fray to control express terms that confer 'permanent' entitlements in favour of employees. In circumstances where employees refuse consent to a variation removing such indefinite entitlements, an implied term in fact will operate to prevent employers from exercising their power to 'fire and rehire' as an avoidance mechanism if it is exercised contrary to good faith, arbitrarily, capriciously, or irrationally, or for an improper purpose.[96] Seen from that perspective, numerous – and, I would argue, a sufficient range of – legal doctrines that empower employees to counter the imposition of varied terms without their agreement are already available in both contract and employment law.

However, it is my third justification to oppose the reform of employment law in a worker-protective direction that is the most material of all, and that is that it would be potentially counterproductive. This might appear to be a confused argument, but it begins to make sense when considered in light of the doctrinal reality that the laws governing both the variation and termination of the contract of employment are inextricably linked together in a sort of symbiotic relationship. To that extent, the respective territories that they occupy edge back and forth, reacting to movements in the other.[97] And the interdependence between them in the case of the law of the contract of employment is acute. By way of explanation, the more restrictions or prohibitions imposed by the law on unilateral employer variations without employee consent, the greater the importance of the law of termination: the more difficult it is for the employer to vary, the more attractive the: (i) dismissal, (ii) dismissal and replacement, or (iii) dismissal and reemployment, of the employee (incorporating the rejected terms) becomes. Of course, the opposite is also true. In other words, if the law regulating the variation of the terms of the employment contract is simplified and lax, then the law governing the termination of the employment contract becomes less relevant: if it is easier to vary, there is less need for the employer to either dismiss, dismiss and replace, or dismiss and reengage an employee to achieve its commercial ends. And this is concerning in light of the recent high-profile use by management of the strategy of dismissal and reengagement – ie 'fire and rehire' or 'fire and replace' – in response to employees who consistently refuse to consent to employer-proposed changes to their terms and conditions.

Of course, political anxiety over the use of 'fire and rehire' and 'fire and replace' reached its zenith at the time of the P&O Ferries scandal. And as evidenced by the UK Government's proposed legislative 'ban' on 'fire and rehire' and 'fire and replace' in the Employment Rights Bill,[98] it has not subsided. Here, P&O sacked

adds to the implied term of mutual trust and confidence is not immediately clear to me and has been under-theorised.

[96] [2024] UKSC 28, [2025] ICR 107.

[97] Freedland (n 5) 40.

[98] See Employment Rights HC Bill (2024–25) [5]. Clause 26 introduces section 104I into the ERA to make any dismissal in terms of a 'fire and rehire' or 'fire and replace' in response to an employee's refusal to agree to a proposed employer-initiated variation an automatically unfair dismissal.

800 workers with immediate effect by video call or text message and then offered to rehire them on the basis of less favourable terms and conditions if they agreed to work as agency staff via an employment agency. This controversial episode highlighted the inadequacy of the employment laws protecting workers from the practice of fire and rehire, where employees have withheld consent to proposed employer-initiated variations of contractual terms, and none of the exceptions (available to effect direct or indirect modifications) apply. As such, the 'counter-productive' point that I am making is an irony: by tightening up the rules that currently enable employer-led variations in the absence of employee consent, the reformed law will simply incentivise employers to either dismiss or dismiss and immediately reengage their employees on a new employment contract containing the varied term(s) that the employee had previously rejected.

Any reform of the law in this way would be diametrically opposed to existing policy to rein in the practice of fire and rehire, as currently articulated in the DBT CoP and the Labour Government's impending 'ban' in the Employment Rights Bill. In relation specifically to the latter, ie, the UK Government's proposed 'ban' on 'fire and rehire' and 'fire and replace', the new section 104I of the ERA to be inserted by clause 26 of the Employment Rights Bill directs that if the employer dismisses employees or engages in such practices in response to their rejection of a proposed variation, this will entitle them to treat themselves as automatically unfairly dismissed.[99] By cutting off these options from the armoury available to the employer to effect workplace changes, the law regulating the variation of the employment contract will become significantly more important: if reining in the power of employers to vary the terms of the contract of employment in the absence of employee consent heightens the status of the law of termination and dismissal, then, by the same token, the harder it is made to fire and rehire, the greater the vitality of the law of variation. And, in recognition of the dynamism of the contract of employment discussed above, the more important it is to enable employers to adjust contractual terms and working practices without employee consent. The change in the 'fire and rehire' policy position radically changes the calculus and

This will replace the existing statutory Code of Practice of the UK Government Department for Business and Trade ('DBT CoP') on dismissal and re-engagement which employers ought to currently adhere to, failing which employment tribunals and courts are empowered to uplift a successful employee's compensation award for unfair dismissal by up to 25% if the employer's failure to honour the terms of the Code was unreasonable: see Department for Business and Trade, *Code of practice on dismissal and re-engagement issued by the Secretary of State under section 203 of the Trade Union and Labour Relations (Consolidation) Act 1992* (Statutory Guidance, 2024) www.gov.uk/government/publications/dismissal-and-re-engagement-code-of-practice/code-of-practice-on-dismissal-and-re-engagement-issued-by-the-secretary-of-state-under-section-203-of-the-trade-union-and-labour-relations-consolidat.

[99] As such, the legal technique adopted to 'ban' 'fire and rehire' or 'fire and replace' has been to make it an automatically unfair dismissal, albeit that other options were available, such as: (i) increasing the compensatory award in a case of 'fire and rehire' or 'fire and replace', or (ii) relaxing the eligibility requirements for an unfair 'fire and rehire' or 'fire and replace', or (iii) removing the SOSR reorganisation/restructuring reason for a fire and rehire, or (iv) treating the 'fire' as a nullity and void, albeit see n 101 on this point.

justifies leaving the law governing the variation of the contract of employment well alone and keeping it as it currently stands. Otherwise, taken in combination with the policy articulated by clause 26,[100] any law reform to constrain the ability of employers to vary without employee consent (by removing or diluting the exceptions discussed above in section III) will simply channel employers down the route of layoffs and/or insolvency, eg, via mass redundancies or compelling them to enter into liquidation or administration. And this would represent a spectacular case of regulatory/policy backfire. Ultimately, looked at in the round, it is unwise and often counterproductive for well-meaning policymakers to tighten up discrete parts of employment law here and there without taking a holistic view of the subject, including the unintended consequences. Hence, there is a more coherent case for the law to remain static, since fire and rehire is being made an automatically unlawful dismissal.[101]

For each of the aforementioned doctrinal and other reasons, any consideration of the imposition of additional legal controls on the ability of employers to vary the employment contract on a non-consensual basis should proceed with caution, cognisant of the fact that any reform proposals must account for the employer's ultimate power of dismissal and the potency of the law of termination.

The preceding discussion of fire and rehire can be contrasted with the position of the functionally equivalent 'nuclear' option discussed in section II in the case of the commercial contract.[102] Here, the connection between the law of variation and termination is much looser. There is much less interdependence for the reason that if a contracting party B rejects contracting party A's proposed variation, A must be extremely cautious to pursue the option of

[100] Admittedly, section 104I(3) of the ERA to be inserted by clause 26(4) provides for an exception where employers can dismiss or fire and rehire without a finding of an automatically unfair dismissal, but the scope of this is untested. For commentary, see A Bogg and M Ford, 'From "Fairness at Work" to "Making Work Pay": A Preliminary Assessment of the Employment Rights Bill' (*UK Labour Law*, 14 October 2024) uklabourlawblog.com/2024/10/14/from-fairness-at-work-to-making-work-pay-a-preliminary-assessment-of-the-employment-rights-bill-by-professor-alan-bogg-and-professor-michael-ford-kc.

[101] Owing to the fact that the conceptual apparatus of English law is incapable of recognising an invalid or void dismissal or a dismissal as a nullity (see *Wilson v St Helens' Borough Council* [1999] 2 AC 52, 78A (Lord Slynn) in the context of the Transfer of Undertakings (Protection of Employment) Regulations 2006 (SI 2006/246)) (unlike continental Civilian jurisdictions) and the stringent rules on injunctions and specific performance, any 'ban' on fire and rehire or fire and replace inevitably will be nothing of the sort, since it will always be possible for the employer to terminate the employment contract on paying damages (in the case of a wrongful dismissal) or statutory compensation (if an automatically unfair dismissal under clause 26 of the Employment Rights Bill (inserting section 104I of the ERA)) to the departed employee. And the ultimate irony is that clause 26 is likely to be a 'dead letter' in practice: for those employees who are dismissed and reject the offer to rehire and subsequently claim automatic unfair dismissal, they are left wide open to the charge that they have failed to mitigate their loss (see *Wilding v BT Plc* [2002] IRLR 524). Their failure to accept the offer will radically reduce any compensation award in any successful unfair dismissal claim they may have, resulting in a Pyrrhic victory for the employee.

[102] To recap, this is where a contracting party A decides to terminate a commercial contract on the service of reasonable notice on B and the immediate service of an offer on B to enter into a fresh commercial contract containing the rejected adjusted terms.

termination with an offer to immediately enter into a new commercial agreement with B. There is a comparatively higher risk that B will reject A's offer in the case of a commercial relationship than in the equivalent employment context. For example, the contracting party B will have the benefit of a much wider range of better options available to them in the commercial market than the suitable alternative employment possibilities open to the employee in the labour market. And for the employee, the other jobs may be no improvement as regards the salary package and working conditions, or may be even less appealing, such as being blacklisted or unemployment. In this way, there is much greater pressure on the employee to accept the rehire offer than on the contracting party B in the commercial context. In conclusion, the rules governing variation exert less of a grip over those relating to termination in the case of commercial dealings insofar as any reform of general contract law to make it harder for contracting parties to modify contractual terms without the express consent of their counterparties are less likely to incentivise them to pursue the cul-de-sac of the 'nuclear' option of termination and re-contracting.

Another non-doctrinal motive for my scepticism is rooted in the impracticability of using the common law, rather than legislation, as the basis for law reforms of the kind proposed, ie, involving an extended role for explicit employee consent. This harks back to the caveat noted in an essay penned by Lord Justice Elias,[103] who writing extra-judicially, reminded us of the limits of the common law in forging a set of more worker-protective employment laws:

> [J]udges' freedom of action may be limited by a variety of constraints, such as contract doctrine – for example, the duty to give effect to express contractual terms, precedent or legislation … [and we must] appreciate the proper limits of the judicial function … [there is] the principle that the courts cannot rewrite the contract; they cannot strike down a bargain because they would prefer it to have been formulated in a different way or because they think it in some general sense inequitable … There is a limit to how far they can develop or modify established doctrines. It must be in a principled way – the rule of law demands no less, even where the common law's application may be unjust in a particular case or class of cases. There is a potential remedy for such injustice, but it lies with Parliament, not with the courts.

Alan Bogg has built on this theme, noting how 'legal arguments will be most attractive to courts where they cohere with existing doctrinal categories … [which means that] labour lawyer[s] must be constantly alive to more general tendencies in private law'.[104] In that vein, it is not obvious to me that expanding the requirement for express employee consent tracks recent developments in private

[103] P Elias, 'Changes and Challenges to the Contract of Employment' (2018) 38 *OJLS* 869, 873 and 885–886. See also P Sales, 'The Common Law: Context and Method' (2019) 134 *Law Quarterly Review* 47, 47–48 and 54–55.

[104] A Bogg, 'Can We Trust the Courts in Labour Law? Stranded Between Frivolity and Despair' (2022) 38 *International Journal of Comparative Labour Law and Industrial Relations* 103, 132.

law. Instead, recent innovations in private law have focused on constraining the exercise of express or implied powers via the *Braganza* criterion and the *Yam Seng* implied term, rather than by fine-tuning the common law rules governing the ability of contracting parties with greater bargaining power to secure contractual variations without the express approval of their counterparty. Moreover, it does not seem appropriate to track private law since it is in a developmental phase with competing views on the best direction that reconciliation between the *Braganza* criterion and the *Yam Seng* implied term should take. In this way, before employment law rules are finessed by analogy with private law, the latter will first have to get its own house in order and the legal position settle.

A pertinent question is whether and how the courts might respond and whether they would or should decide to adapt the common law rules by analogy with the statutory abolition of 'fire and rehire'? On the one hand, if we return to the idea expressed by Lord Justice Elias and Alan Bogg of any common law adaptation 'running with the grain' of evolutions in private law, they also said that where any common law reform occurs, it generally also tracks statutory developments. As Lord Hoffmann famously remarked: 'the common law has adapted itself to the new attitudes [about the employment relationship], proceeding sometimes by analogy with statutory rights'.[105] Hence, there would be some justification in the courts taking the common law down a worker-protective path to expand the requirement for explicit employee consent to variations of contractual terms in light of the legislative abolition of fire and rehire. One option would be to place greater restrictions or a prohibition on the employer's use of flexibility or unilateral variation clauses. Another would be for the courts to tighten up the implied assent rules. Seen from that perspective, there is a compelling case for the judiciary to at least consider marshalling the common law to extend the need for employee consent in relation to employer-initiated variations of the employment contract. Whilst compelling, on the other hand, we should not overlook the conservative tendency of the judiciary, ever mindful of their confined role in law-making within the context of the constitutional settlement. By that account, the courts may take the attitude that if Parliament has decided to outlaw fire and rehire and has failed to clarify the effect of that ban on the practice and law of variation, then their silence is telling. And this is likely to be fortified in light of the discussion above regarding the unintended consequences and self-defeating nature of proceeding with a tightening up of the need for employee consent alongside a legislative 'ban' on 'fire and rehire'. In that way, the courts are likely to conclude that there is no justification to modify the common law in a way that moulds the rules on variation so that they are consistent with the legislative purpose of the ban on fire and rehire.

[105] *Johnson v Unisys Ltd* [2001] UKHL 13, [2003] 1 AC 518, 539C.

V. Conclusion

In resisting calls for the law of variation to depart from traditional contract law rules and compress the power of employers to effect change without employee consent, some may detect a counsel of despair in my position. Some may even brand it as overly conservative and dismiss it as lacking in ambition. However, I would disagree. Although none of the recent developments in private law can be used to found any changes to the rules governing the variation of terms of the contract of employment, I accept that there are legislative developments afoot that are of sufficient note to justify analogical evolution of the common law, ie, the treatment of fire and rehire and fire and replace as an automatically unfair dismissal. However, in this chapter, I have explained how it would be a mistake and self-defeating to the interests of workers for the courts to develop the common law in a way that deviates from orthodox contractual principles to limit the capacity of employers to unilaterally modify the terms of the employment contract without the employee's consent. By doing this, the courts would simply be fast-tracking employers down the route of large-scale redundancies and business insolvencies. And this is in nobody's interests.

4

Substantial Performance in Employment Contracts

JORDAN ENGLISH*

I. Introduction

The central thesis of this chapter is that something has gone wrong in the law relating to substantial performance in contracts of employment. As the law stands, cases such as *Wiluszynski v Tower Hamlets London Borough Council*[1] suggest that an employee's entitlement to be paid is conditional on complete and exact performance of each and every obligation by the employee (or, at the very least, a readiness and willingness to provide complete and exact performance). In that case, the Court of Appeal held that an employee engaging in action short of strike, who had performed most but not all of their contractual duties, in addition to being in breach of contract, was not entitled to be paid for any work done because they were not 'ready, willing, and able' to perform and therefore had not satisfied a condition of payment. The Court also held that it was no answer to the employer's denial of liability that the employee had substantially performed their obligations – the 'doctrine of substantial performance' was applicable only to mitigate 'the hardship of the old law as to entire contracts'.[2]

This chapter argues that the so-called doctrine of substantial performance is simply a matter of ascertaining the relevant conditions of payment. The question is whether the condition of one party's obligation to pay the price is complete and exact performance by the other party or substantial performance by the other party. In the context of commercial contracts, it has been said that 'the courts lean against a construction of the contract which would deprive the contractor of any payment at all simply because there are some defects or omissions'.[3] The result,

* I am grateful to Jonas Atmaz Al-Sibaie, Alan Bogg, Paul Davies, Amy Rogers, and Robert Stevens for their comments on earlier drafts of this chapter and to the participants at the UCL Private Law Perspectives on the Contract of Employment conference for their comments and questions.

[1] *Wiluszynski v Tower Hamlets London Borough Council* [1989] ICR 493.

[2] ibid 499.

[3] *Hoenig v Isaacs* [1952] 2 All ER 176, 180.

then, of cases like *Wiluszynski* is that the law in relation to substantial performance in employment contracts is out of kilter and counterintuitively harsher on the employee than the approach taken to the construction of commercial contracts.

The decision in *Wiluszynski* has been criticised for shifting the balance between employer and employee in favour of the employer,[4] being contrary to various human rights protections,[5] and being contrary to orthodox contract doctrine.[6] Picking up the last of these criticisms, this chapter argues that *Wiluszynski* is wrongly decided both in result and in reasoning. The mistake is that it treats substantial performance as a doctrine rather than a question of construction, and it assumes that questions of substantial performance have no application to contracts of employment because employment contracts are not 'entire'.

This chapter proceeds in five sections. Section II ('The current law') sets out the decision in *Wiluszynski* and an important precursor: the decision of the House of Lords in *Miles v Wakefield Metropolitan District Council*.[7] Section III ('The "doctrine" of substantial performance') explains that the issue of substantial performance is not a doctrine but simply a question of construction relevant to ascertaining the conditions of payment. It also explains the closely related concept of an 'entire contract'. This phrase, unfortunately, is used in different senses in contract law, which has led directly to the mistake made in *Wiluszynski*, namely, assuming that the so-called doctrine of substantial performance was inapplicable because employment contracts are not 'entire'. Section IV ('Application to employment contracts') then explains the mistake in *Wiluszynski* and outlines what, in principle, the position should be; namely, that there should be no rule that substantial performance is irrelevant to contracts of employment, this being a question of construction, and that ordinarily, it would be expected that substantial performance, rather than complete and exact performance, is the condition of payment. Section V ('No deductions?') explains that this does not mean that, at common law, an employer faced with an employee rendering substantial, but not complete and exact, performance can make no deduction. Rather, following the approach in *Sim v Rotherham Metropolitan Borough Council*,[8] employers are, in practice, able to make a proportionate deduction from an employee's salary or wages by way of counterclaim and set-off for the lost value of the performance: the difference between what they were promised and what they got. Such a claim is a claim for 'general damages' that does not depend upon the employer having suffered a

[4] G Mead, 'Employer's Right to Withhold Wages' (1990) 106 *Law Quarterly Review* 192, 195.

[5] D Mead, 'We're Miles Apart Disproportionate Deductions from Wages, Industrial Action and Human Rights' (2023) 52 *Industrial Law Journal* 1; A Bogg and M Ford, 'Striking, Pay Deductions, and Reasonable Orders: A Legal Analysis' (*UK Labour Law Blog*, 6 October 2022): www.uklabourlawblog.com/2022/10/06/striking-pay-deductions-and-reasonable-orders-a-legal-analysis-by-alan-bogg-and-michael-ford-kc.

[6] Mead (n 4) 193; S Deakin, 'Logical Deductions? Wage Protection Before and After *Delaney v Staples*' (1992) 55 *Modern Law Review* 848, 852; Z Adams, C Barnard, S Deakin, and SF Butlin, *Deakin and Morris' Labour Law*, 7th edn, (Oxford, Hart Publishing, 2021) 302.

[7] *Miles v Wakefield Metropolitan District Council* [1987] AC 539.

[8] *Sim v Rotherham Metropolitan Borough Council* [1987] Ch 216.

counterfactual loss.[9] Finally, section VI ('The limits of private law') makes clear that the claims made in this chapter are not a panacea for the problems faced by an employee engaging in action short of strike and that if further restrictions on an employer's ability to withhold pay are desirable, they must come from Parliament.

The claims made in this chapter are particularly relevant to recent controversies surrounding pay deductions made by employers for actions short of strike.[10] They also show the importance of the doctrinal law of contract to issues that are at the heart of labour law disputes. Almost 50 years ago, Professor Mark Freedland claimed that lawyers needed to take a 'new look at the obligations to work and to pay for work'.[11] In words that ring no less true today, he said: 'It may be said that the law of the contract of employment has lost most of its practical importance and has been superseded by statute law. This is only partly true; it is astonishing how often, and in how many diverse ways, we come back to the contract of employment.'[12]

II. The Current Law

The problem with the current state of the law in relation to substantial performance in employment contracts arises primarily from the decision of the Court of Appeal in *Wiluszynski v Tower Hamlets London Borough Council*.[13] But in order to understand *Wiluszynski*, it is necessary to give an account of the leading decision in this area, the decision of the House of Lords in *Miles v Wakefield Metropolitan District Council*.[14]

In *Miles v Wakefield*, the plaintiff, a superintendent registrar of births, deaths, and marriages, engaged in industrial action short of strike by refusing to conduct civil wedding ceremonies on Saturday mornings. The plaintiff worked a 37-hour week, three of which were on a Saturday morning, the most popular time for such weddings. Conducting civil wedding ceremonies was one of the superintendent registrar's most important functions.[15] The defendant council responded to the industrial action by making clear that so long as the plaintiff was not willing to perform the full range of his duties, he was not required to attend work and would not be paid.[16] The plaintiff did, in fact, attend work on Saturday mornings

[9] R Stevens, *The Laws of Restitution* (Oxford, Oxford University Press, 2023) 295–296.

[10] See generally, Bogg and Ford (n 5); Mead (n 5).

[11] M Freedland, 'The Obligation to Work and to Pay for Work' (1977) *Current Legal Problems* 175, 186.

[12] ibid 186.

[13] [1989] ICR 493. Applying the obiter observations of Scott J in *Sim v Rotherham Metropolitan Borough Council* [1987] Ch 216, 252–253.

[14] [1987] AC 536. For a useful discussion of this case, see P Sales, 'Contract and Restitution in the Employment Relationship: No Work, No Pay' (1988) 8 *Oxford Journal of Legal Studies* 301.

[15] [1987] AC 536, 554.

[16] ibid 554.

during the period of the dispute and performed his other functions, but he did not conduct civil wedding ceremonies on Saturdays.

The council refused to pay him at all for his Saturday work during this period and withheld 3/37ths of his salary. After the industrial dispute ended, the plaintiff brought a claim for his unpaid salary. Although he was not employed under a contract of employment, the nature of the superintendent's office was sufficiently analogous to a relationship of employment that the claim for salary was treated in the same way as if there had been a contract of employment.[17]

The House of Lords, rejecting the plaintiff's claim, held that the plaintiff's salary was 'not an honorarium for the mere tenure of an office but had the character of remuneration for work done'.[18] As the plaintiff was unwilling to perform his full range of duties on the Saturday morning, he was not entitled to be paid. Lord Bridge said that '[i]f an employee refuses to perform the full duties which can be required of him under his contract of service, the employer is entitled to refuse to accept any partial performance'.[19] The council's refusal to accept the plaintiff's partial performance accordingly had the effect that despite the plaintiff attending work on Saturdays, he was to be treated as if he had not worked at all. And in this respect, Lord Templeman said:

> It cannot be right that an employer should be compelled to pay something for nothing whether he dismisses or retains a worker. In a contract of employment wages and work go together. The employer pays for work and the worker works for his wages. If the employer declines to pay, the worker need not work. If the worker declines to work, the employer need not pay. In an action by a worker to recover his pay he must allege and be ready to prove that he worked or was willing to work.[20]

In the result, the plaintiff was unable to claim the apportionable part of his salary that would ordinarily accrue[21] because he had 'declined to work on Saturday morning in accordance with his duty'.[22] Lord Oliver explained that this was because the council's obligation to pay salary was 'dependent' (or, as is more commonly said today, 'conditional')[23] on 'the plaintiff's willingness at least to perform his contractual duties'.[24] He could see 'no ground upon which the employee who declines to perform that condition upon which payment depends can successfully sue for the remuneration which is dependent upon its performance'.[25]

[17] ibid 556, 567.
[18] ibid 551.
[19] ibid 551. See also at 552–553 (Lord Brightman), 568 (Lord Oliver).
[20] ibid 561.
[21] This is the effect of the Apportionment Act 1870, ss 2, 5, which deems a salary to accrue day by day. See (n 46) below.
[22] [1987] AC 536, 561.
[23] For an explanation of the 'old law' of independent and dependent promises, see J English, 'The Nature of Promissory Conditions' (2021) 137 *Law Quarterly Review* 630, 631–637.
[24] [1987] AC 536, 561, 570. See also at 553 (Lord Brightman).
[25] ibid 561, 570.

Miles v Wakefield illustrates that an employee does not need to be dismissed, nor does the contract of employment need to be terminated, in order for that employee to be precluded from claiming wages.[26] This is because, ordinarily, the condition of an employee's entitlement to be paid is either that they do the work,[27] or that they are, at least, ready, willing, and able to do the work.[28] As Dixon J explained in the decision of the High Court of Australia in *Automatic Fire Sprinklers Pty Ltd v Watson*,[29] 'a refusal to work on the part of a servant, who neither leaves [their] master's service nor is discharged, may disentitle [them] to wages for the period of the refusal. That is for non-fulfilment of the conditions by which wages are earned'.

It is also important to note that there was no doubt in *Miles v Wakefield* that the plaintiff had failed substantially to perform his obligations. Conducting civil wedding ceremonies, especially on Saturdays, was one of his most important functions. But in observations that were expressly said to 'travel outside the ambit of this case',[30] Lord Brightman and Lord Templeman both expressed the view that even where industrial action took the form of an employee merely working inefficiently, the position would be the same, namely, that the employer can refuse to accept the work and pay nothing, albeit that they thought the employee may be able to recover for the value of his services on a quantum meruit basis.[31] Lord Templeman, for example, said that 'a worker who, in conjunction with his fellow workers, declines to work efficiently with the object of harming his employer is no more entitled to his wages under the contract than if he declines to work at all'.[32] Lord Bridge, Lord Brandon, and Lord Oliver, by contrast, preferred to express no view on the matter.[33]

It was against this background that *Wiluszynski* was decided. The plaintiff was an estate officer employed by the council. His work involved dealing with issues in relation to the council's housing estates. This work primarily concerned 'repairs, tenant's problems, vacant properties and re-letting, illegal occupants and squatters

[26] Sales (n 14) 303; J English, 'Employment Contracts, Conditions, and the Relationship of Employment' (2024) 140 *Law Quarterly Review* 521, 523–526.

[27] See, eg, *Browning v Crumlin Valley Collieries Ltd* [1926] 1 KB 522, 528; *Miles v Wakefield Metropolitan District Council* [1987] AC 539, 561, 570.

[28] It is a question of construction whether the condition of an employee's entitlement to be paid is the actual doing of the work or merely being ready, willing, and able to do the work: *Petrie v Mac Fisheries Ltd* [1940] 1 KB 258, 269–270; *O'Grady v M Saper Ltd* [1940] 2 KB 469, 473; *Automatic Fire Sprinklers Pty Ltd v Watson* (1946) 72 CLR 435, 452. See further T Chitty, A Denning, and C Harvey, *A Selection of Leading Cases on Various Branches of the Law with Notes by John William Smith*, vol 2 (London, Sweet & Maxwell, 1929) 49; P Elias, 'The Structure of the Employment Contract' [1982] *Current Legal Problems* 95, 102; English (n 26).

[29] *Automatic Fire Sprinklers Pty Ltd v Watson* (1946) 72 CLR 435, 466.

[30] [1987] AC 536, 553.

[31] ibid 553 (Lord Brightman), 561 (Lord Templeman). The possible claim in restitution is not discussed further in this chapter but see Stevens (n 9) 131.

[32] [1987] AC 536, 561.

[33] ibid 552 (Lord Bridge), 552 (Lord Brandon), 576 (Lord Oliver).

and so on'.[34] One of the plaintiff's duties was also to answer 'members' inquiries' – inquiries from local councillors in relation to housing estate matters. The evidence was that, on average, the plaintiff would receive one or two of these a week.[35] As part of an industrial dispute, the plaintiff and other members of his union resolved not to answer member inquiries. The plaintiff was informed in writing by the council that if he did not perform his contractual duties in full, he would not be paid and that any work undertaken would be done so in a purely voluntary capacity. During the one-month period of the dispute, the plaintiff refused to answer members' inquiries but otherwise 'performed his duties normally and conscientiously'.[36] After the dispute ended, it took the plaintiff only two to three hours to respond to the 10 members' inquiries he had received. The council nonetheless refused to pay him any salary.

At first instance, in an action for his salary, it was held that the plaintiff had substantially performed his obligations and was, therefore, entitled to be paid.[37] But, the Court of Appeal (Fox LJ, Nicholls LJ, and Mann J) allowed the council's appeal and held that the plaintiff was not entitled to be paid at all. Fox LJ (with whom Mann J agreed)[38] saw *Miles v Wakefield* as establishing the principle that 'an employee is not entitled to remuneration under the contract of employment unless he is willing to perform that contract'.[39] The council was entitled to refuse to accept the plaintiff's partial performance and although the council had not physically prevented him from working, the Court held that it had not accepted or acquiesced in the partial performance of his duties.[40]

One argument put on behalf of the plaintiff was that he had substantially performed his obligations and '[t]he work actually done represented … virtually complete performance of the contract'.[41] But this argument was given short shrift. In an important passage, Fox LJ said:

> I do not think that we are here concerned with any question of the application of the doctrine of 'substantial performance.' That doctrine was concerned with the mitigation of the hardship of the old law as to entire contracts. I agree with the observations to that effect of Scott J in *Sim v Rotherham Metropolitan Borough Council* … The present case is not concerned with entire contracts.[42]

In any event, Fox LJ did not think 'that the breach was in fact insubstantial'.[43] Nicholls LJ, who expressed no view on the applicability of the doctrine of

[34] *Wiluszynski v Tower Hamlets London Borough Council* [1988] IRLR 154, 154 [2] (High Court).
[35] *Wiluszynski v Tower Hamlets London Borough* [1989] ICR 493, 495.
[36] ibid 497.
[37] *Wiluszynski v Tower Hamlets London Borough Council* [1988] IRLR 154.
[38] Mann J agreed with both judgments.
[39] [1989] ICR 493, 499. See also 503 (Nicholls LJ).
[40] ibid 500. But compare the finding at first instance: 1988] IRLR 154, 156 [10]–[11].
[41] [1989] ICR 493, 499.
[42] ibid 499.
[43] ibid 499.

substantial performance, similarly thought that responding to members' inquiries was a 'material part' of the plaintiff's obligations.[44]

These two decisions – *Miles v Wakefield* and *Wiluszynski* – appear to establish the following propositions.[45] First, it is a condition of an employee's entitlement to be paid that they either perform all of their contractual duties or are ready, willing, and able to do so over the period in which the right to payment accrues. The result of sections 2 and 5 of the Apportionment Act 1870, as interpreted by courts, is that this period will ordinarily be a day.[46] Secondly, an employer who is faced with an employee who is not willing to perform their contractual duties in full can refuse to accept the employee's partial performance, but they need not dismiss or suspend the employee or terminate the contractual relationship. Thirdly, provided that this refusal of acceptance is made clear (and it need not amount to a physical exclusion),[47] an employer will come under no obligation to pay the employee's wages. Finally, it is no answer to the employer's denial of the obligation to pay wages that the employee has 'substantially performed' their obligations or was ready, willing, and able to substantially perform – the 'doctrine' of substantial performance was only concerned to mitigate 'the hardship of the old law as to entire contracts'.[48]

The position at common law has been criticised from several different perspectives. For example, the cases have been said to leave workers seeking to take industrial action 'in a very precarious position',[49] giving employers a 'powerful weapon'[50] and 'a quite enormous power'[51] in response to actions short of strike. One contemporaneous commentator wrote that '[t]he decision in *Wiluszynski* shifts the power relationship between employer and worker very much in favour of the employer'.[52] It has also been suggested that the law, as presently understood, might contravene various human rights protections, specifically, an employee's right to strike and take industrial action, derived from the right to freedom of association in Article 11 of the European Convention on Human Rights.[53]

[44] ibid 503.

[45] For similar summaries, see J McMullen, 'The Legality of Deductions from Strikers' Wages' (1988) 51 *Modern Law Review* 234, 237–239; V Shrubsall, 'Industrial Action: Limited Industrial Action and Entitlement to Pay' (1989) 18 *Industrial Law Journal* 241, 243–244; M Freedland and J Adams-Prassl, 'Employment' in H Beale (ed), *Chitty on Contracts*, 35th edn, (London, Sweet & Maxwell, 2023) 1585, 1652–1653 [43-097].

[46] See *Sim v Rotherham Metropolitan Borough Council* [1987] Ch 216, 254–255; *Hartley v King Edward VI College* [2017] 1 WLR 2110; Sales (n 14) 305–306.

[47] See, especially *Wiluszynski v Tower Hamlets London Borough* [1989] ICR 493, 500.

[48] *Wiluszynski v Tower Hamlets London Borough* [1989] ICR 493, 499. See also *Sim v Rotherham Metropolitan Borough Council* [1987] Ch 216, 252–253.

[49] Mead (n 6) 7.

[50] G Smith, '"Part Work No Pay?' The Obligation to Pay Wages for Part Performance in Contracts of Employment' (1989) 2 *Australian Journal of Labour Law* 91, 92.

[51] KD Ewing, *The Right to Strike* (Oxford, Oxford University Press, 1991) 39.

[52] Mead (n 6) 195.

[53] Mead (n 6); Bogg and Ford (n 5).

A further concern has been raised as to whether the law as currently understood is consistent with general contract law principles.[54] Professor Simon Deakin, for example, has written:

> The doctrinal basis of the wider version of 'no work, no pay' is far from clear. General contractual principles would suggest that an employer is not entitled to receive the benefit of substantial performance without paying for it, and that he only has a set-off or a counterclaim for damages if he can prove loss.[55]

This last criticism is particularly significant not just because this chapter appears in a book on private law perspectives on the contract of employment but because, if right, it suggests that the position at common law should not be quite as precarious as the cases suggest. This chapter therefore takes on the mantle of proving that this criticism is right and that the decision in *Wiluszynski* is wrongly decided as a matter of contract law both in result and in reasoning. In the section after the next, it will be argued that the mistake in *Wiluszynski* was to treat substantial performance as a doctrine rather than a question of construction and to assume that questions of substantial performance have no application to contracts of employment because employment contracts are not 'entire'. But before getting there, it is necessary to explain the so-called doctrine of substantial performance. It is to this task that the chapter now turns.

III. The 'Doctrine' of Substantial Performance

The aim of this section is to explain that there is no doctrine of substantial performance, merely a question of construction relevant to ascertaining the conditions of payment. The question is whether 'complete and exact' performance of one party's duty is the condition of the other party's obligation to pay or whether 'substantial performance' is the condition. But it is commonly supposed, albeit much criticised, by academic writers that there is judicial support for a doctrine of substantial performance that applies where a person has 'substantially performed' an 'entire contract' or an 'entire obligation'.[56] The substantial performance doctrine then entitles such a person to bring 'an action to recover the price, subject to a counterclaim for damages which will go in diminution of the price'.[57]

[54] Mead (n 6) 193; Deakin (n 6) 852; Adams, Barnard, Deakin, and Butlin (n 6) 302.302.

[55] Deakin (n 6) 852.

[56] E McKendrick, 'Performance' in H Beale (ed), *Chitty on Contracts*, 35th edn (London, Sweet & Maxwell, 2023) 1967, 1983–1984 [25-031]. See also B McFarlane and R Stevens, 'In defence of *Sumpter v Hedges*' (2002) 118 *Law Quarterly Review* 569, 585–586; E Peel, *The Law of Contract*, 15th edn (London, Sweet & Maxwell, 2020) 924 [17-040]; N Andrews, A Tettenborn, and G Virgo, *Contractual Duties: Performance, Breach, Termination and Remedies*, 4th edn (London, Sweet & Maxwell, 2023) 361 [15-017].

[57] McKendrick (n 56) (2023) 1967, 1983–1984 [25-031].

A. Entire Contracts

The idea that there is a doctrine of substantial performance is closely linked to the idea of an 'entire contract'. Unfortunately, like the word 'condition',[58] the phrase 'entire contract' is used in different senses in contract law, and it is not always easy to pin down the sense which different writers have in mind. As will be seen, this ambiguity has led to a great deal of confusion about substantial performance and is directly linked to the mistake made by the Court of Appeal in *Wiluszynski* discussed in the next section.

The phrase an 'entire contract' can be used in at least two different senses.[59] First, it can refer to a contract where there is a single obligation to pay the price on one side in exchange for a single, indivisible obligation to perform on the other (ie a lump sum contract).[60] It was this sense Professor Glanville Williams had in mind when he wrote that '[a] contract is entire … if the consideration is a lump sum and is neither agreed to be paid *pro rata* nor split up and appropriated to different portions of the contract'.[61] Various cases have used the concept in this way when stating that complete performance is a condition precedent to payment. In *Sumpter v Hedges*,[62] A L Smith LJ said: 'The law is that, where there is a contract to do work for a lump sum, until the work is completed the price of it cannot be recovered.' And in *Bolton v Mahadeva*,[63] Cairns LJ said that '[t]he rule which was laid down many years ago in *Cutter v Powell* … in relation to lump sum contracts was that unless the contracting party had performed the whole of the contract, he was not entitled to recover anything.'

In *Cutter v Powell*,[64] the concept of an entire contract was also used in this first sense. The defendant had promised to pay a sailor 30 guineas for a voyage of approximately two months from Jamaica to Liverpool. The usual wage for a sailor on a trip of this kind was four pounds per month. The sailor went onboard the ship but died around a month and a half into the voyage. The sailor's representatives sought to recover a proportion of his wages. The Court rejected the claim because the contract was 'entire'. The obligation to pay was subject to a condition precedent that the sailor complete the voyage and could not be considered divisible.

[58] See SJ Stoljar, 'The Contractual Concept of a Condition' (1953) 69 *Law Quarterly Review* 485, 486–488.

[59] Putting to one side the concept of an 'entire agreement' clause, designed to indicate that the written contract represents the entirety of the parties' agreement.

[60] This appears to be the sense used in Andrews, Tettenborn, and Virgo (n 56) 357 [15-001].

[61] G Williams, 'Partial Performance of Entire Contracts' (1941) 57 *Law Quarterly Review* 373, 374. Although note the criticism of this in A Beck, 'The Doctrine of Substantial Performance: Conditions and Conditions Precedent' (1975) 38 *Modern Law Review* 413, 413 fn 3; McFarlane and Stevens (n 56) 595–596.

[62] *Sumpter v Hedges* [1898] 1 QB 673, 674. Although the Queen's Bench report only refers to a 'lump sum' contract, not an 'entire contract', the Law Journal Reports version of the case refers to both phrases interchangeably: see *Sumpter v Hedges* (1898) 67 LJQB 545.

[63] *Bolton v Mahadeva*[1972] 1 WLR 1009, 1011.

[64] *Cutter v Powell* (1795) 6 Term Rep 320, 101 ER 573.

The result was that the sailor was bound to perform the whole voyage before he could recover anything under the contract. Nor could he recover in restitution – '[h]e stipulated to receive the larger sum [of thirty guineas] if the whole duty were performed, and nothing unless the whole of that duty were performed: it was a kind of insurance'.[65] The Court was particularly influenced by the fact that the contract was for nearly four times the amount he would have made if he had been paid by the month. It was, as we might say today, an 'if and only if' contract.[66]

The second sense, however, in which the concept of an entire contract can be used is to describe a contract where the condition of the obligation to pay is complete and exact performance by the other party of their contractual duty. This is the sense in which it was used in *Hoenig v Isaacs*.[67] In that case, the plaintiff was hired to decorate and furnish a flat for a sum of £750, payment to be made 'net cash, as the work proceeds; and balance on completion'.[68] The defendant had paid the plaintiff £400 but refused to pay the balance of £350 on the basis that the plaintiff had 'failed to perform his contract'.[69] It was found that the door of a wardrobe required replacing, a bookshelf would have to be remade, and that this would also require alterations to be made to a bookcase. The defendant had argued that this was an 'entire contract' that had not been performed.[70] The Court of Appeal (Somervell, Denning, and Romer LJJ) held that the work had been 'substantially performed' and the plaintiff was entitled to recover the contract price, subject to the defendant having a counterclaim in damages.

Somervell LJ said '[t]he question here is whether in a contract for work and labour for a lump sum payable on completion the defendant can repudiate liability under the contract on the ground that the work though "finished" or "done" is in some respects not in accordance with the contract'.[71] He referred to '[t]he principle that fulfilment of *every* term is not necessarily a condition precedent in a contract for a lump sum',[72] and added that 'if there was a substantial compliance with the contract', then 'the price must be paid subject to set-off or counterclaim'.[73] Denning LJ said:

> [T]he first question is whether, on the true construction of the contract, entire performance was a condition precedent to payment. … When a contract provides for a specific sum to be paid on completion of specified work, the courts lean against a construction of the contract which would deprive the contractor of any payment at all simply because there are some defects or omissions. The promise to complete the work is, therefore,

[65] *Cutter v Powell* (1795) 6 Term Rep 320, 325; 101 ER 573, 576 (Lord Kenyon CJ).
[66] See *Barton v Morris* [2023] UKSC 3 [35]–[36].
[67] [1952] 2 All ER 176. See also Sales (n 14) 305 fn 17.
[68] [1952] 2 All ER 176, 177.
[69] ibid 177.
[70] ibid 177.
[71] ibid 179.
[72] ibid 178 (emphasis added).
[73] ibid 179.

> construed as a term of the contract, but not as a condition. It is not every breach of that term which absolves the employer from his promise to pay the price, but only a breach which goes to the root of the contract, such as an abandonment of the work when it is only half done. Unless the breach does go to the root of the matter, the employer cannot resist payment of the price.[74]

The plaintiff's claim for the price therefore succeeded because the contract was not 'entire' in the sense that complete and exact performance of every contractual term was the condition of the defendant's obligation to pay.

These two senses of 'entire contracts' are not the same – what is an entire contract in one sense is not necessarily an entire contract in the other sense. As Denning LJ said in *Hoenig v Isaacs*,[75] '[i]t was a lump sum contract, but that does not mean that entire performance was a condition precedent to payment.' Similarly, commenting on *Cutter v Powell*, Somervell LJ in the same case said:

> It clearly decided that his continuing as mate during the whole voyage was a condition precedent to payment. It did not decide that if he had completed the main purpose of the contract, namely, serving as mate for the whole voyage, the defendant could have repudiated his liability by establishing that in the course of the voyage the sailor had, possibly through inadvertence, failed on some occasion in his duty as mate whereby some damage had been caused.[76]

It is probably too late to insist that judges, academics, and practitioners only use the phrase 'entire contract' in one sense.[77] But it is paramount that the distinction between these two senses is made clear lest mistakes be made. The fact that a contract is a contract for a lump sum, does not mean that exact and literal performance is required.

Even here, a criticism still remains, for it is often said – in a proposition attributed to Sir Guenter Treitel – that the concept of an entire contract is misleading because 'what is entire or severable is a particular *obligation* arising under the contract'.[78] Thus, it is said: 'A building contract may provide for payments as the work progresses, subject to a "retention fund" to be paid over on completion. There is then a series of severable obligations to complete each stage as well as an entire obligation to complete the whole.'[79] The idea is that, in an example such as this, the 'contract' is neither wholly entire nor severable. Instead, the focus must be on the obligations that trigger the duty to pay the price, some of which may be entire and some of which may be severable.

[74] ibid 180–181.
[75] ibid 180.
[76] ibid 178.
[77] cf Beck (n 61) who attempted in 1975 to insist that only the second sense is used.
[78] Peel (n 56) 921 [17-037] (emphasis in original). See also McFarlane and Stevens (n 56) 571; McKendrick (n 56) 1967, 1981 [25-027]; Andrews, Tettenborn, and Virgo (n 56) 357–358 [15-002]–[15-005].
[79] Peel (n 56) 922 [17-037].

But with respect, this criticism is slightly off the mark. To be clear, it is not off the mark in concluding that the language of an 'entire contract' may mislead (which it clearly can) but rather because the concept has nothing to do with the obligations of the parties at all. Instead, it is about the *conditions* of the parties' obligations. As Professors Ben McFarlane and Robert Stevens have pointed out, '[t]hose acts which a party needs to perform if he wants to trigger a duty of counter-performance can be categorised as entire or severable, even if there is no contractual obligation on that party to perform at all.'[80] Thus, in *Cutter v Powell*, if the sailor had been promised payment if and only if he proceeded from Liverpool to Jamaica but being under no obligation to do so (ie, a unilateral contract), the result would be no different. It would still be an entire contract in the first sense identified above. The claim failed not because of any breach of duty,[81] but because he could not satisfy the condition of payment. It would be better to explain the concepts without reference to the parties' obligations at all.[82] This is because there is an important distinction between obligations (ie duties) and conditions.

The reason all this matters is because failing to clarify the concepts in play leads to confusion. So while in *Wiluszynski* Fox LJ said that the 'doctrine [of substantial performance] was concerned with the mitigation of the hardship of the old law as to entire contracts',[83] it is also often said that there is no room for questions of substantial performance in relation to entire contracts.[84] These two statements appear to contradict each other, but this is because they are using the same phrase in different senses. The latter proposition, for example, is clearly false when the concept of an entire contract is used in the first sense to refer to a lump sum contract. As we saw in *Cutter v Powell*, even if he had remained alive until the completion of the voyage, questions of substantial performance may have remained if his work was so poor as to deprive his employer of substantially the whole benefit of the contract. By contrast, when the concept of an entire contract is used in the second sense, to indicate a contract where the condition of the obligation to pay is complete and exact performance by the other party, it is clearly right – there is no room for questions of substantial performance. But this is to beg the question of construction: whether complete and exact performance is the condition of payment or whether substantial performance is the condition.

[80] McFarlane and Stevens (n 56) 571.

[81] Indeed, there was no breach of duty: 'All contracts for personal services which can be performed only during the lifetime of the party contracting are subject to the implied condition that he shall be alive to perform them' (*Hall v Wright* (1859) El Bl & El 765, 793; 120 ER 695, 706 (Pollock CB)). See also *Poussard v Spiers & Ponds Ltd* (1876) 1 QBD 410, 414, dealing with illness.

[82] McFarlane and Stevens (n 56) 571.

[83] *Wiluszynski v Tower Hamlets London Borough* [1989] ICR 493, 499.

[84] McFarlane and Stevens (n 56) 585–586; J Beatson, A Burrows, and J Cartwright, *Anson's Law of Contract*, 31st edn (Oxford, Oxford University Press, 2020) 452; Peel (n 56) 924 [17-040]; McKendrick (n 56) 1967, 1984 [25-031].

B. Substantial Performance: A Question of Construction

As *Hoenig v Isaacs* makes clear, even when the concept of an entire contract is used in the second sense, there is no doctrine of substantial performance. Instead, there is only a question of construction: is the condition of one party's obligation to pay the price complete and exact performance by the other party (sometimes expressed by the idea that the contract or obligation is 'entire') or substantial performance by the other party? The mistake has been to suggest that there is a doctrine that renders substantial, but not complete, performance of a condition sufficient.[85] When stated in these terms, the doctrine is obviously objectionable, for it assumes that a condition requiring complete and exact performance can be satisfied by something less than that. Conditions do not work in that way. They are binary: either they are performed, or they are not. Just as it is no defence to an action for breach of duty to claim that the promisor has 'substantially performed',[86] a condition requiring complete and exact performance cannot be satisfied by substantial performance. Cases where substantial performance has been sufficient to trigger the duty to pay are not cases in which there has operated a doctrine of substantial performance; they are cases in which '"substantial performance" *is* the condition – the fact that must exist before payment is due'.[87]

When understood in this way, the process of construction and application of the relevant condition becomes clear. First, it must be asked whether complete and exact performance is the condition of a party's obligation to pay the price. If it is, then questions of substantial performance are irrelevant. But, as we have seen, 'courts lean against a construction of the contract which would deprive the contractor of any payment at all simply because there are some defects or omissions'.[88] If, therefore, complete and exact performance is not the condition of that party's obligation to pay the price, the second question to be asked is whether substantial performance is the condition.[89] Where substantial performance is the condition, the promisor will only come under an obligation to pay where they have received substantially the whole benefit of the contract – in other words, where there has been substantial performance.

One final point to make is that where substantial performance is the condition, the question is not whether a substantial part of the performance has been rendered or whether the party seeking to claim the price has 'performed to a

[85] See, eg, Beck (n 61) 427; F Wilmot-Smith, 'Reconsidering "Total" Failure' (2013) 72 *Cambridge Law Journal* 414, 428.

[86] A Corbin, *Corbin on Contracts: A Comprehensive Treatise on the Rules of Contract Law* (Eagan, Minnesota, West Publishing Company, 1960) vol 3A, 315–316 §702.

[87] ibid 314 §701 (emphasis in original).

[88] *Hoenig v Isaacs* [1952] 2 All ER 176, 180.

[89] It is of course possible that the obligation to pay the price is not conditional on either exact and complete performance or substantial performance – often referred to as an 'independent' or 'unconditional' promise. But this will be rare, to say the least.

substantial degree'.[90] This runs the risk of putting the bar too low, enabling satisfaction of the condition where one party has provided a material part, but not substantially all, of the consideration. The better way of putting the question is to ask whether the party liable to pay has received 'substantially the whole benefit which it was the intention of the parties as expressed in the contract that [they] should obtain as the consideration for [their payment]'.[91] If a shorthand is needed: did the party under the obligation to pay get substantially what they bargained for?

IV. Application to Employment Contracts

A. The Problems with *Wiluszynski*

Having explained the so-called doctrine of substantial performance, the mistake in *Wiluszynski* can be seen more clearly. As we have seen, Fox LJ thought that questions of substantial performance were irrelevant because '[t]hat doctrine was concerned with the mitigation of the hardship of the old law as to entire contracts. … The present case is not concerned with entire contracts.'[92] In reaching this conclusion, he relied on the obiter observations of Scott J in *Sim v Rotherham Metropolitan Borough Council*,[93] another case (discussed in the next section) concerned with an action short of strike, in which Scott J had stated: '[T]he doctrine of substantial performance does not, in my view, have anything to do with these four [test] cases. The question whether there has or has not been substantial performance of a contract only arises, in my view, where the contract is an entire contract.'[94]

It is clear that both judges are using 'entire contracts' in the first sense identified in the previous section – to identify a lump sum contract in which there is a single obligation to pay the price on one side in exchange for a single, indivisible obligation to perform on the other. They cannot be referring to the second sense – to describe a contract where the condition of the obligation to pay is complete and exact performance by the other party of their contractual duty – because then no question of substantial performance could ever arise. Their reasoning then appears to be as follows.

First, they conclude that an employment contract is not an entire contract in the sense of a lump sum contract. This is because in each case the worker was paid a salary, which meant that by virtue of the Apportionment Act 1870, their right to

[90] McMullen (n 45).

[91] *Hongkong Fir Shipping Co Ltd v Kawasaki Kisen Kaisha Ltd* [1962] 2 QB 26, 66 (Diplock LJ). For the relationship between substantial performance and the doctrine in *Hongkong Fir*, see J English, *Discharge of Contractual Obligations* (Oxford, Oxford University Press, 2025) ch 3.

[92] *Wiluszynski v Tower Hamlets London Borough* [1989] ICR 493, 499.

[93] [1987] Ch 216.

[94] *Sim v Rotherham Metropolitan Borough Council* [1987] Ch 216, 252–253.

payment was deemed to accrue day by day.[95] Secondly, because the contract is not an entire contract in this sense, then the 'doctrine' of substantial performance is inapplicable. The result is that exact and literal performance of the employee's duty is the condition precedent to payment, and substantial performance is not sufficient. Following *Sim* and *Wiluszynski*, the position appears to be that substantial performance 'is unlikely to come into play in relation to personal work or employment contracts in so far as the obligations of work and remuneration are regarded as divisible into daily units'.[96]

But this is an obvious mistake. It assumes that because a contract is not entire in the first sense (ie, it is a divisible rather than a lump sum contract), it must be entire in the second sense so as to require literal and exact performance in order to satisfy the condition of payment. This is to beg the question of construction. The question still remains as to whether, on a proper construction of the contract, for each period over which the right to payment accrues, the employee must render exact and complete performance of their contractual duty or substantial performance. In other words, what is the condition of each payment obligation? Whether the payment obligation accrues by day, by month, or by year, this question needs to be answered. Substantial performance is not a doctrine designed to mitigate some perceived unfairness but a simple question of construction: is complete and exact performance or substantial performance the condition of the obligation to pay?

The effect of *Wiluszynski* is that employment law cases are now (counter-intuitively) harsher on employees than the approach taken in cases involving commercial contractors. In the context of commercial contracts, 'courts lean against a construction of the contract which would deprive the contractor of any payment at all simply because there are some defects or omissions'.[97] The effect of this is that unless made clear, the default assumption is that substantial performance, rather than complete and exact performance, is the condition of the promisor's obligation to pay. *Wiluszynski* and the cases following it[98] take precisely the opposite approach. While there might be room for proper debate about whether there should exist an autonomous law of employment contracts,[99] or whether 'we should keep the contract of employment firmly within the harbour which the common law has solidly constructed for the entire fleet of contracts',[100] it would seem wrong for employment contracts to develop in a way that produces harsher effects on employees.

[95] See, eg, [1987] Ch 216, 255.

[96] M Freedland, *The Personal Employment Contract*, Paperback edn (Oxford, Oxford University Press, 2005) 204.

[97] *Hoenig v Isaacs* [1952] 2 All ER 176, 180.

[98] *Cooper v Isle of Wight College* [2007] EWHC 2831; *Spackman v London Metropolitan University* [2007] IRLR 744.

[99] D Brodie, 'The Autonomy of the Common Law of the Contract of Employment from the General Law of Contract' in M Freedland (ed), *The Contract of Employment* (Oxford, Oxford University Press, 2016) 124.

[100] *Geys v Société Générale* [2013] 1 AC 523, 561 [97].

What should the position be? In principle, there should be no rule that questions of substantial performance are irrelevant to contracts of employment. It is always a question of construction as to whether the condition of the employer's obligation to pay salary or wages is complete and exact performance by the employee or substantial performance by the employee. In line with the approach taken to commercial contracts, ordinarily, it would be expected that substantial performance, rather than complete and exact performance, is the relevant condition.[101] If substantial performance is the condition, then as Philip Sales has observed: '[T]he proper approach is, first, to determine the period over which the employee must work before a right to receive pay for that period accrues and, secondly, to determine whether or not [they have] substantially performed [their] obligations under the contract over that period.'[102]

Moreover, where substantial performance is the condition of the obligation to pay, an employer should only have a 'right to refuse to accept services which do not substantially comply with the contract'.[103] When the House of Lords in *Miles v Wakefield* said that unless an employee is willing to perform their duties in full, the employer is entitled to refuse to accept any partial performance, they were dealing with a case in which the superintendent had failed substantially to perform. Even assuming that in a contract of employment an employer must 'accept' an employee's services before they are under a duty to pay (like in a contract for the sale of goods where the goods must be 'accepted' before the obligation to pay the price falls due),[104] it cannot be right that, as suggested in *Wiluszynski*,[105] an employee must be ready and willing to provide complete and exact performance before an employer is under a duty to accept their service. If the performance being tendered would be sufficient to trigger the duty to pay, it should also trigger the duty to accept.

Again, the approach taken in *Wiluszynski* is not the approach taken in commercial contexts. In *Shipton Anderson & Co v Weil Bros & Co*,[106] for example, the plaintiffs had sold to the defendants a cargo of wheat that was to weigh 10 per cent more or less than 4,500 tons. The plaintiffs tendered a cargo that was 55 lbs more than the maximum permitted weight (4,950 tons), following which the defendants rejected the goods. The defendants relied upon section 30(2) of the Sale of Goods

[101] Sales (n 14) 305 fn 17 ('the usual precondition to the right to payment implied is substantial performance of the payee's obligations'). See also AT Denning, 'Wages During Sickness' (1939) 54 *Law Quarterly Review* 353, 354; B Napier, 'Aspects of the Wage-Work Bargain' (1984) 43 *Cambridge Law Journal* 337, 342, 344.

[102] Sales (n 14) 305.

[103] ibid 305.

[104] It seems doubtful that an employer must 'accept' an employee's work before coming under an obligation to pay. The real role of an employer refusing to 'accept' non-conforming work seems to be to negate any inference that a condition has been waived or to prevent any restitutionary or implied contract claim arising from the acceptance of non-conforming work.

[105] [1989] ICR 493, 499.

[106] *Shipton Anderson & Co v Weil Bros & Co* [1912] 1 KB 574.

Act 1893,[107] which entitled a buyer to reject a delivery of the wrong quantity. Lush J held that the defendants could not rely upon this section and that the plaintiffs were entitled to substantial damages. He said:

> I think that the question is whether there has been a substantial departure from the contract. … [T]he right to reject is founded upon the hypothesis that the seller was not ready and willing to perform, or had not performed, his part of the contract. The tender of a wrong quantity evidences an unreadiness and unwillingness, but that, in my opinion, must mean an excess or deficiency in quantity which is capable of influencing the mind of the buyer. In my opinion, this excess is not.[108]

As *Shipton Anderson* shows, when courts speak of readiness and willingness, they usually mean readiness and willingness to substantially perform or to perform the 'essential' obligations contained within the contract, not readiness and willingness to provide complete and exact performance. So in the Australian case of *Foran v Wight*,[109] Brennan J said that a party seeking to terminate for anticipatory breach must show 'not only the other's repudiation but his own readiness and willingness up to the time of rescission to perform his *essential* obligations under the contract'.

A further example can be found in the context of specific performance. A claimant seeking specific performance of a contract must show that they are ready, willing, and able to perform their contractual obligations. But they only need to show that they are ready, willing, and able to provide substantial performance, not complete and exact performance.[110] As Barwick CJ observed in the High Court of Australia in *Mehmet v Benson*,[111] in a statement that has been applied by Mr Justice Briggs (as he then was) in *Frasers Islington Ltd v Hanover Trustee Co Ltd*:[112]

> The question as to whether or not the plaintiff has been and is ready and willing to perform the contract is one of substance not to be resolved in any technical or narrow sense. It is important to bear in mind what is the substantial thing for which the parties contract and what on the part of the plaintiff in a suit for specific performance are his essential obligations.[113]

It therefore seems that both in reasoning and result, the decision in *Wiluszynski* is wrongly decided. In terms of reasoning, it assumes that because contracts of employment are not 'entire' in the sense that they are not lump sum contracts, questions of substantial performance have no application. This is mistaken and begs the question of construction as to whether substantial performance is the condition of payment. It also results in the approach taken to employment

[107] See now Sale of Goods Act 1979, s 30(2).
[108] [1912] 1 KB 574, 577.
[109] *Foran v Wight* (1989) 168 CLR 385, 424 (emphasis added), citing *Rawson v Hobbs* (1961) 107 CLR 466, 480–481.
[110] See Andrews, Tettenborn, and Virgo (n 56) 684 [27-055]–[27-056].
[111] *Mehmet v Benson* (1965) 113 CLR 295.
[112] *Frasers Islington Ltd v Hanover Trustee Co Ltd* [2010] EWHC 1514 (Ch) [17].
[113] *Mehmet v Benson* (1965) 113 CLR 295, 307.

contracts being out of kilter with the approach taken to commercial contracts. As for the result, the Court of Appeal concluded that, in any event, the breach was 'substantial' because it was important 'in terms of the responsibility of councillors to their constituents and of the rights of constituents to be properly informed in relation to matters affecting them'.[114] But the question that should have been asked was whether the council had received substantially the whole benefit that it was intended that they should obtain from the contract. They hired an estates officer, whose principal role was to deal with complaints from tenants, repairs, relations with neighbours, and other matters.[115] The plaintiff had even dealt with any problems that arose from a member's inquiry (he just did not inform the member of the answer to the inquiry).[116] The backlog of inquiries, built up over the month-long dispute, only took him two to three hours to clear. It was, as has been observed by Professor Keith Ewing, 'virtually complete performance of the contract'.[117] The council may not have gotten complete and exact performance, but they had received substantially the whole benefit that it was intended they should obtain in consideration for their promise to pay.

B. The Obligation to Render Faithful Service and Follow Lawful Instructions

It might be argued that there is another explanation for the result in *Wiluszynski* and the strict approach it takes to an employee's entitlement to be paid, which would also explain the wider comments of Lord Brightman and Lord Templeman in *Miles v Wakefield* about employees 'working to rule'. It will be recalled, for example, that Lord Templeman said: 'a worker who, in conjunction with his fellow workers, declines to work efficiently with the object of harming his employer is no more entitled to his wages under the contract than if he declines to work at all'.[118] Similarly, in *Secretary of State for Employment v ASLEF (No 2)*,[119] Lord Denning MR said: 'Is a man to be entitled to wages for his work when he, with others, is doing his best to make it useless? Surely not. Wages are to be paid for services rendered, not for producing deliberate chaos.'

Employees are under an implied obligation to render faithful service to their employers and to follow all lawful and reasonable instructions.[120] A breach of this obligation can give the employer the ability to terminate the relationship of

[114] [1989] ICR 493, 499.
[115] ibid 495.
[116] *Wiluszynski v Tower Hamlets London Borough Council* [1988] IRLR 154, 155 [3].
[117] KD Ewing, *The Right to Strike* (Oxford, Oxford University Press, 1991) 32.
[118] [1987] AC 536, 561.
[119] *Secretary of State for Employment v ASLEF (No 2)* [1972] ICR 19, 56.
[120] See, eg, *Laws v London Chronicle (Indicator Newspapers) Ltd* [1959] 1 WLR 698; *Secretary of State for Employment v ASLEF (No 2)* [1972] ICR 19.

employment; that is, to dismiss the employee.[121] In this sense, it is a condition of the employer's ongoing obligation to maintain the employment relationship. Can it be argued that performance of this obligation is also a condition of an employee's entitlement to be paid? The effect of this would be that an employee who refuses to follow their employer's lawful instructions during a period of industrial action falling short of a strike fails to satisfy the condition of payment during that period and is, therefore, in the same position as a worker who refuses to work at all.[122]

That this is not the case is shown by the cases concerned with claims for salary or wages following a justified dismissal for misconduct.[123] These cases show that the dismissal 'does not relate back to the time of the antecedent misconduct'.[124] A particularly illustrative case is *Healey v Société Anonyme Française Rubastic*.[125] In that case, the plaintiff was justifiably dismissed by his employer in October 1915 for submitting false and misleading reports from January to April 1915. The employee was paid up until May 1915 but was not dismissed until October 1915. He sought to recover his unpaid salary for the months up to his dismissal. The defendants argued that 'it was a condition precedent to the right of payment of the salary that the plaintiff should truly and faithfully serve his employers and that as he had failed in the performance of this condition was not entitled to recover.'[126] The Court rejected this argument and held that he was entitled to recover for the months that he had served.[127]

It therefore seems implausible to argue that performance of the obligation to render faithful service is also a condition of an employee's entitlement to be paid: the consideration for the payment obligation is simply the doing of or the readiness and willingness to do the work. The law has long since abandoned the 'simple notion of obedience as the identifying feature of the obligation to work'.[128] But this is not to say that no instance of working to rule would ever disentitle an employee to payment: the question is whether the action has deprived the employer of substantially the whole benefit that it was intended that they should obtain for payment in the period in question. If the effect of a railway employee, for example, taking action short of strike is that the trains cannot run, then irrespective of the minor nature of the duty not performed, the effect of that breach will have been to

[121] Chitty, Denning, and Harvey (n 28) 48.
[122] Z Adams, '"Wage", "Salary" and "Remuneration": A Genealogical Exploration of Juridical Terms and their Significance for the Employer's Power to Make Deductions from Wages' (2019) 48 *Industrial Law Journal* 34, 58.
[123] *Button v Thompson* (1869) LR 4 CP 330; *George v Davies* [1911] 2 KB 445; *Healey v Société Anonyme Française Rubastic* [1917] 1 KB 946.
[124] Chitty, Denning, and Harvey (n 28) 48.
[125] [1917] 1 KB 946.
[126] ibid 947.
[127] In fairness, the claim for salary was for the months of June to October, which was *after* the period in which the misconduct had occurred. But there was no suggestion that the salary for January to April 1915 (the period in which the misconduct did occur) should be recoverable on the grounds that the condition for its payment had not occurred and therefore it was not due.
[128] Freedland (n 11) 176.

deprive the employer of substantially the whole benefit that it was intended they should obtain as the consideration for their payment obligation. But this is a question that will turn upon the contract in question and the facts of each case. The fact that the work was done, as will usually be the case in actions short of strike with the intention of inflicting economic damage on the employer, is a red herring. The focus is on the action's effects.

It should also be emphasised that the fact that an employee's obligation to act faithfully and loyally to their employer is not a condition of their entitlement to be paid does not mean that it cannot be a condition of other obligations in the contract. As has already been mentioned, the duty to act loyally *is* a condition of the employer's ongoing obligation to maintain the relationship of employment; failure to comply with this condition permits the employer to bring that relationship to an end, that is to dismiss the employee.

Similarly, there is a line of cases that suggest that where an employer is under a specific duty to provide work to the employee,[129] that obligation is conditional on the employee complying with their obligation of loyalty.[130] In *SG & R Valuation Service Co v Boudrais*,[131] for example, the question for Cranston J was whether, in the absence of an express contractual power, two defendant employees, who had breached their duties of good faith and fidelity and who sought to join a rival employer, could be placed on 'garden leave' while they served out their notice period. This was dealt with by asking whether the employees had a 'right to work'. Cranston J held that they did, but because of their prior breaches of duty, the employer was under no obligation to provide them with work.[132] But importantly, and underscoring the point being made in this section, although the obligation to provide work was conditional on there not being a prior breach of the duty of loyalty, the obligation to pay their salary was not – the employees were still entitled to be paid.[133]

Boudrais was applied in similar circumstances by the Court of Appeal in *Standard Life Health Care Ltd v Gorman*.[134] Waller LJ (with whom Longmore and Jacob LJJ agreed) said it was 'strongly arguable' that:

> where the employer discovers that the employee has been in serious breach of duty and in breach of his duty of good faith … then the employer has, even if he keeps the contract alive, no obligation to provide work; that obligation to provide work being interdependent with the obligation of the employee to act loyally.[135]

[129] *cf Collier v Sunday Referee Publishing Co* [1940] KB 647, 650 ('[A] contract of employment does not necessarily, or perhaps normally, oblige the master to provide the servant with work. Provided I pay my cook her wages regularly she cannot complain if I choose to take any or all of my meals out.').

[130] *SG & R Valuation Service Co v Boudrais* [2008] EWHC 1340 (QB); *Standard Life Health Care Ltd v Gorman* [2009] EWCA Civ 1292.

[131] [2008] EWHC 1340 (QB).

[132] ibid [24].

[133] ibid [33].

[134] [2009] EWCA Civ 1292.

[135] ibid [27]. See also at [21].

The key difference in this case was that the employees were paid by commission. The effect then of the employer not being under a duty to provide work was that the employees could lawfully be prevented from earning their commission and thus satisfying the conditions of payment. But even here, this is not because it was a condition of their entitlement to be paid that they render faithful service, but simply because it was a condition of the employer's obligation to provide work that they render faithful service. Practically speaking, the employer could prevent the employees from satisfying the condition of payment. If the employer had chosen to provide work and this had been done, there is no suggestion that the employees would not have been entitled to payment. And if, as in *Boudrais*, they were not paid on a commission basis, then they would have been entitled to their salary. The obligation to render faithful service is not a condition of an employee's entitlement to remuneration.

V. No Deductions?

In a case where substantial, but not complete and exact, performance has been rendered and the employee is thus entitled to payment of their salary or wages, does this mean that, at common law, an employer is not entitled to make any deduction and instead must either choose to dismiss the employee or keep the employment relationship on foot with little to no sanction? The answer is no, and this follows from the important distinction between duties and conditions. While the employee may have satisfied the condition of payment by rendering substantial performance, this is no defence to an action for breach of duty. The employee is, therefore, liable to pay damages to their employer, representing the value of the lost performance to the employer.[136] Although the employee's salary or wages have fallen due and are payable, an employer can withhold a proportionate amount and, when sued by the employee for their salary or wages, set up a counterclaim by way of setoff for the damage the employer has suffered – 'effectively [they] can, in practice, make a deduction from the employee's [salary or] wages'.[137]

This was the approach taken in *Sim v Rotherham Metropolitan Borough Council*,[138] decided a few months before *Miles v Wakefield*. In that case, as part of industrial action, teachers refused to provide teaching cover for colleagues who were absent. The local authority in each case (four test cases were brought) had deducted a small amount from each of their salaries, which represented the 'failure of the teacher to take the class for the period in question'.[139] Scott J held that each teacher had not been dismissed and was therefore entitled to their salary,

[136] *Miles v Wakefield Metropolitan District Council* [1987] AC 539, 559–560 (Lord Templeman) 566–568 (Lord Oliver). See also Sales (n 14) 310.
[137] ibid 566.
[138] [1987] Ch 216.
[139] ibid 229.

partly because of a view, then-prevailing and pre-*Miles v Wakefield*,[140] that a salary was, in essence, an unconditional payment, conditional only upon the continuation of the employment relationship.[141] Nonetheless, he held that the teachers were in breach of their contractual duties in not providing the cover teaching and that the local authorities were able to set up a counterclaim for damages and set this off against the amount owing by way of salary. It was agreed that the value of the deductions was at least the value of the services of which the local authorities had been denied.[142]

A similar, albeit not quite the same, approach was taken in *Royle v Trafford Borough Council*.[143] There, an assistant teacher, as part of industrial action, refused to teach more than 31 students in his class. He was instructed to teach 36 students. Nonetheless, he continued to teach the 31 students in his class and otherwise fulfilled his duties conscientiously. Park J held that any breach did not go 'to the very root of the consideration',[144] (in other words, it did not deny the employer of substantially the whole benefit of the contract), and so the teacher was entitled to his salary but held that a deduction of 5/36ths should be made to reflect 'the notional value of the services he ha[d] not rendered'.[145] The reason this approach is not quite the same as that taken in *Sim v Rotherham Metropolitan Borough Council* is that Park J did not make the deduction by allowing the defendant's counterclaim for damages for breach of contract but rather somehow deducted the amount directly from the salary that was held to be due and owing. But the result is clearly justifiable on the same basis as that in *Sim v Rotherham Metropolitan Borough Council*.

One difficulty with this approach might be thought to be: 'What if an employer … suffers no proven financial damage as a result of the industrial action?'[146] However, an answer to this problem has already been given by Lord Templeman and Lord Oliver in *Miles v Wakefield*.[147] Lord Templeman said:

> My Lords, an employer always suffers damage from the industrial action of an individual worker. The employer suffers the loss of the services of the worker. The value of those services to the employer cannot be less than the salary payable for those services …[148]

Lord Oliver also said:

> The simple fact would be that the council had suffered damage to the extent that it was liable to pay for what was, in effect, a period of voluntary absence from work and I see

[140] Adams (n 122) 42–44. See also Sales (n 14) 303–304.
[141] [1987] Ch 216, 253.
[142] ibid 230.
[143] *Royle v Trafford Borough Council* [1984] IRLR 184.
[144] ibid 188 [34].
[145] ibid 190 [53].
[146] Bogg and Ford (n 5).
[147] See generally, Sales (n 14) 310.
[148] *Miles v Wakefield Metropolitan District Council* [1987] AC 539, 560.

> no particular difficulty in quantifying that damage, since the employee could hardly contend successfully that that of which his employer had been deprived by his absence (i.e. his services) was worth less than the sum which he was claiming to be paid for them.[149]

The key to understanding this claim is to draw a distinction between a claim for 'general damages' and 'special damages'.[150] General damages, in this context, are, broadly speaking, damages for the difference between what the employer was promised and what they got – the value of the lost performance to the employer. Special damages, by way of contrast, are claims for proven, consequential, financial loss. An employer should be entitled to general damages, 'even if it can be shown that [they have], as a counterfactual matter, suffered no loss'.[151] This is not just an approach unique to employment contracts. It is the approach taken in contracts for the sale of goods,[152] contracts of carriage,[153] time charters,[154] and contracts to provide services.[155] A number of different labels have been used to describe this sort of claim,[156] but the key point is that it does not depend, in this context, on the employer showing that they are worse off counterfactually. Rather, the employer is claiming general damages for the lost performance by the employee due to their breach of duty.

It does not follow then that an employer faced with an employee who is taking action short of strike is left without any form of recourse. If the employee does not render substantial performance of their obligations, then the employer need not pay them anything at all. If the employee does render substantial performance, then the employer is still able to withhold an amount representing the value of the lost performance. If and when sued by the employee for their full salary or wages, the employer can then counterclaim or set-off by way of general damages (or special damages if they have suffered consequential loss) for the lost value of the performance: the difference between what they were promised and what they got. Of course, the downside of this approach for the employer is that if they do make a deduction, they 'must be prepared to justify the deduction by reference to the damage which [they have] suffered'.[157] But this provides a protection for the

[149] ibid 568.
[150] For an explanation, see Stevens (n 9) 295–296, 333–337; R Stevens, 'Damages and the Right to Performance: A Golden Victory or Not?' in J Neyers, R Bronaugh, and S Pitel (eds), *Exploring Contract Law* (Oxford, Hart Publishing, 2009) 171.
[151] Stevens (n 9) 296.
[152] See Sale of Goods Act 1979, s 51(3); *William Bros v Ed T Agius Ltd* [1914] AC 510; *Slater v Hoyle Smith Ltd* [1920] 2 KB 11; *Clark v Macourt* (2013) 253 CLR 1.
[153] *Rodocanachi, Sons & Co v Milburn Bros* (1886) 18 QBD 67.
[154] *Fultons Shipping Inc of Panama v Globalia Business Travel SAU* [2017] 1 WLR 2581.
[155] See *Alfred McAlpine Construction Ltd v Panatown Ltd* [2001] 1 AC 518, 547 (Lord Goff). This is the 'broad ground' in *Panatown*, adopted by Lord Goff and Lord Millett (admittedly both dissenting); cf Lord Jauncey and Lord Clyde. Lord Browne-Wilkinson, in the majority, appeared inclined to adopt it but for the existence of the duty of care deed on the facts: at 577–578. Thus three members of five in the House of Lords were supportive of this ground of recovery.
[156] Stevens (n 9) 296–297.
[157] *Miles v Wakefield Metropolitan District Council* [1987] AC 539, 566–567.

employee: it ensures that it is in the employer's own interest to only make proportionate deductions to avoid being found ultimately liable to the employee.

VI. The Limits of Private Law

The purpose of this chapter has not been to present a panacea to the problems faced by an employee who engages in an action short of strike but rather to suggest that the position at common law is not quite as precarious as the cases have sometimes suggested. Naturally, however, there are limits to what doctrinal private law can do for labour law and it would be a mistake to read this chapter as suggesting otherwise. Although this chapter argued that an employee who renders or is ready, willing, and able to provide substantial performance – contrary to the decision in *Wiluszynski* – should be entitled to payment, this only applies to employees who do, in fact, render substantial performance of their obligations over the period in which the right to payment accrues. If the effect of an employee's (in)action is that an employer has not received substantially the whole benefit that it was intended they should obtain as the consideration for performance of their payment obligation then, in accordance with common law principle, the employer would be entitled to withhold all payment. This is the case even if the employer, economically, is affected only minimally. Any further restrictions on an employer's ability to withhold payment must come from Parliament, where a proper balancing of the social, economic, and political factors can take place.

It would, however, equally be a mistake to assume that private law is completely powerless to protect itself from attempts to circumvent the operation of its rules. In particular, one response to the claims made in this chapter might be that even if courts accepted that in contracts of employment, ordinarily substantial performance, rather than complete and exact performance, is the condition of payment, then one would expect lawyers acting for employers to immediately insert a clause into all contracts to state expressly that complete and exact performance is the condition of payment, not substantial performance. If this clause were genuinely intended to take effect, then it is true that courts, absent legislative intervention, would give effect to that intention. But it must seriously be questioned whether such clauses would represent the genuine intentions of the parties to such an agreement. Would the employer genuinely intend, if the employee were five minutes late to work in breach of the agreement, to withhold the full day's pay? Courts have already developed tools to disregard clauses that have been inserted merely as a 'smoke screen' or 'pretence' to evade the operation of a legal rule, particularly where there exists between the parties an inequality of bargaining power. This is the 'pretence doctrine' that has been applied in relation to leases,[158] and was applied

[158] *AG Securities v Vaughan* [1990] 1 AC 417.

by the Supreme Court in the employment context in *Autoclenz Ltd v Belcher*.[159] If such drafting practices were to occur, the doctrine may have a renewed role to play.

VII. Conclusion

This chapter has been concerned with substantial performance in employment contracts. It has been argued that the decision of the Court of Appeal in *Wiluszynski* is wrongly decided both in result and in reasoning. The mistake it makes is that it assumes substantial performance is a doctrine that has no application to contracts that are not entire, in the sense of contracts that are not lump sum contracts. But the question of substantial performance is not a doctrine. It is a question of construction: what is the condition of the obligation to pay for services rendered? In commercial contracts, courts typically assume that the parties did not intend for complete and exact performance by one party to be the condition of the other's obligation to pay. Employment contracts should be no different. Yet the current state of the law treats employees more harshly than commercial contractors. Something has gone wrong.

The suggested solution in this chapter has been to recognise that *Wiluszynski* is wrongly decided and should no longer be followed. The effect would be that an employee who engages in industrial action short of a strike but nonetheless still renders substantial performance would ordinarily (unless, exceptionally, complete and exact performance were the condition of the obligation to pay) be entitled to their salary or wages. Substantial performance, however, is still no defence to a claim for breach of duty. An employer faced with an employee who is breaching their contractual duty can, in practice, make a proportionate deduction from their salary or wages. This deduction reflects the employer's claim for general damages, which it can set off against any claim by the employee for unpaid salary or wages. It is not dependent upon proving counterfactual loss. The employer is entitled to the difference between what was promised and what it got – in other words, the value of the lost performance. This does not solve all the problems raised by pay deductions in the context of actions short of strike, but it is an improvement, and one which coheres with general contractual principles.

[159] *Autoclenz Ltd v Belcher* [2011] 4 All ER 745.

5

Remedies in Workplace Discrimination Law: Private Law Perspectives on Damages

ALYSIA BLACKHAM*

I. Introduction

Damages for successful discrimination claims are generally very low,[1] and are rarely high. In my empirical research on age discrimination law in the UK and Australia, damages were described by experts in the field as 'very, very low', 'a pittance' and 'modest'.[2] This can act as a disincentive to claiming. As I found in that study, expert respondents reported that 'feeling that you're not going to get anything out of it is … one of the big reasons people don't want to pursue [a claim]'.[3] This has systemic consequences: if individuals are unwilling to bring a complaint, and discrimination law relies largely on individual complaints for enforcement, discriminatory treatment is likely to go unchallenged. At the same time, compared to unfair dismissal law, damages in discrimination law can offer benefits to claimants, as compensation is generally not capped under discrimination law,[4] and compensation for injury to feelings can be awarded.

* This research was funded by the Australian Government through the Australian Research Council's Discovery Projects funding scheme (Project DE170100228). The views expressed herein are those of the author and are not necessarily those of the Australian Government or Australian Research Council. I am grateful to Alan Bogg, Paul Davies, Nadia Motraghi KC, Lord Burrows and the Private Law Perspectives on the Contract of Employment Conference participants for their formative comments on this chapter.

[1] B Gaze and B Smith, *Equality and Discrimination Law in Australia: An Introduction* (Cambridge, Cambridge University Press, 2017) 196.

[2] A Blackham, *Reforming Age Discrimination Law: Beyond Individual Enforcement* (Oxford, Oxford University Press, 2022) 152. This research had ethics approval from the Human Research Ethics Committee of the University of Melbourne (ID number 1748973.4). To maintain source anonymity, each interview respondent is identified with A or UK and a number (eg, Respondent A1).

[3] ibid 153, Respondent A104.

[4] Note, though, that compensation is capped in some Australian states and territories: Western Australia, at AU$40,000: Equal Opportunity Act 1984 (WA) s 127(b); the Northern Territory, at

There is a need, then, to reconsider how we assess and award damages in discrimination law. Damages in discrimination claims are compensatory and appear to be analogous to damages in tort.[5] Tort law may therefore offer an important means of critiquing, supplementing, and developing discrimination law jurisprudence. In Australia, the courts embraced this approach in the case of *Richardson v Oracle Corporation Australia Pty Ltd*,[6] where tort (and, in particular, negligence) cases were used to recalibrate general damages awarded in discrimination claims.

This chapter considers the impact of *Richardson* in the Australian context and the extent to which private law perspectives have strengthened the award of damages in employment discrimination cases. It considers, too, the implications of these developments for the UK context, where discrimination damages are also generally low. This chapter draws on the findings of a multi-year mixed-methods empirical study of the enforcement of age discrimination law in Australia and the UK[7] to illustrate the implications of the law in practice. In particular, it draws on qualitative expert interviews conducted with 101 respondents in the UK and Australia, exploring the effectiveness of age discrimination law and barriers to its enforcement, including those relating to remedies.

II. The Australian Legislative Remedial Regime

Courts and tribunals in Australia have broad remedial powers in discrimination claims, but these powers are generally exercised conservatively. In the federal jurisdiction, for example, for discrimination claims, the Australian Human Rights Commission Act 1986 (Cth) section 46PO(4) (AHRC Act) says:

> (4) If the court concerned is satisfied that there has been unlawful discrimination by any respondent, the court may make such orders (including a declaration of right) as it thinks fit, including any of the following orders or any order to a similar effect:
>
> (a) an order declaring that the respondent has committed unlawful discrimination and directing the respondent not to repeat or continue such unlawful discrimination;
>
> (b) an order requiring a respondent to perform any reasonable act or course of conduct to redress any loss or damage suffered by an applicant;
>
> (c) an order requiring a respondent to employ or re-employ an applicant;
>
> (d) an order requiring a respondent to pay to an applicant damages by way of compensation for any loss or damage suffered because of the conduct of the respondent;

AU$60,000: Anti-Discrimination Act 1992 (NT) s 88(1)(b), Anti-Discrimination Regulations 1994 (NT) reg 2; and New South Wales, at AU$100,000: Anti-Discrimination Act 1977 (NSW) s 108.

[5] Gaze and Smith (n 1) 195.

[6] *Richardson v Oracle Corporation Australia Pty Ltd* [2014] FCAFC 82.

[7] The full method is detailed in Blackham (n 2).

(e) an order requiring a respondent to vary the termination of a contract or agreement to redress any loss or damage suffered by an applicant;

(f) an order declaring that it would be inappropriate for any further action to be taken in the matter.

Under the Fair Work Act 2009 (Cth) (FWA), the federal industrial law, following contravention of a civil remedy provision (including an adverse action claim), a court can 'make any order the court considers appropriate', including an injunction, compensation, or an order for reinstatement.[8] A court may also 'order a person to pay a pecuniary penalty that the court considers is appropriate'.[9] This penalty is in addition to other orders;[10] the penalty can be paid to the Commonwealth, an organisation, or a person.[11]

Australian states and territories have discrimination laws that generally operate concurrently with federal discrimination laws, and with similarly broad remedial powers. In the State of Victoria, for example, the Equal Opportunity Act 2010 (Vic) section 125 says:

> After hearing the evidence and representations that the parties to an application desire to adduce or make, the Tribunal may—
>
> (a) find that a person has contravened a provision of Part 4, 6 or 7 and make any one or more of the following orders—
>
> (i) an order that the person refrain from committing any further contravention of this Act;
>
> (ii) an order that the person pay to the applicant, within a specified period, an amount the Tribunal thinks fit to compensate the applicant for loss, damage or injury suffered in consequence of the contravention;
>
> (iii) an order that the person do anything specified in the order with a view to redressing any loss, damage or injury suffered by the applicant as a result of the contravention; or
>
> (b) find that a person has contravened a provision of Part 4, 6 or 7 but decline to take any further action; or
>
> (c) find that a person has not contravened a provision of Part 4, 6 or 7 and make an order that the application or part of the application be dismissed.

Despite the breadth of these remedial provisions, remedies in discrimination law often focus on compensation; in Victoria, to 'compensate the applicant for loss, damage or injury' and, at the federal level, 'by way of compensation for any loss or damage'. Understandably, then, damages in discrimination law are generally compensatory, and include special damages (which are economically quantifiable) and general damages (including for pain and suffering).[12]

[8] Fair Work Act 2009 (Cth) (FWA) s 545.
[9] FWA 2009, s 546(1).
[10] FWA 2009, s 546(5).
[11] FWA 2009, s 546(3).
[12] *cf* Gaze and Smith (n 1) 195.

Damages in discrimination claims appear to be broadly analogous to damages in tort.[13] That said, the courts have recognised that discrimination remedies are creatures of statute and will therefore not follow common law principles if they are inconsistent with the relevant statute.[14] In *Hall v A &A Sheiban Pty Ltd*, Lockhart J noted that:

> Although in my view it cannot be stated that in all claims for loss or damage under the [Sex Discrimination] Act the measure of damages is the same as the general principles respecting measure of damages in tort, it is the closest analogy that I can find and one that would in most foreseeable cases be a sensible and sound test. I would not, however, shut the door to some case arising which calls for a different approach.[15]

French J was more hesitant about relying on tortious principles to assess discrimination law damages, emphasising instead the primacy of statute:

> [The] measure is to be found, not in the law of tort, but in the words of the statute … There are decisions on anti-discrimination legislation which treat its contravention as a species of tort and approach the measure of damages accordingly …. Whether that classification is strictly correct or not, the measure of damages is to be governed by the statute and the rules applicable in tort can be of no avail if they conflict with it.[16]

Thus, while tortious principles might inform an assessment of damages in Australian discrimination law, this analogy cannot be stretched too far; remedies in discrimination law must defer to their statutory foundation.

III. The Legislative Regime in Great Britain

Under section 124(2) of the Equality Act 2010 (EqA), Employment Tribunals (ETs) may, following a contravention of the EqA,

> (a) make a declaration as to the rights of the complainant and the respondent in relation to the matters to which the proceedings relate;
> (b) order the respondent to pay compensation to the complainant;
> (c) make an appropriate recommendation.

An 'appropriate recommendation' is defined by section 124(3) as a recommendation that, within a specific period, 'the respondent takes specified steps for the purpose of obviating or reducing the adverse effect [on the complainant] of any matter to which the proceedings relate'. This is a more limited power to make recommendations than that which was originally included in the EqA; when the EqA was enacted, this power enabled the making of recommendations that related to any person. Following the Deregulation Act 2015 (c 20), section 2, however, the

[13] ibid.
[14] ibid; *Qantas Airways Limited v Gama* [2008] FCAFC 69 [94], [96] (French and Jacobson JJ).
[15] *Hall v A &A Sheiban Pty Ltd* [1989] FCA 65; 20 FCR 217 [72] (Lockhart J).
[16] ibid [60]–[61] (French J).

power to make recommendations has been limited to recommendations relating to the complainant specifically, rather than a broader power.

Under the EqA, section 119(2)(a), the County Court can grant any remedy that could be granted in the High Court in proceedings in tort, and, under section 124(6), the compensation an ET can award is the same as what a County Court can award under section 119. An award of damages may include compensation for injured feelings, irrespective of whether there is any other form of compensation.[17] There is no upper bound to the amount of compensation that can be awarded. An employer's unreasonable failure to follow the ACAS Code of Practice on Disciplinary and Grievance Procedures may lead to a 25 per cent uplift in compensation.[18]

Compensation in a discrimination claim is based on tortious principles.[19] The aim, then, is to put the claimant in the position they would have been in if the discrimination had not occurred;[20] any loss must 'flow "directly and naturally"' from the discrimination but need not be reasonably foreseeable[21] so long as there is a real causal link.[22] Compensation does not seek to punish the respondent. The ET is to assess the claimant's loss; when this arises from dismissal, the ET must assess how long the claimant would likely have been employed but for the dismissal.[23] As noted in *Chagger v Abbey National*,[24]

> It is necessary to ask what would have occurred had there been no unlawful discrimination. If there were a chance that dismissal would have occurred in any event, even had there been no discrimination, then in the normal way that must be factored into the calculation of loss.[25]

In assessing future loss of earnings, the ET is required to assess the chances of the claimant, for example, remaining in work until retirement age.[26] As noted in *Vento v Chief Constable of West Yorkshire Police* (*Vento*), 'The question requires a forecast to be made about the course of future events. It has to be answered on the basis of the best assessment that can be made on the relevant material available to the court'[27] which might include – but is not necessarily dictated by – statistics.[28] This is inevitably a process that is uncertain and somewhat speculative.[29]

[17] EqA, ss 119(4), 124(6).
[18] Trade Union and Labour Relations (Consolidation) Act 1992, s 207A. Or, conversely, a 25% reduction for an employee's unreasonable failure to follow the Code.
[19] *Chagger v Abbey National* [2010] ICR 397 [11] (determined under the Race Relations Act 1976).
[20] ibid [11], citing *Livingstone v Rawyards Coal Co* (1880) 5 App. Cas 25, 29.
[21] ibid [12], citing *Essa v Laing Ltd* [2004] IRLR 313 [37] (Pill LJ).
[22] ibid [13], citing *Essa v Laing Ltd* [2004] IRLR 313 [53] (Clarke LJ).
[23] In relation to unfair dismissal, see similarly *Software 2000 Ltd v Andrews* [2007] ICR 825 [54] (Elias J).
[24] *Chagger v Abbey National* (n 19).
[25] ibid [57].
[26] *Vento* v *Chief Constable of West Yorkshire Police* (2003) EWCA Civ 1871 [32].
[27] ibid [33].
[28] ibid [43].
[29] In relation to unfair dismissal, see similarly *Software 2000 Ltd v Andrews* [2007] ICR 825 [54] (Elias J).

The compensation that may be awarded for injured feelings has been developed following the Court of Appeal decision in *Vento*. In that case, the complexity of quantifying injury to feelings as a monetary sum was clearly recognised:

> It is self evident that the assessment of compensation for an injury or loss, which is neither physical nor financial, presents special problems for the judicial process, which aims to produce results objectively justified by evidence, reason and precedent. Subjective feelings of upset, frustration, worry, anxiety, mental distress, fear, grief, anguish, humiliation, unhappiness, stress, depression and so on and the degree of their intensity are incapable of objective proof or of measurement in monetary terms. Translating hurt feelings into hard currency is bound to be an artificial exercise.[30]

While it is impossible to quantify exactly such hurt, some principles are used to guide such awards, as set out in *HM Prison v Johnson*,[31] and endorsed in *Vento*.[32] Awards for injury to feelings:

- are compensatory, not punitive;
- should not be too low ('as that would diminish respect for the policy of the anti-discrimination legislation. Society has condemned discrimination and awards must ensure that it is seen to be wrong'), but should be 'restrained';
- should be broadly similar to damages in personal injury cases;
- should be determined by reference to the sum's 'value in everyday life', by reference to earnings or purchasing power; and
- bear in mind the need for public respect of damages awards.[33]

Clearly, then, awards for injury to feelings have been developed with reference to private law damages, illustrating the links between discrimination and private law.[34]

The Court of Appeal in *Vento* identified three 'bands' of compensation for injury to feelings.[35] There is flexibility within each band, but any award below the lower band should be avoided.[36] The *Vento* bands have been updated to reflect the changing value of money based on the RPI All Items Index.[37] For ET claims presented on or after 6 April 2024 in England, Wales, and Scotland, the *Vento* bands are:

- a lower band of £1,200 to £11,700 (less serious cases);
- a middle band of £11,700 to £35,200 (cases that do not merit an award in the upper band); and

[30] *Vento* (n 26) [50].
[31] *HM Prison v Johnson* [1997] ICR 275, 283 (Smith J).
[32] *Vento* (n 26) [53].
[33] *HM Prison v Johnson* (n 31) (Smith J), endorsed in *Vento* (n 26) [53].
[34] *HM Prison v Johnson* (n 31) (Smith J); see also A McColgan, 'Paying for Discrimination?: Compensation in the Courts' (1998) 3 *International Journal of Discrimination and the Law* 135, 138.
[35] *Vento* (n 26) [65].
[36] ibid [65], [66].
[37] These bands also include the *Simmons v Castle* uplift: see *De Souza v Vinci Construction (UK) Ltd* [2017] EWCA Civ 879.

- an upper band of £35,200 to £58,700 (the most serious cases), with the most exceptional cases capable of exceeding £58,700.[38]

In Great Britain, the courts distinguish between awards for injury to feelings and awards for psychiatric injury; by contrast, the Australian case law tends to amalgamate these two heads under 'general damages'. As noted by the Court of Appeal in *De Souzav Vinci Construction (UK) Ltd*,[39]

> It has long been the practice of employment tribunals to make awards in discrimination cases in respect of both injury to feelings and, where the evidence supports it, psychiatric injury. Those two heads are regarded as conceptually distinct, and attracting separate awards, though the authorities point out that they are liable in practice to overlap and warn against double-counting .... As regards the assessment of compensation for injury to feelings, the leading authority is *Vento* .... As regards the assessment of compensation for psychiatric injury, the tribunal will in principle (and subject to the issue raised by this appeal) follow the level of damages for equivalent injury in the civil courts. As to that, the Judicial College publishes regularly updated "Guidelines for the Assessment of General Damages in Personal Injury Cases", which include a chapter covering psychiatric and psychological damage.[40]

Thus, awards for psychiatric injury are consciously linked to damages in the civil courts via the Judicial College Guidelines.[41] However, the *Vento* bands for injury to feelings remain distinct. As the House of Commons Women and Equalities Committee (WEC) has recognised, in discrimination claims, the bulk of a claim for damages might be for injury to feelings;[42] the *Vento* bands are, therefore, a critical part of the overall damages awarded.

Aggravated damages are an aspect of damages for injury to feelings.[43] Aggravated damages are compensatory; they are not designed to punish like exemplary damages.[44] Rather, they recognise that some 'aggravating features' of a case might increase the impact of discrimination and – as a result – any injury to feelings.[45] Such damages may be awarded in three categories of cases, relating

[38] Judge Susan Walker and Judge Barry Clarke, 'Presidential Guidance: Employment Tribunal Awards for Injury to Feelings and Psychiatric Injury Following De Souza v Vinci Construction (UK) Ltd [2017] EWCA Civ 879': www.judiciary.uk/wp-content/uploads/2023/06/Vento-bands-seventh-presidential-guidance-April-2024-addendum.pdf.

[39] *De Souza v Vinci Construction (UK) Ltd* [2017] EWCA Civ 879.

[40] ibid [15].

[41] Judicial College, *Guidelines for the Assessment of General Damages in Personal Injury Cases*, 17th edn (Oxford, Oxford University Press, 2024). The Australian courts have no equivalent to the Guidelines, though it has been suggested they should create an equivalent publication: 'Review of the Law of Negligence: Final Report' (2002) 187–88: treasury.gov.au/sites/default/files/2019-03/R2002-001_Damages.pdf.

[42] *Enforcing the Equality Act: The Law and the Role of the Equality and Human Rights Commission* HC 1470 (2017–19): www.publications.parliament.uk/pa/cm201719/cmselect/cmwomeq/1470/1470.pdf. See also McColgan (n 34) 135–6.

[43] *Commissioner of Police of the Metropolis v Shaw* [2012] ICR 464 [21].

[44] ibid [20].

[45] ibid [21].

to: the manner in which the wrong was committed,[46] and the distress that occasioned; the motive for the conduct, if that exacerbated the claimant's distress; and subsequent conduct, including the way in which a complaint of discrimination was handled by the respondent.[47]

IV. The Exercise of Court and Tribunal Remedial Powers

While the remedial powers of Australian courts and tribunals are expressed broadly, where a discrimination claim is – exceptionally – successful, remedies generally reflect an individualised model of discrimination law, with an emphasis on compensating the individual for harm caused rather than achieving structural or behavioural change.[48] Remedies generally focus only on the individual case[49] and rarely relate to systems change or education.[50] As Sturm argues, 'first generation' discrimination law remedies seek 'clarity, uniformity, and simplicity … [They do not] examine or directly encourage revision of the intra-organizational culture and decision processes that entrench bias, stereotyping, and unequal access'.[51] This individualised focus has led to a predominant emphasis on financial compensation as a remedy;[52] the usual order is for damages.[53] Similarly, in Great Britain, where the remedial powers of courts and tribunals are more limited, the primary remedy granted in a discrimination claim is compensation. This approach has five key limitations.

First, the harm that is recognised by discrimination law – and the harm that is remedied through compensation – is a fairly limited conception of the damage that discrimination does. As one respondent in this study noted, 'I think the damage that is caused by discrimination is not just about hurt feelings, and it's really important that that is acknowledged.'[54] It is questionable whether the law is able to recognise broader forms of damage, at least in the way legal provisions are currently framed. Indeed, expert respondents often felt that discrimination law – as presently framed – could not provide the remedy or outcome that claimants desired.[55] This might act as a significant deterrent to claiming.

Second, while systemic outcomes are often agreed upon at conciliation,[56] courts and tribunals are more limited in the remedies that they can and do award. For

[46] *Alexander v Home Office* [1988] IRLR 190, 193 (May LJ).
[47] *Commissioner of Police of the Metropolis v Shaw* [2012] ICR 464 [22]; *Vento* (n 26) [67].
[48] L Dickens, 'The Road Is Long: Thirty Years of Equality Legislation in Britain' (2007) 45 *British Journal of Industrial Relations* 463, 480.
[49] Gaze and Smith (n 1) 195.
[50] ibid.
[51] S Sturm, 'Second Generation Employment Discrimination: A Structural Approach' (2001) 101 *Columbia Law Review* 458, 467–8.
[52] Dickens (n 48) 480.
[53] Gaze and Smith (n 1) 195.
[54] Respondent A100.
[55] Respondent A100.
[56] Respondents A101, A106.

example, in Great Britain, ETs can no longer make broader recommendations that do not relate to the claimant specifically.[57] Even where courts and tribunals have a broad discretion in relation to remedies (as in many Australian jurisdictions), this discretion is rarely exercised. Instead, remedies typically focus solely on financial compensation. This limits the systemic impact of discrimination law remedies.

Third, to obtain compensation, it is necessary to prove harm, loss, or damage. Higher income earners with a large projected future salary will receive the highest levels of compensation for financial loss.[58] Conversely, it is difficult for some older workers, in particular, to prove financial harm, especially if they are approaching the age at which they planned to retire.[59] The highest awards of compensation will be for claimants who are the most 'broken'.[60] This means, then, that the strongest and most resilient claimants, with a 'tougher skull',[61] who are most likely to be able and willing to bring a claim, are also likely to receive the smallest compensatory remedy.[62] While Australian courts are increasingly awarding higher levels of general damages, this recognises a significant level of individual harm:

> [such a claim has] to be supported by a significant psychological injury and this significant bearing of one's soul of the impact that discrimination had on you and how it ruined you. … what is the price of a significantly disrupted life?
>
> Now what if your life wasn't significantly disrupted but … you still experienced discrimination … [which] is wrong [and] socially unacceptable behaviour. … it's a disincentive to those that might be able to withstand the blow …
>
> [P]eople who bring these claims are not weak in any way. They're very strong and … have endured a lot and … have to endure a lot to bring their claims. But that we calculate our damages on those kind of metrics about how broken are you, rather than what did they do and what do we say to society is so wrong or could potentially be so wrong about that regardless of what impacts it had on you.[63]

Rather than focusing on the harm caused to the claimant, a remedy could instead focus on punishing or deterring the respondent, or the *societal* harm that has been caused. Indeed, some interviewees felt that this was how claimants already viewed compensation, even if it is not the way the law is framed:

> compensation I think is, is more about the respondent than the complainant. I mean, obviously there are [complainants] that come and money is all that they want, but really when they're asking for money, it goes back to that, you know, sense of punishment. It's more about punishing the respondent than that they think they've got a legitimate claim to, you know, $130,000 or whatever it is that they're asking for. It's because they want the respondent to hurt.[64]

[57] Deregulation Act 2015 (c. 20) s 2.
[58] Respondent A118.
[59] Respondent A169.
[60] Respondent A118.
[61] Respondent A118.
[62] Respondent A118.
[63] Respondent A118.
[64] Respondent A99.

For claimants, then, compensation is a proxy for achieving a sense of justice or vindication. Punitive or vindicatory damages might be a better means of achieving these aims rather than compensatory damages.[65] Alternatively, civil penalties could be imposed, which consider the impact on the individual as just one factor to be taken into account, alongside the impact on society and the protective function of discrimination law.[66] This would 'be less about requiring the stereotypical broken woman to sit there in the box and cry',[67] and more about considering the broader impact of discrimination and the conduct of the respondent.[68] These are suggestions I return to in section VIII.

Fourth, as noted above, damages for discrimination complaints 'are very, very low',[69] 'a pittance'[70] and 'modest'.[71] As one respondent noted in a survey of advocates,

> It's my view that age discrimination still attracts less compensation than such matters usually warrant. There also seems to be a sense that it's not as significant or egregious as some other types of discrimination.

Such low compensation may prove a disincentive to claiming,[72] especially when damages may be entirely consumed by legal fees:[73]

> They're really low paying jurisdictions … so it's really hard to encourage vulnerable people to enter … that process … when their outcome that they can expect is really … a pittance really for what they've experienced.[74]

Further, with such low awards, some respondents do not fear a discrimination complaint; instead, complaints are just a cost of doing business.[75] Low damages awards therefore do little to achieve systemic change or to deter or disincentivise repeat respondents:[76] 'They know that they're not going to be hit very hard, you know; especially large companies.'[77] Without a significant monetary penalty for discriminating, some employers are unlikely to change their behaviour.[78]

[65] See, eg, Justice Edelman, 'Vindicatory Damages' (Private Law in the 21st century, Brisbane, 15 December 2015): www.fedcourt.gov.au/digital-law-library/judges-speeches/speeches-former-judges/justice-edelman/edelman-j-20151215.

[66] Respondent A118.

[67] Respondent A118.

[68] Respondent A118.

[69] Respondent A99.

[70] Respondents A7, A100.

[71] Respondent UK97.

[72] Respondent A112.

[73] Respondent UK97.

[74] Respondent A100, also Respondent A7.

[75] Respondent A99.

[76] Respondents A99, A107.

[77] Respondent A155.

[78] Respondent A99.

Fifth, compensation rarely reflects the complex and compounding harms occasioned by intersectional discrimination.[79] This limits the law's ability to recognise intersectional discrimination, and dampens any incentive to bring a claim on multiple grounds.[80]

V. Remedial Awards in Practice

To illustrate how courts and tribunals utilise their remedial powers in practice, it is helpful to consider a case study of age discrimination claims. This choice of case study is partly pragmatic: there are few successful age discrimination cases, making this analysis practically possible. Further, this builds on my work considering all Australian age discrimination cases relating to work until 2017,[81] and a two-year period of UK ET decisions relating to age discrimination.[82] This consideration of remedies can helpfully build on those findings. That said, a focus on court and tribunal decisions may undersell the outcomes achieved in conciliation: indeed, strong claims may be more likely to settle, and for higher amounts of compensation.[83] However, public court and tribunal decisions offer important guidance and background to conciliation, as negotiation is often conducted 'in the shadow of the law'.[84]

Compensation in discrimination claims in courts and tribunals is rarely high. In ETs in Great Britain, for example, 16 age discrimination cases had compensation awarded in 2022–23.[85] In 2022–23, the median compensation awarded in the age jurisdiction was £5,675, with an average award of £14,210. This implies, then, that there are a number of high awards, which distort this average picture. This is also evident in Table 5.1: the maximum award – of £84,723 – far exceeds the majority of awards, which are under £10,000.

[79] Respondent A112.

[80] Respondent A112. See S Atrey, *Intersectional Discrimination*, 1st edn (Oxford, Oxford University Press, 2019) 197–207.

[81] A Blackham, 'Why Do Employment Age Discrimination Cases Fail? An Analysis of Australian Case Law' (2020) 42 *Sydney Law Review* 1.

[82] A Blackham, 'Enforcing Rights in Employment Tribunals: Insights from Age Discrimination Claims in a New "Dataset"' (2021) 41 *Legal Studies* 390.

[83] A Blackham and D Allen, 'Resolving Discrimination Claims Outside the Courts: Alternative Dispute Resolution in Australia and the United Kingdom' (2019) 31 *Australian Journal of Labour Law* 253; D Allen and A Blackham, 'Under Wraps: Secrecy, Confidentiality and the Enforcement of Equality Law in Australia and the UK' (2019) 43 *Melbourne University Law* Review 384; Blackham (n 2).

[84] Blackham and Allen (n 83). See generally RH Mnookin and L Kornhauser, 'Bargaining in the Shadow of the Law: The Case of Divorce' (1979) 88 *The Yale Law Journal* 950.

[85] GOV.UK, 'Tribunal Statistics Quarterly: April to June 2023' (*GOV.UK*, 14 September 2023): www.gov.uk/government/statistics/tribunal-statistics-quarterly-april-to-june-2023. Note that, in these tables, compensation is allocated to the lead jurisdiction only; where age discrimination is a non-lead claim, any compensation awarded will not appear in these tables.

Table 5.1 Compensation awarded, age discrimination ET decisions, 2022–23

Compensation band	**No.**	**%**
<£500	0	*0*
£500–£999	0	*0*
£1,000–£1,999	1	*6*
£2,000–£2,999	2	*13*
£3,000–£3,999	1	*6*
£4,000–£4,999	2	*13*
£5,000–£5,999	2	*13*
£6,000–£6,999	1	*6*
£7,000–£7,999	0	*0*
£8,000–£8,999	1	*6*
£9,000–£9,999	0	*0*
£10,000–£12,499	0	*0*
£12,500–£14,999	2	*13*
£15,000–£19,999	0	*0*
£20,000–£29,999	3	*19*
£30,000–£39,999	0	*0*
£40,000–£49,999	0	*0*
£50,000+	1	*6*
All	**16**	***100***
Maximum award	**£84,723**	
Median award	**£5,675**	
Average (mean) award	**£14,210**	

Source: Employment Tribunal and Employment Appeals Tribunal Annual Tables, 2023, GOV.UK.

In my study of 1,208 UK ET age discrimination decisions handed down from February 2017 to 17 April 2019,[86] of 43 successful claims, a remedy was recorded in 30 cases. Compensation was awarded in all 30 cases. The median award for the age discrimination jurisdiction was £8,800, with a minimum of £1,000 and a maximum of £386,059.73.[87] Six cases involved an award below £5,000. Only two decisions included non-compensatory remedies.[88] In 19 cases, the claimant was also successful in other jurisdictions, not just on the basis of age. In these decisions, compensation for age discrimination ranged from 10 per cent

[86] Blackham (n 2).

[87] These calculations use gross figures.

[88] *McCloud v The Lord Chancellor* [2020] UKET 2201483/2015 (10 January 2020); *Amu v Department for Work and Pensions* [2018] UKET 1600465/2017 (22 February 2020).

to 97 per cent of the total award. This typically reflected whether loss of earnings was awarded in the age discrimination jurisdiction (leading to a higher percentage of compensation being awarded in the age jurisdiction), or a different jurisdiction (leading to a lower percentage). Where specified, most cases (22) included awards for injury to feelings;[89] that said, the highest awards were typically for loss of earnings (awarded in the age discrimination jurisdiction in 11 cases).[90]

In a further study of those successful claims where unfair dismissal was also alleged (22 of 43 claims),[91] it is possible to map the differences – and potential advantages and drawbacks – of the age discrimination and unfair dismissal jurisdictions. In 13 of the 22 cases alleging both unfair dismissal and age discrimination, the claim for unfair dismissal was also successful. In nine of those cases, a remedy had been determined. In those cases, compensation for injury to feelings (awarded in eight of the nine cases) often represented a substantial component of compensation awarded in the discrimination jurisdiction, representing over 85 per cent of the compensation awarded in the discrimination jurisdiction in seven cases.

Overall, though, this sample of ET cases – and their relatively low damages awards – indicate that remedies are unlikely to recognise the social benefit of enforcing discrimination law, will likely not act as a deterrent to respondents, and are unlikely to achieve broader change.[92] The WEC has therefore recommended that: the *Vento* bands be significantly increased; exemplary damages for discrimination claims be made more widely available; ETs be given the power to make wider recommendations and to made orders requiring organisational change;[93] and punitive damages be available.[94] As the WEC summarises,

> compensation awards [in discrimination claims] must be significantly increased to incentivise employers to do more to prevent discrimination and harassment in the workplace. This can be done through the introduction of punitive damages and by increasing the current awards available for non-financial losses such as injury to feelings and psychiatric harm.[95]

The WEC further argues that the 'bands in the Vento guidelines should be increased significantly to take into account the non-financial impact of discrimination'.[96]

[89] The exception was *Fogarty v Colman Greaves Fabrications Ltd* [2019] UKET 2410534/2018, where the claimant did not seek an award for injury to feelings.

[90] *cf Shirin v Wilson Barca LLP* [2019] UKET 2208035/2016, where £46,908.38 was awarded for injury to feelings and aggravated damages; the claimant sought over £1million.

[91] A Blackham, 'Older Workers, Unfair Dismissal, and Age Discrimination Law: Strengthening Employment Protection? Comparative Perspectives from Australia and the UK' in JJ Votinius and M Rönnmar (eds), *Older Workers, Active Ageing, and the Future of Work: Discourses and Legal Advancements* (Alphen, Kluwer Law International, 2025).

[92] *Enforcing the Equality Act* (n 42) 62–3.

[93] ibid.

[94] *The Use of Non-Disclosure Agreements in Discrimination Cases* HC 1720 (2017-19) [67].

[95] ibid 5.

[96] ibid.

In considering Australian age discrimination case law (to the end of 2017), I found only 12 successful substantive age discrimination cases, across all Australian jurisdictions, and across discrimination and industrial law.[97] The damages awarded in those cases were generally low, with six decisions resulting in compensation for the age discrimination claim equal to or less than AU$5000. Further, there was limited evidence of creative remedial outcomes, though an apology was granted in some cases. As I concluded in that study, then,

> Even when claims are successful, damages for loss of a chance to be employed are likely to be low. While one successful claim achieved a high damages payout, this reflected the loss of a career, recognising that few older workers will be re-employed after experiencing age discrimination.[98]

VI. Using Tort to Transform Equality Law Damages: Australian Discrimination Law and *Richardson v Oracle*

Overall, then, the approach to discrimination law remedies in Australia and Great Britain appears limited: focused on individualised compensation and adopting a narrow view of the harms effected by discriminatory conduct. There is a need, then, to reconsider and transform discrimination law remedies; one approach might be to integrate private law perspectives on damages to critique, supplement, and develop discrimination law jurisprudence.

In the Australian context, in *Richardson v Oracle Corporation Australia Pty Ltd*,[99] analogy with tort was used to challenge and transform general damages in sexual harassment law. The case flagged two potential ways in which tort might inform the development of discrimination law: first, in informing the rules and tests that should be applied (such as causation) under statutory discrimination law; and, second, in recalibrating the quantum of damages awarded in sexual harassment cases, by analogy with personal injury negligence cases (particularly those relating to workplace bullying and harassment).

In *Richardson*,[100] the claimant was awarded AU$18,000 as compensation for sexual harassment in the workplace under the Sex Discrimination Act 1984 (Cth) (the SDA) at first instance. The clamant appealed to the Full Court of the Federal Court of Australia regarding the quantum of damages. On appeal, the claimant was awarded AU$130,000, plus interest.

[97] Blackham (n 81). On the complexity of this federal framework, see A Blackham, 'Promoting Innovation or Exacerbating Inequality? Laboratory Federalism and Australian Age Discrimination Law' (2023) 51 *Federal Law Review* 347.

[98] Blackham (n 81).

[99] *Richardson* (n 6).

[100] ibid.

A. The Use of Tortious Principles

The decision of the Federal Court at first instance was appealed on the basis that the judge applied tortious principles of damages. Instead, the claimant argued that the Court should have deferred to the provisions of the AHRC Act, section 46PO(4)(d) (as extracted above). At first instance, the trial judge said that:

> The applicant and Oracle agreed that, generally speaking, assessment of damages by way of compensation for sexual harassment under the [Sex Discrimination] Act would normally follow principles for the assessment of damages in tort. While the principle is not to be strictly applied where a particular case calls for a different approach, I see no reason in the present case to depart from that approach.[101]

This approach was challenged on appeal; instead, the claimant argued that damages should be assessed having regard to 'the purpose, nature and scope of the AHRC Act and the SDA'.[102] As Kenny J noted, though, in awarding 'damages by way of compensation' under the Act, and 'In giving content to the concept of compensatory damages in this context, the authorities establish that the court **may** be guided, at the assessment stage, by the general principles governing the assessment of damages in tort'.[103] Tortious principles can therefore inform the assessment of damages under the AHRC Act.[104]

At first instance, the trial judge found that common law causation was not established between the sexual harassment and Ms Richardson's claim for economic loss. The question arose, then, whether common law principles of causation should be applied in this case. It was unnecessary to address this question on appeal, as Besanko and Perram JJ held that the trial judge had erred in finding that common law causation was not established.[105] It remains an open question, then, whether the test for causation should be different under discrimination statutes than under the common law.

B. Recalibrating General Damages to Meet Community Expectations

In assessing whether the damages awarded at first instance were 'manifestly inadequate' (with Besanko and Perram JJ agreeing with Kenny J on this point),[106]

[101] *Richardson v Oracle Corporation Australia Pty Ltd* [2013] FCA 102; 232 IR 31 [208].
[102] *Richardson* (n 6) [25] (Kenny J).
[103] ibid [27] (Kenny J) (emphasis in original).
[104] ibid [30] (Kenny J).
[105] ibid [137] (Besanko and Perram JJ).
[106] ibid [119] (Besanko and Perram JJ).

the Full Court had regard to other cases of 'analogous non-pecuniary injury',[107] including those in tort. These cases were contrasted with the prevailing range of damages in sex discrimination and sexual harassment cases, which sat 'between [AU]$12,000 and $20,000 for general damages awards'.[108] Considering cases relating to personal injury compensation, Kenny J noted that the courts had recognised that 'there is reason to believe that community standards now accord a higher value to compensation for pain and suffering and loss of enjoyment of life than before'.[109]

In particular, Kenny J referred to the unsuccessful appeal against the award of AU$1,150,000 in damages (AU$730,000 for pain and suffering and loss of enjoyment of life) in the Victorian Court of Appeal negligence case of *Amaca Pty Ltd v King* (*Amaca*),[110] a mesothelioma case.[111] In that case, the Court of Appeal opined that, as wages and remuneration have increased, and contemporary society increasingly values quality of life, 'who doubts that modern society may place a higher value on the loss of enjoyment of life and the compensation of pain and suffering than was the case in the past?'[112] While that case differed from *Richardson*, Kenny J emphasised that the key idea – 'that the community may place a higher value on the loss of enjoyment of life and the compensation of pain and suffering than in the past' – also applied to this case.[113]

As Kenny J noted, subsequent personal injury cases in negligence have echoed this sentiment and increased personal injury damages accordingly. In particular, Kenny J cited a stream of negligence cases relating to workplace bullying and harassment, where damages far outstripped the first instance award in *Richardson*. In *Willett v Victoria*,[114] for example, Tate and Priest JJA relied on *Amaca* to substitute damages of AU$250,000 for a jury verdict of AU$108,000 for pain and suffering and loss of enjoyment of life occasioned by workplace bullying and harassment.[115] In *Swan v Monash Law Book Co-operative*[116] Ms Swan was awarded AU$300,000 as damages for pain and suffering and loss of enjoyment of life following workplace bullying and harassment.

For Kenny J, these cases illustrate 'that awards of damages today place a significant value on the loss of enjoyment of life and the experience of pain and suffering',[117] even if Ms Richardson's pain and suffering and loss of enjoyment of life differed from the claimants in the other cases. There was no difference in principle between the harm in these, negligence, cases and the harm in sexual

[107] ibid [82] (Kenny J).
[108] ibid [89] (Kenny J).
[109] ibid [96] (Kenny J).
[110] *Amaca Pty Ltd v King* [2011] VSCA 447.
[111] *Richardson* (n 6) [96]–[97] (Kenny J).
[112] *Amaca* (n 110) [177] (Nettle, Ashley and Redlich JJA).
[113] *Richardson* (n 6) [98] (Kenny J).
[114] *Amaca* (n 110) [79]–[80] (Tate and Priest JJA).
[115] See the reference in *Richardson* (n 6) [99] (Kenny J).
[116] *Amaca* (n 110).
[117] *Richardson* (n 6) [102] (Kenny J).

harassment cases.[118] Reference to tortious principles was also important for the coherence of the law:

> The need for coherence in the law means that, in attempting to compensate victims for comparable kinds of injuries, interconnected fields of law look to one another in establishing a "reasonable" sum by way of compensation. The analogy between sums awarded for pain and suffering and loss of enjoyment of life caused by unlawful discrimination with sums awarded in the tortious context is particularly obvious.[119]

By contrast, arguing by analogy with defamation cases was seen as less useful.[120]

Overall, the 'comparison demonstrates that the award for general damages in this case was disproportionately low and failed adequately to compensate Ms Richardson for the loss and damage she suffered because of Mr Tucker's conduct'.[121] Thus, while the award of AU$18,000 was not out of step with other sexual harassment cases, it was 'disproportionately low' if 'judged by prevailing community standards'.[122] The general damages were therefore increased to AU$100,000, and an award was made for economic loss of AU$30,000, plus AU$31,572.24 interest. This meant, too, that Ms Richardson was no longer liable for Oracle's costs – previously, Oracle had made an offer of AU$55,000 to settle the proceedings, and Ms Richardson faced the prospect of paying Oracle's costs on an indemnity basis after the date of that offer.[123] Instead, Oracle was ordered to pay Ms Richardson's costs until her offer of compromise (of AU$106,500) on a party-party basis, and on an indemnity basis thereafter.[124]

VII. The Legacy of *Richardson* in Australian Discrimination Law

The legacy of *Richardson* – and the tortious recalibration of discrimination law damages – could be significant. In the subsequent sexual harassment case of *Hughes v Hill*,[125] on appeal the respondent challenged the award of AU$120,000 in general damages as manifestly excessive. (Ms Hill was also awarded AU$50,000 in aggravated damages.) As Perram J concluded (the other judges agreeing):

> What is the ruin of a person's quality of life worth? I flatly reject the Appellant's contention that it was not worth $120,000 and the allied submission that such a finding was

[118] ibid [108] (Kenny J).
[119] ibid [110] (Kenny J).
[120] ibid [112] (Kenny J).
[121] ibid [114] (Kenny J).
[122] ibid [117] (Kenny J).
[123] ibid [234]–[235] (Besanko and Perram JJ).
[124] *Richardson v Oracle Corporation Australia Pty Ltd (No 2)* [2014] FCAFC 139. By reference to the then *Federal Court Rules 1979* (Cth) Order 23 rule 11(4), later replaced by the *Federal Court Rules 2011* (Cth).
[125] *Hughes v Hill* [2020] FCAFC 126; 277 FCR 511.

> not open on the evidence. It seems to me to have been entirely within the range of available awards for general damages in a case of this seriousness where actual psychological harm was occasioned to the Respondent by the Appellant's repeated and self-indulgent actions. The Court's decision in *Oracle* involved an award of $100,000 ….[126]

Further, Perram J rejected the argument that the Court should have referred to decisions prior to *Richardson* (with their lower damages awards):

> [*Richardson*] effected a substantial increase in the general damages which could be awarded in a case of sexual harassment. As comparators, decisions involving awards of general damages pre-dating *Oracle* are not useful, as this Court there explained. It is not clear to me why a submission directly contrary to a recent Full Court decision was advanced.[127]

This appears, then, to be the Federal Court drawing a line in the sand, with damages awarded prior to *Richardson* no longer being seen as a helpful reference point for subsequent decisions.

The impact of *Richardson* on subsequent decisions is also illustrated by the comprehensive study of sexual harassment and discrimination case law undertaken by Thornton and others, commissioned by the federal Attorney-General's Department.[128] The annexure to that report offers a table of cases, including any damages awarded, which enables us to track the quantum of damages awarded in the federal jurisdiction since *Richardson* (15 July 2014 to the end of 2021) (see Table 5.2). That said, the vast majority of cases included in the authors' table were unsuccessful or did not have damages awarded; only the successful claims with a compensatory remedy are extracted below. The authors' table includes, but is not limited to, cases relating to employment; only employment cases are included below.

Table 5.2 Successful sexual harassment and discrimination cases, federal jurisdiction, 2014 to 2021 (AUD)

Year	Case	General damages	Other remedies
	Sexual harassment		
2019	*Morton v Commonwealth Scientific and Industrial Research Organisation (No 2)* [2019] FCA 1754 (adverse action, sexual harassment and sex discrimination)	$1,000 for CSIRO's contravention of the FWA	

(continued)

[126] ibid [47] (Perram J).
[127] ibid [49] (Perram J).
[128] M Thornton, K Pender and M Castles, 'Damages and Costs in Sexual Harassment Litigation: A Doctrinal, Qualitative and Quantitative Study' (2022): www.ag.gov.au/sites/default/files/2022-12/damages-and-costs-in-sexual-harassment-litigation.pdf.

Table 5.2 ***(Continued)***

2019	*Hill v Hughes* [2019] FCCA 1267	$120,000	$50,000 in aggravated damages
	Race discrimination		
2021	*Ferguson v Martin* [2021] FedCFamC2G 58 (adverse action)	$50,000	Declaration Written apology
2016	*Murugesu v Australia Post (No 2)* [2016] FCCA 2355	$40,000	
	Disability discrimination		
2015	*Huntley v State of NSW, Department of Police and Justice (Corrective Services NSW)* [2015] FCCA 1827	$75,000	Economic loss: $116,241.97 (including interest) Recredit leave entitlements
2015	*Pop v Taylor* [2015] FCCA 1720	$5,000	Economic loss: $5,000
	Age discrimination		
2021	*Gutierrez v MUR Shipping Australia Pty Limited* [2021] FedCFamC2G 56	$20,000 (Note: increased on appeal)	Apology Declaration

Source: Thornton et al, 2022, annexure A.

While *Richardson* might have recalibrated the assessment of damages in the Australian federal jurisdiction, success in discrimination law in the courts is so exceptional that it is difficult to quantitatively track the impact of *Richardson* in subsequent cases, even after 10 years. This likely reflects the prevalence of conciliation in Australian discrimination law; most cases are settled or withdrawn.[129]

However, the reasoning in the cases themselves illustrates the importance of *Richardson*. In *Gutierrez v MUR Shipping Australia Pty Ltd* (*Gutierrez*),[130] for example, at first instance the claimant was awarded an apology and damages for non-economic loss of AU$20,000 plus interest.[131] This decision was appealed to the Federal Court of Australia on the question of remedy. The appeal was upheld, and Mr Gutierrez was awarded AU$90,000 in general damages,[132] and economic loss of AU$142,215.56 plus interest. MUR Shipping was required to pay Mr Gutierrez's costs of the appeal, and Mr Gutierrez was no longer exposed to paying MUR Shipping's costs of trial.[133]

[129] Blackham and Allen (n 83); Blackham (n 2).
[130] *Gutierrez v MUR Shipping Australia Pty Ltd* [2021] FedCFamC2G 56.
[131] ibid [177].
[132] *Gutierrez v MUR Shipping Australia Pty Ltd* [2023] FCA 399 [5].
[133] K Pender, 'Landmark Win in Age Discrimination Case' *The Saturday Paper* (Melbourne, 6 October 2023) www.thesaturdaypaper.com.au/news/law-crime/2023/06/10/landmark-win-age-discrimination-case.

At first instance, the trial judge in *Gutierrez* distinguished the higher damages awarded in cases such as *Richardson* on the basis of 'the significant findings of the conduct towards the victim'.[134] As I have argued elsewhere, this implicitly devalues Mr Gutierrez's experiences of age discrimination,[135] implying that age discrimination is less 'valuable' than experiences of sexual harassment. However, on appeal, this approach was rejected. Burley J held that:

> to suggest, as the primary judge appears to, that the seriousness of the conduct of a defendant towards a victim, separately from a consideration of the damage caused by that conduct, is relevant to the assessment of general damages reflects error. At the point of the assessment of damages, the question is the amount which can fairly be regarded as reasonable compensation for the injuries and disabilities which a plaintiff has sustained, not the manner in which the harm was caused or egregiousness by which it was inflicted.[136]

That is, the issue is the harm caused, not its manner of infliction.[137] At first instance, the trial judge did not adequately engage with expert evidence relating to the harm inflicted on Mr Gutierrez.[138] The trial judge classed Mr Gutierrez's adjustment disorder as 'mild', though this was not consistent with the expert evidence presented.[139] On appeal, then, with reference to *Richardson* (and the negligence cases cited in *Richardson*), the damages in *Gutierrez* were increased significantly. Overall, Burley J concluded:

> Having regard to the particular facts of this case, the [expert] evidence … and the evidence of Mr and Mrs Gutierrez, in my view the general damages that ought to be awarded are considerably less than those awarded in a case such as *Willett*, but the harm that he suffered might properly be regarded to be comparable with that identified in *Oracle* and *Walker*. Although there is necessarily an element of imprecision in the analysis, I consider that the appropriate award should also be $90,000.[140]

VIII. Comparison with Tort as a Way Forward?

Compensation for successful discrimination claims is generally low. The WEC has therefore advocated for awarding higher compensation in discrimination claims, including through the award of exemplary or punitive damages, and increasing the

[134] *Gutierrez* (n 130) [157].
[135] A Blackham, 'Federal Age Discrimination Law Finally Coming of Age: Gutierrez v MUR Shipping Australia Pty Ltd' (2023) 36 *Australian Journal of Labour Law* 289.
[136] *Gutierrez* (n 132) [52] (references omitted).
[137] Though this may be relevant to assessing aggravated damages: see further N Rees, S Rice and D Allen, *Australian Anti-Discrimination and Equal Opportunity Law*, 3rd edn (Alexandria, The Federation Press, 2018) 825–6.
[138] *Gutierrez* (n 132) [63].
[139] ibid [69], [80].
[140] ibid [92].

Vento bands.[141] But, perhaps, could reference to tort law and private law perspectives offer another route to increasing damages in discrimination claims?

One of the challenges in using tort to inform discrimination law relates to how we keep damages recalibrated over time. For example, since *Richardson*, damages in tort have continued to increase in Australia; but discrimination claims continue to use *Richardson* as their touchstone. For example, in *Mathews v Winslow Constructors (Vic)*,[142] a claim in negligence for abuse, sexual harassment, and bullying at work, the claimant was awarded damages of AU$1,360,027, including general damages of AU$380,000, past economic loss of AU$283,942, and future economic loss of AU$696,085 until the claimant would reach retirement age (23 years). This case was one where the conduct led to a serious chronic psychiatric illness; it is possible that it is better seen as an exceptional case, with less relevance to later decisions. However, it is notable that later discrimination cases do not cross-refer to new decisions in tort; rather, they refer to *Richardson* to inform their assessment of damages. Any recalibration of damages with tort may therefore become less connected over time.

A better approach, then, might be to adopt clear guidelines for personal injury damages, which can be referred to and regularly updated over time. For example, in Great Britain, awards for psychiatric injury in discrimination claims are consciously linked to damages in the civil courts via the Judicial College Guidelines, which are regularly updated.[143] The Australian courts have no equivalent to the Judicial College Guidelines, though it has been suggested they should create an equivalent publication.[144] Guidelines can ensure clear coherence and consistency between discrimination law and private law, though there is still significant scope within the guidelines for judicial discretion.

It may be, too, that discrimination law has lessons for private law; for example, the development of tort and contract might be informed by discrimination law, particularly in relation to damages for mental distress.[145] For Burrows, the *Vento* bands might offer an example of how to better assess damages for mental distress in private law,[146] particularly in seeking consistency between decisions and across areas of law.[147] That said, Burrows expresses concern that aggravated damages and damages for injury to feelings are assessed separately in discrimination law (not combined); and that the *Vento* bands 'appear high' when compared to damages for psychiatric injury, for example.[148] By contrast, the WEC has argued that the *Vento*

[141] *Enforcing the Equality Act* (n 42) 62–63; *The Use of Non-Disclosure Agreements* (n 94) 24.
[142] *Mathews v Winslow Constructors (Vic)* [2015] VSC 728.
[143] Judicial College (n 41).
[144] 'Review of the Law of Negligence: Final Report' (n 41) 187–88.
[145] A Burrows, *Remedies for Torts, Breach of Contract, and Equitable Wrongs* (Oxford, Oxford University Press, 2019).
[146] ibid 289.
[147] ibid 290.
[148] ibid.

bands are too low, therefore recommending that they be significantly increased.[149] Again, there is clear potential for mutual learning between discrimination law and private law – in both directions – though it is unclear whether these disparities can be reconciled. Indeed, it may be that there is a need to first increase damages for personal injury before considering increasing damages in discrimination law.[150]

That said, this process of mutual learning and cross-pollination is not without difficulty. There is a risk that by focusing on a comparison with tort, the breadth and remedial scope of statutory discrimination law is ignored or lost. As noted in section II, the remedial powers of Australian courts and tribunals in discrimination law are particularly wide. There is significant scope for creative and adapted remedial outcomes in discrimination law. At present, though, these broad remedial powers are rarely utilised to their full potential. Where these broad powers are used, though, it is often in cases where claimants are represented by practitioners skilled in discrimination law.[151] Perhaps, then, the priority is to *disentangle* discrimination and tort law, rather than to promote their cross-fertilisation of ideas.

Relatedly, then, there may be a need to move beyond a focus on compensation in discrimination law, to encompass a broader range of damages. As noted above, compensation is a limited proxy for achieving a sense of justice or vindication, which is often sought in the context of discrimination law. If we recognise the public interest in addressing discrimination and inequality, and the social harms of discrimination,[152] we might also seek remedial alternatives that better reflect the social effects of discrimination, and the public interest in preventing discrimination. This might involve, for example, awarding punitive or vindicatory damages.[153] In tort law, for example, Varuhas has put forward a case for normative damages (at least for torts actionable per se).[154] That said, any head of vindicatory damages in tort has been rejected by the Australian High Court,[155] and the UK

[149] *Enforcing the Equality Act* (n 42) 62–3.

[150] See, eg, *Damages for Personal Injury: Non-Pecuniary Loss* (Law Com No 257, 1999); R Lewis, 'Increasing the Price of Pain: Damages, The Law Commission and Heil v Rankin' (2001) 64 *The Modern Law Review* 100.

[151] See, eg, *Slattery v Manningham City Council* [2014] VCAT 1442, where the claimant was represented by the specialist Victorian Legal Aid Equality Law Program. Remedies in that case included an order to revoke a discriminatory Proscribed Prohibited Person Declaration; providing training on the Charter of Human Rights and Responsibilities Act 2006 (Vic) for Councillors, the Chief Executive Officer and Directors; compensation of AU$14,000; and a declaration.

[152] A Blackham, 'Faces of Inequality: Reflections on Exceptional Developments' (2024) 63 *Dialogue: Canadian Philosophical Review / Revue canadienne de philosophie* 85, 93.

[153] See, eg, Edelman (n 65).

[154] For Varuhas, 'normative' damages 'redress a wrongful interference with a protected interest'. Their availability 'in itself furthers the vindicatory goal of the law, attesting to, affirming and reinforcing the fundamental nature of the interest and its inherent value': JNE Varuhas, 'The Concept of "Vindication" in the Law of Torts: Rights, Interests and Damages' (2014) 34 *Oxford Journal of Legal Studies* 253, 255.

[155] *Lewis v Australian Capital Territory* [2020] HCA 26 [2] (Kiefel CJ and Keane J), [22] (Gageler J), [51], [118] (Gordon J), [172] (Edelman J).

Supreme Court,[156] which both regard nominal damages as adequate vindication of the right. While punitive damages might be awarded for discrimination claims in the US, exemplary damages (which aim to punish the defendant) are seen as beyond the statutory remedies available in discrimination law in Australia, which focus on redressing 'loss and damage'.[157] The WEC has recommended that exemplary damages should be made more widely available for discrimination claims[158] and that punitive damages should be available.[159] A different remedial approach to damages in this area is likely to require statutory change.

Another remedial option might take the form of civil penalties, which consider the impact of discrimination on society, and the protective function of discrimination law.[160] This might be modelled, for example, on the power to impose penalties for a breach of industrial laws, including adverse action on the basis of a protected characteristic, under the Australian Fair Work Act 2009 (Cth).[161] A court can impose a maximum penalty for a general protections contravention of AU$18,780 per breach for individuals, and AU$93,900 per breach for a company, in addition to any compensation awarded. If civil penalties are paid to the government, there may be little incentive for individuals to seek them; under the Fair Work Act 2009 (Cth), then, the penalty can be paid to the government, an organisation or a person.[162] A similar provision in discrimination law might better reflect the social condemnation of discrimination; again, this requires statutory change and would require us to better consider how we value (and quantify) the social harm of discrimination.

IX. Conclusion

This chapter flags the normative limits of applying private law perspectives to the employment contract. For discrimination law, which is increasingly seen as having public and social functions and addressing public and social wrongs, there is a need to embrace remedies that also address public and social ends. Private law, with its primary focus on compensatory remedies at common law, is perhaps a helpful starting point for reconsidering discrimination law remedies. More is required, though, to embrace the full transformative potential of discrimination law. This

[156] *R (Lumba) v Secretary of State for the Home Department* [2012] 1 AC 245 [97]–[101] (Lord Dyson), [222]–[237] (Lord Collins), [253]–[256] (Lord Kerr).

[157] See, eg, Equal Opportunity Act 2010 (Vic) s 125; AHRC Act 1986, s 46PO(4).

[158] *Enforcing the Equality Act* (n 42) 62–3.

[159] *The Use of Non-Disclosure Agreements* (n 94) [67]. Though see the discussion of *Ministry of Defence v Fletcher* [2010] IRLR 25 in A Bogg, 'Labour Constitutionalism: Effective Judicial Protection as a Constitutional Principle in UK Labour Law' (2022) 43 *Comparative Labor Law and Policy Journal* 59.

[160] Respondent A118.

[161] FWA 2009, ss 546, 539; *cf* the Employment Tribunals Act 1996, s 12A, where the penalty is paid to the Secretary of State.

[162] FWA 2009, s 546(3).

does not mean that we should abandon individual claims and individual enforcement of discrimination law in favour of, say, the criminalisation of discrimination. Indeed, the experience of other jurisdictions, which have criminalised discrimination, is that enforcement is rare or non-existent.[163] Individual claims, while only a partial means of addressing discrimination,[164] remain a critical part of the legal framework.[165] Using private law to recalibrate discrimination law remedies could be one part of the puzzle for strengthening the enforcement of discrimination law and better advancing equality.

[163] See the discussion of Finland in A Blackham, *Extending Working Life for Older Workers: Age Discrimination Law, Policy and Practice* (Oxford, Hart Publishing, 2016).
[164] Blackham (n 2).
[165] A Blackham, 'Abandoning Individual Enforcement? Interrogating the Enforcement of Age Discrimination Law' (2023) 43 *Legal Studies* 3.

6

Damages for Breach of the Contract of Employment: Valuing the Loss of a Chance

GABRIELLE GOLDING*

I. Introduction

This chapter is concerned with an employee's ability to claim damages for loss of a chance in the event of a wrongful dismissal by their employer.[1] It pursues the potential for an extension of the understanding of a 'lost chance' to account for the value of maintaining an employment relationship.[2] I go so far as to say that there is scope for a revitalised category of damages for loss of a chance in the form of damages for the value of the lost chance of maintaining an employment relationship. It is envisaged that these damages will have the purpose of compensating the wronged employee for the loss of the chance that they might otherwise have gained from an ongoing employment relationship with their employer.

While the law on loss of a chance has been a vexed issue in both the law of tort and contract,[3] this chapter focuses on damages for loss of chance in the law of contract – and, even more closely, on the law of the contract of employment.[4] The

* I thank attendees of the Private Law Perspectives on the Contract of Employment Conference at University College London (7 June 2024) for their insightful comments on an earlier draft. I am especially grateful to Adam Kramer KC for his detailed commentary and to Professors Alan Bogg and Paul S Davies for their invaluable editorial feedback.

[1] Academic literature and case authorities tend to use the labels 'loss of a chance' and 'loss of opportunity' interchangeably. For consistency, this chapter refers primarily to 'loss of a chance'.

[2] I first explored the potential for 'relational damages' to account for the value of the chance of maintaining that relationship in G Golding, 'Employment as a Relational Contract and the Impact on Remedies for Breach' (2021) 30(2) *Griffith Law Review* 270. The present chapter builds on that initial suggestion, especially in section IV.

[3] See, eg, *Hotson v East Berkshire Area Health Authority* [1987] AC 750 (HL), 789, wherein it was branded a 'difficult area of the law'.

[4] Some of the earliest examples of such claims concerning contracts of employment include *Manubens v Leon* [1919] 1 KB 208 (EWHC), which concerned a hairdresser's claim for lost tips and it was held to be clearly within the contemplation of the parties that the plaintiff would receive the tips, and *Herbert Clayton and Jack Waller Ltd v Oliver* [1930] AC 209 (HL), in which a performing artist made a successful claim for damages in respect of the lost chance to derive fame and reputation.

focus is further narrowed to the jurisdictional responses in England and Australia. It seeks to connect and bring together various themes in the common law from both jurisdictions, with a view to pursuing a meaningful recommendation when it comes to the potential for a revitalised category of damages, which recognises and accounts for the value of maintaining an employment relationship. The spirit of this exercise is not to ask which jurisdiction's approach is superior, but rather to enrich the 'supply of solutions'.[5] It recognises the consideration of the approaches taken in both legal systems as an *écolé de vérité*, drawing normative conclusions from the comparison undertaken.

To frame this Introduction, it is helpful to commence with a working example of how and when damages have previously been awarded for loss of a chance in the context of wrongful termination of a contract of employment. I therefore turn to *Barker v Commonwealth Bank of Australia* – a first instance decision of the Federal Court of Australia.[6] Even though this decision was later appealed twice by the Commonwealth Bank, it is the trial judge's decision regarding Mr Stephen Barker's initial award of damages for loss of a chance that is most captivating in the context of this chapter.

At first instance, Mr Barker was awarded damages in the amount of AU$317,500 for the loss of the chance to be redeployed within the bank during his notice period pursuant to the bank's Redeployment Policy.[7] That figure was said to represent a 25 per cent chance that Mr Barker otherwise would have had in successfully applying for and working in one of the four available and suitable other positions with the bank,[8] an organisation in which he had already worked for close to 30 years.[9]

According to Besanko J, by not following its Redeployment Policy, not only had the bank breached that policy, but, at that stage in proceedings, had also breached an implied duty of mutual trust and confidence.[10] When the bank later appealed to the Full Court of the Federal Court of Australia,[11] followed by a further and final appeal to the High Court of Australia,[12] it was ultimately successful. At this moment, it is worth mentioning that because of the High Court of Australia's decision, we now know that the duty of mutual trust and confidence does not exist in Australian contracts of employment.[13] But that is a whole other conundrum, and not a focus of this chapter.

[5] K Zweigert and H Kötz, *An Introduction to Comparative Law*, 3rd edn (Oxford, Oxford, Clarendon Press, 1998) 15.

[6] *Barker v Commonwealth Bank of Australia* (2012) 229 IR 249 (FCA).

[7] ibid [369]–[372].

[8] ibid.

[9] ibid [32].

[10] ibid [352].

[11] *Commonwealth Bank of Australia v Barker* (2013) 233 IR 31 (FCAFC).

[12] *Commonwealth Bank of Australia v Barker* (2014) 253 CLR 169 (HCA).

[13] For more detailed commentary on the High Court of Australia's decision, see further, G Golding, *Shaping Contracts for Work: The Normative Influence of Terms Implied by Law* (Oxford, Oxford University Press, 2023) 87–99.

Having regard to the subject matter of the present exercise, it is curious that, at first instance, Besanko J found that by denying Mr Barker the chance to be redeployed into one of the four available and suitable other positions within the bank during his notice period in accordance with its Redeployment Policy, he had lost the chance of future earnings.[14] Mr Barker's chance was said to last up until an estimated retirement age of 65, while also incorporating a slight reduction in terms of his earning capacity and existing contractual termination rights.[15] Based on his level of experience and expertise, he might have otherwise had the chance of being offered one of those four available positions and working in it until the nominal retirement age of 65, the likelihood of which was estimated at 25 per cent.[16]

In arriving at that estimate, Besanko J acknowledged candidly that it was 'difficult to assess Mr Barker's chances of redeployment'.[17] His Honour made it apparent that he was simply 'doing the best' that he could,[18] having regard to the evidence and applicable case law.[19] As we shall see, this speculative quality of damages for loss of a chance in the context of wrongful termination of contracts of employment is precisely what makes this category of damages especially interesting to consider more deeply. The theme of judges 'doing the best that they can' is all-pervading in such cases.

This chapter thus pursues the potential for an employee to receive damages for loss of a chance in the event of the wrongful termination of their contract of employment. In that sense, what is referred to is contractual 'wrongful termination' (which can be treated as synonymous with 'wrongful dismissal')[20] by the employer specifically. That focus is not to diminish claims that may be made by employers as against employees. While uncommon, such claims are certainly possible. The present focal point is on claims for damages for loss of a chance by employees in the event of a breach of contract by the employer. As demonstrated by the admittedly imperfect method applied when calculating such damages at first instance in *Barker*, that focus has been, and remains, a topic of contention in employment contract law. As such, this chapter analyses and normatively evaluates the concept of damages for loss of a chance in the event of wrongful termination of the contract of employment. Its underlying aim is to substantiate the remedial dimension of employees' lost chances, especially those arising from the very fact of being in an employment relationship, since that status attracts a unique value.

[14] *Barker* (n 6) [369].
[15] ibid [370].
[16] ibid [372].
[17] ibid [369].
[18] ibid.
[19] ibid.
[20] See, eg, the similar suggestion regarding this synonymity in A Bogg and M Freedland, 'The Wrongful Termination of the Contract of Employment' in M Freedland et al. (eds), *The Contract of Employment* (Oxford, Oxford University Press, 2016) 537, 537.

Before embarking upon a more nuanced discussion, section II consists of an account of the general legal framework governing damages for loss of a chance, setting the scene for the remainder of this chapter. Section III then invokes a more dedicated focus on the law governing an employee's loss of a chance in the event of an employer's wrongful termination of their contract. That discussion is followed by section IV's consideration of both English and Australian case law, which serves to demonstrate instances in which damages for loss of a chance have been recoverable in the event of unlawful termination of the contract of employment across both jurisdictions. Section V recognises that given the increased recognition of the contract of employment as 'relational',[21] there may be some plausibility in recognising a category of 'relational damages' in the event of wrongful termination of the contract of employment. However, considering the present uncertainty associated with classifying contracts of employment as relational, the discussion expands to consider the underlying value of maintaining employment being linked to 'human flourishing' – a concept, with philosophical underpinnings, that will be expanded upon in section V. It is envisaged that an award of damages for loss of a chance to maintain an employment relationship would play an important role in compensating a wrongfully dismissed employee for the value of the opportunity to flourish – an opportunity they otherwise would have had, had their employment relationship been maintained. There is, after all, real, tangible, and lasting value in the chance of maintaining an employment relationship, given its enablement of human flourishing. Overarching conclusions are then drawn.

II. The General Legal Framework

To lay the foundation for the remainder of this chapter, this opening summarises the current legal framework regarding damages for loss of a chance in general breach of contract claims. In doing so, I acknowledge that there exists an ongoing debate concerning the extent to which the law governing the contract of employment should continue to borrow from the general law of contract.[22] However, in recognition of the importance and need for the general principles of orthodox contract law to continue to 'play a pivotal role in the development of the law of the employment contract and the resolution of hitherto unresolved controversies',[23] this discussion remains general in nature. Such a general approach occurs with a view to playing its own pivotal role in guiding the remainder of this chapter, which

[21] For further background to contracts of employment being understood as 'relational', both academically and judicially, see, eg, Golding (n 2) 272–80 (and the sources cited therein).

[22] For a summary of the early academic literature concerning this debate, see, eg, M Freedland, *The Contract of Employment* (Oxford, Clarendon Press, 1976) 3–7.

[23] D Brodie, 'The Autonomy of the Common Law of the Contract of Employment from the General Law of Contract' in M Freedland et al. (eds), *The Contract of Employment* (Oxford, Oxford University Press, 2016) 124, 124.

is specifically dedicated to the contract of employment. Indeed, as will become clearer in section III, employment contract law has borrowed heavily from the general law of contract insofar as damages for loss of a chance are concerned.

Damages are the standard remedy for breach of contract. Their overarching purpose is to place the injured party in the same position that they otherwise would have been in had their contract been properly performed.[24] Though the loss suffered by the injured party must not be too remote, it must be in the parties' reasonable contemplation at the time they entered the contract.[25] When considering damages in the broadest sense, they must be proved with reasonable certainty.[26] This requirement of certainty applies to the fact of the damages, but not the amount.[27] In fact, the quantification of damages may be uncertain for a whole range of reasons, including how the quantifiable loss might necessarily occur from a breach of contract. Even so, courts in common law jurisdictions, including England and Australia, have routinely shown a willingness to award damages for loss of a chance.[28]

It has been said that, at common law, there is no valid reason as to why a party cannot contract for the benefit of a chance.[29] Consequently, if a contract – including a contract of employment – includes a promise to provide a chance, then breaching that contract will result in damages for the loss of that chance.[30] A plaintiff can receive more than nominal damages if they are unjustly deprived of the chance they contracted for. Loss of chance damages help to uphold the core objectives of orthodox contract law by protecting the parties' reasonable expectations and the interests of those who have reasonably relied on the promises or actions of others.[31]

In the event of a breach of contract, damages will be assessed according to the difference between the promised and actual outcomes. To repeat a point already made, in some situations, it is simply impossible to know what the outcome will be, even if the contract had been performed. However, there do exist situations

[24] *Robinson v Harman* (1848) 1 Exch 850 (Exch), 855 (Parke B). This principle has been routinely confirmed in common law jurisdictions, including the United Kingdom and Australia: see, eg, *Golden Strait Corporation v Nippon Yusen Kubishika Kaisha (The Golden Victory)* [2007] 2 AC 353 (HL), [29]; *Tabcorp Holdings Ltd v Bowen Investments Pty Ltd* (2009) 236 CLR 272 (HCA), [13].

[25] *Hadley v Baxendale* (1854) 9 Exch 341 (Exch), 354. On the general principle of remoteness in relation to contractual damages, see, eg, H McGregor, *McGregor on Damages*, 18th edn (London, Sweet and Maxwell, 2009) 769–71.

[26] McGregor (n 25), 325–7.

[27] AG Guest (ed), *Chitty on Contracts*, 24th edn (London, Sweet and Maxwell, 1977) §1562. See also, *Fink v Fink* (1946) 74 CLR 127 (HCA), 143.

[28] See, eg, *Chaplin v Hicks* [1911] 2 KB 786 (CA); *Joseph v National Magazine Co Ltd* [1959] Ch 52 (CA). See generally, R Dunn, *Recovery of Damages for Lost Profits (Vol 1)*, 5th edn (Westport, Connecticut, Lawpress Corporation, 1998).

[29] B Coote, 'Chance and the Burden of Proof in Contract and Tort' (1988) 62 *Australian Law Journal* 761, 771.

[30] The earliest recognition of compensation for loss of a chance occurred in *Richardson v Mellish* (1824) 2 Bing 229 (CPD), which was later approved in *Chaplin* (n 28). See further, McGregor (n 25), 342–3; SM Waddams, *The Law of Damages*, 2nd edn (Toronto, Canada Law Book Inc 1991) [13.280].

[31] PS Atiyah, *An Introduction to the Law of Contract*, 5th edn (Oxford, Clarendon Press, 1995) 34–6.

in which there is far less uncertainty. In those instances, even though a specific outcome may not be ascertainable, its chance may well be. Rather than proving on the balance of probabilities that a certain outcome would have occurred, the plaintiff can show that there was a chance of that outcome, making way for a claim for damages for loss of a chance. The seminal case demonstrating that potential is *Chaplin v Hicks*,[32] which has a well-known, but peculiar, factual matrix. There exist other decisions more specific to the contract of employment, which are discussed in section IV. For now, *Chaplin* sets the scene.

The plaintiff in *Chaplin* was a young woman who, in 1908, entered a beauty contest by submitting her photograph to a local newspaper.[33] She was one of 50 contestants shortlisted from 6,000 applicants. This shortlisting generated a contractual relationship between her and the defendant newspaper. The defendant then interviewed each shortlisted applicant, with a view to then selecting 12 women to gain employment as actresses. The plaintiff was unable to attend the interview on her allocated date and time. By refusing to reschedule her interview, the defendant was found to have breached her contract.

The plaintiff could not claim damages for the lost prize itself. She could not prove on the balance of probabilities that she would have won the competition. However, the court recognised that but for the defendant's actions, the plaintiff would have at least had a chance to compete. This chance was seen as valuable, and losing it was worthy of compensation. The court dismissed the defendant's argument that, due to the uncertainties, it was impossible for the plaintiff to recover any damages for the loss of a chance to win the prize. Instead, it determined that each competitor had an average chance of about one in four. Consequently, the plaintiff was awarded 25 per cent of what she would have gained had she been chosen as an actress.

What this formative decision demonstrates is that, at the most basic level, there are effectively two elements contained within a lost chance: (1) the element of a chance; and (2) the element of a loss. In the law of contract, a 'chance' is the possibility of gaining a certain benefit or avoiding a detriment. It involves a hypothetical expectation, allowing it to materialise into a gain or a loss. A 'loss' must mean that no substantial chance remains. It constitutes its own unique kind of loss-generating recovery. Factually speaking, proof of causation is transformed in terms of the assessment of damages. A 'lost chance' thus functions as a 'normative legal limit for tracing hypothetical consequences', based on the separation of chances and events.[34]

There must consequently exist an approximation that one can recover for loss of a chance, so long as there exists a hypothetical chain of events linked together by human decision-making, which is inherently unreliable. It has been said in a

[32] *Chaplin* (n 28).

[33] See further, the more expansive examination of this decision in B Smith, 'Loss of a Chance' (1999) 29 *Victoria University of Wellington Law Review* 225, 227–8.

[34] N Jansen, 'The Idea of a Lost Chance' (1999) 19(2) *Oxford Journal of Legal Studies* 271, 284.

Chinese proverb that 'The past is before us, only the future is behind us', which stands for the proposition that the past is, theoretically, discoverable, whereas certainty cannot be achieved regarding the future.[35] A similar sentiment was put by Lord Reid in *Davies v Taylor*:[36]

> When the question is whether a certain thing is or is not true – whether a certain event did or did not happen – then the court must decide one way or the other. There is no question of chance or probability. Either it did or did not happen … You can prove that a past event happened, but you cannot prove that a future event will happen, and I do not think that the law is so foolish as to suppose that you can.

Nonetheless, what damages for loss of a chance show us is that sometimes, one *can* prove that a future event will occur. The fundamental question lies in whether the hypothetical chain of events is to be entirely determined by the events that have already taken place. Having now considered the general contractual position, the following discussion moves to consider the potential for damages for loss of a chance in matters involving contracts of employment wrongfully terminated by the employer.

III. Recovery Arising Out of Wrongful Termination of Employment

It is relatively rare to find damages being sought in employment matters, save for instances of wrongful termination, resulting from a breach of the contract of employment.[37] An action for wrongful termination arises only when an employer acts to bring a contract of employment to an end, not where it ends according to its terms, based on its fixed term reaching a natural end, or by certain other means.[38] As this chapter's Introduction highlights, it is actions for wrongful termination that pave the way for employees being able to claim damages for loss of a chance.

In Australia, access to damages for wrongful dismissal is typically available in ordinary courts, rather than an employment tribunal (typically, the Fair Work Commission). In the UK, an employee can make a claim for wrongful dismissal in the Employment Tribunal,[39] provided that claim occurs within three months less one day from the date of termination of their employment or within six years

[35] As quoted in H Reece, 'Losses of Chances in the Law' (1996) 59(2) *Modern Law Review* 188, 206.

[36] *Davies v Taylor* [1972] 3 All ER 836 (HL), 838.

[37] *cf* unfair dismissal, which arises from a dismissal involving infringement of an employee's statutory-based rights.

[38] Eg, by consent of both parties, by reason of frustration, upon a party's death, following the dissolution of a partnership, or upon the resolution of a company for its voluntary winding up. See further, I Neil et al., *The Modern Contract of Employment*, 3rd edn (Pyrmont, NSW, Thomas Reuters, 2023) [10.001]–[10.006], [10.037]–[10.043].

[39] Employment Tribunals Extension of Jurisdiction (England and Wales) Order 1994, SI 1994/1623, Art 6.

if their claim is made in a court in England or Wales (noting that in Scotland, the limitation is five years).[40] In the Employment Tribunal, the maximum amount an employee can claim for wrongful dismissal is £25,000.[41] If the amount is greater, then the claim must be brought before the County or High Court.

The prevalence of such claims will thus be limited to a relatively small number of employees. Even so, that limitation does not, and ought not, diminish the value of the discussion at hand. As Lizzie Barmes has eloquently put it, there are an increasing number of working people who, from an already high base, are 'expected to simply rely on their employers to do the right thing',[42] but that behaviour is by no means guaranteed. After all, it is those employees who can 'more effectively deploy contract law' and 'fashion more substantial protections',[43] with the impact trickling down to those who are less affluent and unrepresented. Those who are in a position to bring such claims play a key role in ensuring that the benefits of these legal developments flow through to those less highly remunerated employees, who can otherwise rarely afford to litigate such claims with adequate representation. Their pursuit of damages for loss of a chance in instances of wrongful dismissal presents an influential opportunity to lead from the top-down.

In matters involving wrongful termination, an action for damages by the employee can only be brought where an employer acts to bring the contract of employment to an end. If a wrongful termination has occurred, when assessing damages, courts will ask not what the parties' legal rights were, but instead, what would have occurred, as a matter of practical reality, if the wrongful termination had not occurred.[44] This assessment requires an evaluation of the likelihood that the employer's right to terminate would have been exercised in a manner that would have reduced the damages for which the employee might otherwise have been entitled. That likelihood is to be assessed in accordance with the circumstances at the time that the employee's contract of employment was terminated.

In terms of assessing damages for wrongful termination, the mere existence of a contractual right of a party to terminate will not automatically operate to restrict the damages that could be awarded.[45] An employee might then succeed in a claim for damages for loss of a chance where their employer's breach of contract causes them to lose a chance to acquire a benefit or avoid a detriment, and the general principles stated above in section II will apply in terms of assessing that loss. Such a claim by an employee can transcend the value of their contract of employment that

[40] ibid Art 3.

[41] ibid Art 10. It is worth noting that in *Mrs S Ugradar v Lancashire Care NHS Foundation Trust* UKEAT/0301/18/BA (EAT) [28], it was suggested that this cap on compensation is outdated.

[42] L Barmes, 'Remedies for Breach and for Wrongful Dismissal' in M Freedland et al. (eds), *The Contract of Employment* (Oxford, Oxford University Press, 2016) 599, 619.

[43] L Barmes, 'The Contract of Employment and the Remedial Dimension' in M Freedland et al. (eds), *The Contract of Employment* (Oxford, Oxford University Press, 2016) 167, 186.

[44] See, eg, MA Eisenberg, 'Probability and Chance in Contract Law' (1998) 45 *UCLA Law Review* 1005, 1048–51.

[45] See, eg *Chaplin* (n 28), 792.

is otherwise limited to either their strict or non-discretionary contractual entitlements or the earliest point at which the employer may have lawfully terminated the contract, whether by reason of an express minimum period of notice of termination or by declining to renew a contract that has expired by virtue of its own terms.

As was the case in *Barker v Commonwealth Bank of Australia* discussed in this chapter's Introduction,[46] it is typical for courts to express the percentage of a possibility or probability in calculating damages to be awarded for loss of a chance. Still, a court may otherwise decide to take a global approach and award a lump sum damages payment.[47] With the above discussion in mind, attention now turns to a combination of English and Australian employment contract cases in which a claim for damages associated with the loss of a chance has been successfully brought by an employee.

IV. Examining English and Australian Case Law

This section identifies that issues regarding an employee's loss of a chance usually arise in four main scenarios, with a potential fifth: (1) missing out on a commission, bonus, or similar discretionary payment; (2) missing the opportunity to have a fixed-term contract renewed; (3) losing the chance to stay employed under a job security clause; and (4) failing to obtain a benefit when a contract of employment includes an express promise of procedural fairness or consultation in case of dismissal. The fifth possible option is for an employee to claim damages for loss of a chance of obtaining future employment.[48] But for the reasons outlined later in this section, that type of loss is not easily quantifiable in the form of damages.

The following discussion considers case authorities relevant to each of these five possibilities in turn, with a view to rationalising the later arguments in section V concerning the potential for damages associated with the loss of a chance of maintaining an employment relationship. The examination here is by no means an exhaustive account of the applicable English and Australian case law. Rather, it serves to highlight a series of notable decisions in which an award of

[46] *Barker* (n 6).

[47] See, eg, *Rakic v Johns Lyng Insurance Building Solutions (Victoria) Pty Ltd* (2016) 259 IR 47 (FCA), [218]–[227], where there were many hypotheticals available to assess the former employee's chances in relation to potential future remuneration, had she not relied upon misleading conduct of her former employer. Rather than endeavouring to explore each hypothetical, the court assessed the most likely answer to the various questions and adjusted the purported loss upwards or downwards according to its assessment of the chances and figures associated with more and less favourable alternatives, arriving at a lump sum award of damages.

[48] An employee who has been wrongfully dismissed is, however, unable to bring a claim for losing the chance to bring an unfair dismissal claim if they are dismissed before acquiring the necessary period of service in which to bring such a claim. If that kind of action were permissible, the effect would be to subvert the requisite period of employment required under statute: see, eg, *Harper v Virgin Net Ltd* [2004] IRLR 390 (CA), noting that the relevant statutory provision is Employment Rights Act 1996, s 97(2).

damages for loss of a chance has already been granted. The below selection of case law also demonstrates a newfound category of damages for loss of the chance of maintaining an employment relationship that is yet to be realised, and nor has it been the subject of an employee's claim. Nonetheless, there is encouragement in the fact that the following lost chances arising out of the wrongful termination of the contract of employment have been compensable.

A. Loss of a Chance to Acquire a Discretionary Benefit

First, in terms of an employee's ability to recover damages where the breach of contract by their employer has resulted in the employee losing a chance to obtain a discretionary benefit (eg, a commission, bonus, or other payment), whether an employee can recover for the loss of benefits other than their salary depends on whether the benefits are ones to which the employee is necessarily entitled to under their contract of employment.[49] A court's task is to assess what position the employee would have otherwise been in had the employer performed its contractual obligation.[50] This process necessarily involves the court assessing the employee's prospect of being granted the discretionary payment, as well as the quantum of that payment.[51] In *Lavarack v Woods of Colchester Ltd*,[52] for instance, a terminated employee successfully sought compensation for the income they could have earned from the opportunity to earn bonuses. These bonuses were initially at the company directors' discretion but had become a contractual obligation for the company to still maintain.

An important aspect of *Lavarack* was the Court of Appeal's finding that an employee can only claim for what they are legally entitled to under their contract of employment, nothing more, thereby generating what is now known as the 'minimum' or 'least burdensome' performance rule.[53] *Lavarack*'s impact was, therefore, such that discretionary bonus payments would typically be disregarded in assessing damages. Only where a contract of employment expressly provided for a guaranteed bonus in the sense of it being a contractual entitlement would it become payable in the event of an employee's wrongful dismissal.

More recent authorities have since done away with the *Lavarack* minimum performance rule, suggesting that the mere possibility of being paid a discretionary benefit will suffice to substantiate a claim for damages for loss of a chance. In *Horkulak v Cantor Fitzgerald International*,[54] for example, the Court of Appeal determined that the principles established in *Lavarack* did not apply to situations

[49] See, eg, M Irving, *The Contract of Employment*, 2nd edn (London, LexisNexis Butterworths, 2019) 1085.
[50] ibid.
[51] See, eg, *Horkulak v Cantor Fitzgerald International* [2005] ICR 402 (CA) [56].
[52] *Lavarack v Woods of Colchester Ltd* [1967] 1 QB 278 (CA).
[53] ibid.
[54] *Horkulak* (n 51).

where there existed a contractual right to a bona fide and rational exercise of the employer's discretion regarding the awarding of bonuses. In such cases, the court reasoned that it ought to assess what decision would have been made regarding the bonus by putting itself into the position of those making it and then decide what figure would have been reached had the discretion been exercised in line with those principles.

Similarly, in *Macdonald v Australian Wool Innovation Ltd*,[55] the employee was entitled to a share of a project's profits, which their employer, in breach of their employment agreement, had opted not to pursue. Given that the project was high risk, there was but a mere possibility that it would have generated a profit. Even though the evidence of the value of the lost chance was limited, the court still concluded that there was some prospect of a profit and awarded the employee AU$50,000 in damages.[56] Given these more recent decisions, it appears that the 'minimum performance' rule from *Lavarack* may well have been abandoned. Indeed, there are legal academics who agree that this is the correct approach.[57]

Even so, there may still be good sense in maintaining the 'minimum performance' rule, particularly insofar as awards of general damages, rather than damages for consequential loss, are concerned. In fact, in the most recent case concerning the rule's application, *Robert MacKenzie v AA Limited*,[58] the Court of Appeal signalled a revival of the *Lavarack* approach. The court confirmed that where an employer has several alternative methods of terminating a contract of employment lawfully, it should be permitted to choose the 'least burdensome' method. It was accepted that while some circumstances called for a derogation from the 'minimum performance' rule, where there are alternative methods for a contract's lawful performance (eg, termination), the 'least burdensome' performance rule will continue to apply. In other words, if the employer has the contractual right to terminate a contract of employment and provide pay in lieu of notice, then that will be the maximum amount payable. If one accepts that this newfound *Lavarack*-infused position is correct, then in assessing damages where an employee has been wrongfully dismissed, the court should not necessarily entertain arguments about the purported loss of other discretionary benefits (eg, bonus payments), especially where their contractual entitlement is otherwise clear.

Separate from the resurfaced application of the 'minimum performance' rule, another consideration is whether an employee's entitlement to benefits

[55] *Macdonald v Australian Wool Innovation Ltd* [2005] FCA 105 (FCA).

[56] ibid [251]–[255]. See also *Shove v Downs Surgical Plc* [1984] ICR 532 (EWHC), where an award of damages for wrongful termination included amounts in respect of the employee's exclusion from the employer's life insurance scheme, the loss of his subscription to a private health care scheme and his loss of being able to use a company car.

[57] See, eg, D Pearce, 'Of Ceilings and Flaws: An Analytical Approach to the Minimum Performance Rule in Contract Damages' (2016) 36(4) *Oxford Journal of Legal Studies* 781; D McLauchlan, 'The Minimum Performance Rule in Contract Damages' (2019) *Lloyd's Maritime and Commercial Law Quarterly* 75.

[58] *Robert MacKenzie v AA Limited* [2022] EWCA Civ 901 (CA).

depends on the maintenance of the employment relationship. For example, in *Micklefield v SAC Technology Ltd*,[59] the employee's dismissal triggered certain share options to lapse when they would have otherwise been available to the employee automatically under the associated company scheme. The result was that the employee was not entitled to compensation in respect of that loss. Likewise, in *Commerzbank AG v Keen*,[60] the employee's contract indicated that no bonus would be payable to them if they were not employed at the bank as of the date the bonus would have fallen due. The English Court of Appeal found that there was no real prospect of success in the employee's claim that the bank had acted irrationally or perversely in not awarding the employee the relevant bonus in relation to the year-long period for which he had worked, particularly given that his employment had been terminated before the date of the payment otherwise falling due.

The maintenance of the relationship between employer and employee was also paramount in *O'Laorie v Jackel International Ltd (No 2)*,[61] in which the employee was entitled to stock options under a scheme that could only be exercised with the board's consent. The employee was wrongfully dismissed and attempted to claim damages for the lost chance of exercising those options. Nevertheless, it was revealed that the employer's board had become so antagonistic towards the employee that the court concluded that there could be no chance of the board granting consent. Ultimately, the value of the employee's lost chance was said to be £0.[62]

B. Loss of a Chance to Renew a Fixed-term Contract

Second, the potential for an employee to claim damages for loss of a chance in relation to having a fixed-term contract renewed was explored in *Martin v Tasmania Development and Resources*.[63] In that case, the employee was engaged on a three-year fixed-term contract, which could be terminated by the employer due to 'operational reasons' after consulting with the employee and providing one month's notice. The employer proceeded to terminate the employee's employment but did not consult with them. It also provided the employee with pay in lieu of notice, rather than notice itself. On appeal, it was relevantly held that no operational reasons existed to justify the employee's termination. It was also held that the employee had lost a valuable opportunity to have their fixed-term contract renewed at the expiration of its term.[64]

59 *Micklefield v SAC Technology Ltd*, [1990] 1 WLR 1002 (EWHC).
60 *Commerzbank AG v Keen* [2007] IRLR 132 (CA).
61 *O'Laorie v Jackel International Ltd (No 2)* [1991] ICR 718 (CA).
62 ibid 730. See also, *Guthrie v News Limited* (2010) 27 VR 196 (VSC), [169]–[170].
63 *Martin v Tasmania Development and Resources* (1999) 89 IR 98 (FCA).
64 ibid [97]–[100].

C. Loss of a Chance to Remain in Employment where a Contractual Job Security Clause Exists

Third, when considering an employee's potential claim for the loss of a chance to remain in employment following the application of a contractually agreed job security clause, it is helpful to look to *WT Partnership (Aust) Pty Ltd v Sheldrick*.[65] In that case, an employee was employed in Malaysia under a contract stipulating that his employer must give him three months' notice of termination. Despite that requirement, when his employer unlawfully terminated his employment without notice, the employee had to leave Malaysia promptly due to the breach, which deprived him of the chance to stay and pursue potentially profitable alternative employment. The Full Court of the Federal Court of Australia granted the employee AU$30,000 in damages for the missed opportunity to secure lucrative employment that he might have otherwise pursued had it not been for the employer's breach.[66]

D. Loss of a Chance to Obtain a Benefit where an Express Contractual Obligation to Provide Procedural Fairness or Consultation During a Disciplinary Process Exists

Fourth, in situations where a contract of employment contains an express promise that an employer will provide an employee procedural fairness or consult with them in the event of a dismissal, such a promise can amount to a chance to obtain a benefit.[67] That kind of opportunity may well prove valuable for an employee if they have not engaged in misconduct. Though, if they have, it may simply be delaying their inevitable dismissal. It should, of course, not be presumed that a contractual term requiring procedural fairness or consultation in the event of a dismissal is invaluable. In Australia, the approach is that damages for the breach of a promise to afford an employee procedural fairness should be assessed by determining the chance of an employee remaining in employment had procedural fairness been afforded to them.[68]

[65] *WT Partnership (Aust) Pty Ltd v Sheldrick* (1999) 96 IR 202 (FCAFC).

[66] ibid [39].

[67] A breach of an express term requiring that procedural fairness be afforded to an employee can give rise to a separate cause of action (ie, separate from a claim of wrongful dismissal): see, eg, *Edwards v Chesterfield Royal Hospital NHS Foundation Trust* [2012] 2 AC 22 (UKSC), [37]–[38], [42], [50]; *Elisha v Vision Australia Limited* [2024] HCA 50 (HCA), where the High Court of Australia awarded AU$1.4 million in damages to compensate an employee for psychiatric injury caused by their employer neglecting to follow an express contractual disciplinary procedure fairly. For an examination of the potential for an implied duty requiring an employer to conduct disciplinary processes fairly, see, eg, P Collins and G Golding, 'An Implied Term of Procedural Fairness During Disciplinary Processes: Into Contracts of Employment and Beyond?' (2023) 53(2) *Industrial Law Journal* 125. *cf*, D Brodie, 'Disavowing an Implied Term of Fairness' (2024) 53(2) *Industrial Law Journal* 157.

[68] See, eg, *Williamson v Commonwealth* (1907) 5 CLR 174 (HCA), 186.

The approach in English law is notably different.[69] In *Gunton v Richmond-upon-Thames London Borough Council*,[70] the employee was engaged under a contract of employment, which contained a disciplinary procedure (including the potential for a hearing and appeal) in the event of allegations of misconduct. Otherwise, the employee's position was terminable upon the provision of one month's notice. However, the employer dismissed the employee without adhering to the necessary disciplinary procedure. The Court of Appeal then decided that damages for that breach were to be equal to the wages that the employee would have received while the disciplinary procedure was being engaged in, with that period now commonly known as the '*Gunton* extension period'.[71] There was no assessment of the employee's chance of remaining in employment had the disciplinary procedure been followed. Though it has since been suggested in academic writing that such an approach is unsatisfactory.[72]

It should also be noted that, in the UK, contractually agreed disciplinary procedures are covered by a dedicated legislative scheme governing dismissals.[73] Considering that legislation, the Supreme Court has otherwise held that where there are express terms in a contract of employment providing for a disciplinary procedure, those terms are not to be treated as ordinary contractual terms.[74] The parties are deemed not to have intended that a failure to comply with binding procedures will give rise to a contractual claim for damages for loss of a chance. There is, however, no similar statutory provision in Australia, meaning that the approach in English law is likely to remain unique to that jurisdiction alone.[75]

E. Loss of a Chance that Accrues by Reason of the Contract's Performance

Fifth and finally, there have been cases in which an employee, as the consequence of a breach of contract, purportedly loses an opportunity that would have accrued by reason of the contract's performance. In such cases, prior to *Addis v Gramophone Co Ltd*,[76] the legal position, following *Maw v Jones*,[77] was that

[69] See, eg, Irving (n 49) 1090.

[70] *Gunton v Richmond-upon-Thames London Borough Council* [1980] ICR 755 (CA).

[71] See, eg, C Barnard and L Merritt, 'Winners and Losers: *Edwards* and the Unfair Law of Dismissal' (2013) 72(2) *Cambridge Law Journal* 313, 330 and 333.

[72] See, eg, Z Adams, C Barnard, S Deakin, and S Fraser Butlin, *Deakin and Morris' Labour Law*, 7th edn (Oxford, Hart Publishing, 2021) [4.42].

[73] For a careful examination of the relevant statutory framework and its history, see, eg, A Bogg, 'Express Disciplinary Procedures in the Contract of Employment: Parliamentary Intention and the Supreme Court' (2015) 131 *Law Quarterly Review* 15.

[74] See, eg, *Edwards* (n 67) [38]–[40], [49], [90], [94], [150]. See also, H Collins, 'Compensation for Dismissal – In Search of Principle' (2012) 41(2) *Industrial Law Journal* 208.

[75] See, eg, Irving (n 49) 1091.

[76] *Addis v Gramophone Co Ltd* [1909] AC 488 (HL).

[77] *Maw v Jones* (1890) 25 QBD 107 (QBD).

'dismissal with an imputation might well be thought by a jury to hurt the plaintiff's prospects of finding another situation, and on that ground alone, might give a legal claim to consequential damages within the ordinary rule'.[78] Yet, following *Addis*, the 'limited damages rule' precluded recovery of damages for the diminution in a dismissed employee's prospects of obtaining new employment arising out of the dismissal. *Addis* was then for a long time treated as authority for the proposition that:[79]

> A contract breaker is not in general liable for any distress, frustration, anxiety, displeasure, vexation, tension or aggravation which his [or her] breach of contract may cause the innocent party.

Addis therefore presents a long-standing English authority that damages for the possibility (or chance) of reputational harms will be irrecoverable in an action for breach of a contract of employment connected to termination by the employer.[80]

In *Shaw v New South Wales*,[81] the New South Wales Court of Appeal conducted a detailed analysis of the case law throughout Australia, as well as in the UK and elsewhere, finding that there was now 'room' to address a claim of damages of this kind.[82] The New South Wales Court of Appeal's reasons for reaching that decision included that: (1) it was arguable that in the UK (especially after the majority judgments in *Malik v Bank of Credit & Commerce International SA*,[83] and Lord Steyn in *Johnson v Unisys Ltd*)[84] that *Addis* no longer precluded the recovery of damages for diminished chances of obtaining new employment; (2) 'neither the High Court of Australia nor any intermediate appellate court in Australia had been called upon to give effect to the particular part of the *Addis* formulation concerning the difficulty of obtaining fresh employment';[85] and (3) *Addis* had otherwise lost support or authority, both in the UK, and elsewhere.[86]

There are four things to say about the impact of *Shaw*.[87] The first is that the reasoning is expressly confined to the Australian position on damages for the diminution a dismissed employee's chance of successfully obtaining damages arising out of their dismissal. It does not affect other aspects of the limited damages rule.

[78] *Addis* (n 76) 500.
[79] *Watts v Morrow* [1991] 1 WLR 1421, 1445. *cf*, N Enonchong, 'Breach of Contract and Damages for Mental Distress' (1996) 16 *OJLS* 617.
[80] For further consideration of the impact of *Addis* (n 76), see generally, Bogg and Freedland (n 20) 537.
[81] *Shaw v New South Wales* (2012) 219 IR 87 (NSWCA).
[82] See further, the related discussion in Neil and others (n 38) [13.022].
[83] *Malik v Bank of Credit & Commerce International SA* [1998] AC 20 (HL).
[84] *Johnson v Unisys Ltd* [2003] 1 AC 518 (HL).
[85] *Shaw* (n 81) [118].
[86] ibid [103].
[87] See further, Neil and others (n 38) [13.023]–[13.026].

The second point to make is that, in *Ramsey v Annesley College*,[88] the South Australian Supreme Court confined the application of *Shaw* to 'the situation where the breach is of a specific term during the currency of the contract (the implied term of mutual trust and confidence)',[89] rather than the principle in *Addis*, which applied to a breach by reason of wrongful termination. Assuming that understanding is correct, the impact of *Shaw* is made less by reason of the mutual trust and confidence duty's demise following the High Court of Australia's appellate decision in *Barker*, along with the ongoing uncertainty that same decision generated with respect to the existence of an implied duty of good faith.[90] Third, the question of whether damages are now available in Australia for the diminution of a dismissed employee's chance of obtaining new employment arising out of their dismissal still requires determination by a court.[91]

The fourth and final matter to note is it is possible that in the UK, the majority's opinions in *Johnson* further bolstered support for the underlying reasoning in *Addis*.[92] As mentioned earlier in this section, the Supreme Court majority in *Edwards v Chesterfield Royal Hospital NHS Foundation Trust* held that damages for breach of contract were not recoverable in relation to the manner of an employee's dismissal, even in a situation where the breach was of an express term of the contract of employment regulating disciplinary procedures giving rise to the relevant dismissal.[93] Curiously, *Edwards* was not cited at all in *Shaw*.

Up until this point, the discussion in this chapter has sought to connect with and bring together the law concerning damages for loss of a chance in contract law generally, followed by its more specific application to contracts of employment. The authorities described above in this section demonstrate that there are already distinct categories of case concerning wrongful termination of the contract of employment, which give rise to an employee being able to claim damages for loss of a chance. In fact, the first of those categories – damages for loss of a chance to acquire a discretionary benefit – represents a form of compensation for loss of a chance, which is obviously prefaced on the value of maintaining an employment relationship. Be that as it may, the remaining categories are arguably just as contingent on the hypothetical existence and maintenance of such a relationship. The discussion that follows accordingly explores whether a separate and distinct category of chance has been lost by an employee in the event of wrongful dismissal by their employer – that being, the loss of the chance of maintaining their employment relationship, which is arguably of substantial value.

[88] *Ramsey v Annesley College* [2013] SASC 72 (SASC).
[89] ibid [449].
[90] For commentary on that ongoing uncertainty in Australian law, see, eg, Golding (n 13) 105–11.
[91] See, eg, Neil et al. (n 38) [13.025].
[92] ibid [13.026].
[93] *Edwards* (n 67) [38].

V. The Prospect of Damages for Loss of a Chance of Maintaining an Employment Relationship

We know from the above discussion that, in terms of legal principle, when judges need to assess damages for loss of a chance in employment, they must determine whether the value of the employee's chance is necessarily one for which they are contractually entitled. If it is, then the likelihood of the employee's chance must be established on the balance of probabilities and reflected in the calculation of damages awarded. That calculation is not an exact science; a court will typically wield a 'broad axe' to do justice as best it can.[94] Therefore, where a chance has been lost, the court must do its best to quantify that loss, the process of which will inevitably involve a determination made from a range of reasonable possibilities. This process begs the question: What of the value of the chance of maintaining an employment relationship where a contract of employment has been wrongfully terminated?

In answering that question, this chapter's central thesis is that in instances of wrongful termination of contracts of employment, there is value in the chance of maintaining an employment relationship. The existence of such a chance is borne out of the formation of the parties' contract of employment with one another. The very existence of their employment relationship carries a substantial and unique value. If there is a chance that the relationship could have otherwise been maintained, the law must operate to protect that chance. After all, when parties form a contract of employment, they surely do so with the inevitable and reciprocal contractual promise of upholding their valuable relationship. Not only is this assertion supported by the existence of the mutually implied duties of cooperation,[95] and trust and confidence (at least in English law)[96] during the life of the contract, but, as I explore below, the value of the chance of maintaining an employment relationship can be rationalised in two further ways, with the second proving more convincing than the first.

[94] For a recent example, see, eg, *Morris-Garner v One Step (Support) Ltd* [2019] AC 649 [37]. See also, *Watson, Laidlaw & Co Ltd v Pott, Cassels & Williamson* (1914) 31 RPC 104 [29–30] where the assessment of damages was described as 'the exercise of a sound imagination and the practice of the broad axe'.

[95] See, eg, Golding (n 13) 69–70, which traces the origins and current status of that mutual duty as it exists in contracts of employment in both England and Australia. *cf*, M Freedland, *The Personal Employment Contract* (Oxford, Oxford University Press, 2003) 146–51, which casts doubt over the existence of the implied duty to cooperate in English contracts of employment.

[96] *Malik v Bank of Credit and Commerce International SA* [1998] AC 20 (HL), 34–5 and 45–6, noting that this decision first unlocked the remedial potential arising from a breach of the mutual trust and confidence term following *Courtaulds Northern Textiles Ltd v Andrews* [1979] IRLR 84 and *Woods v WM Car Services (Peterborough) Ltd* [1981] ICR 666. *cf*, in Australia, *Barker* (n 12) and the related commentary on that decision in Golding (n 13) 87–99.

A. Value Derived from the Contract's Relationality

First, contracts of employment are increasingly being understood as relational, both academically and judicially,[97] a classification that supports the idea that there is value in the chance of maintaining an employment relationship. A 'relational' classification of contracts of employment typically means that such contracts encompass 'more than a discrete transaction of a wage paid in exchange for the employee's performance of work; rather, a relationship exists between the employer and employee that extends along a spectrum beyond a discrete commercial exchange'.[98] In other words, there is value in the employment relationship itself, which extends beyond a discrete exchange of wage for work.

As cases concerning wrongful termination of contracts of employment continue to be brought by employees, one could reasonably 'assume that the classification of those contracts as relational will gather momentum'.[99] In turn, the concept of a 'relational' contract of employment, and the impact that classification may have, will undoubtedly become the subject of increased judicial attention.[100] By extension, eventually, courts may 'be urged to consider how the [relational] classification affects the remedies available for breach'.[101]

Despite burgeoning recognition of contracts of employment as relational, the impact of that classification on associated doctrines and rules – including those concerning remedies – remains unclear at present. I have written elsewhere about the possible remedial impact of a relational classification of contracts of employment.[102] In that earlier work, I suggested that the potential for 'relational damages' may exist in the event of a breach of a contract of employment caused by a wrongful termination. It is, however, impossible to say, in the absence of guiding authority, whether that potential attracts any kind of certainty, or indeed, whether some other replicative remedy may be more appropriate–most obviously, an award of specific performance.

For example, there exists a compelling argument that the employment relationship ought to be maintained through an order of specific performance with a view to continuing its existence wherever possible to truly honour and uphold its status as a relational contract. An award of specific performance requiring the contract of employment's performance may therefore be seen as more closely aligned to its relational status than an award of damages. Saying that, existing case law emphasises that courts are reluctant to award specific performance with respect to contracts for personal service, which obviously includes contracts of employment.[103]

[97] See, eg, (n 21).
[98] Golding (n 2) 270.
[99] ibid 271.
[100] ibid.
[101] ibid.
[102] ibid.
[103] ibid 282–3.

There remains the possibility that any relational classification of the contract of employment will have no remedial impact. Perhaps, even more crucially, there is lingering uncertainty as to whether a contract of employment would necessarily be categorised as relational at all. It may therefore be trite to say that a relational classification, which is uncertain of itself, will give rise to any remedial outcome in the event of wrongful termination.

Last, when considering longer-term commercial contracts by way of comparison, some may be classified as relational, generating the potential to attract 'relational damages' in the event of wrongful termination in the same way as relational contracts of employment. However, it is striking that commercial contracts are not concerned with 'human flourishing' in quite the same way as contracts of employment – a concept which is expanded on in more detail directly below. This outcome gives rise to a notable point of distinction with respect to contracts of employment. It suggests that the ability of contracts of employment to facilitate human flourishing exists beyond their potential relationality, carrying its own unique value. Perhaps then the distinctive value of the chance of maintaining an employment relationship is not necessarily linked to its relational quality but is instead more about the value of employment as it relates to facilitating human flourishing. The absence of a relational classification ought not to stymie the fact that there remains an inherent value in the chance of remaining employed.

A relational classification of the contract of employment may well create a more direct, obvious, formulaic, even doctrinal, route towards the potential for 'relational damages' for loss of the chance of maintaining employment in the event of wrongful termination. However, even in the absence of a relational classification, the very value of remaining employed and its links to human flourishing, enabling what Aristotle understood as 'the good life',[104] remain extant. The potential for an award of damages reflecting the value of the lost chance of maintaining employment must still stand. So, the resultant question is: What exactly comprises the value of the chance of maintaining employment as it relates to human flourishing? I endeavour to answer this question below.

B. Value Derived from Enabling Human Flourishing

Attention thus shifts to the potential value of the chance of maintaining an employment relationship as it relates to enabling human flourishing. Employment is ubiquitous in 'human flourishing',[105] operating as a basic 'human good'.[106] The value of employment has been examined extensively in the philosophical tradition,

[104] See especially, Aristotle's *Nicomachean Ethics*, Book I, (D Ross trans, Oxford, Oxford University Press, 1980).

[105] See, especially, A Veltman, *Meaningful Work* (Oxford, Oxford University Press, 2016) 35, 36.

[106] ibid 62–70.

with an overarching emphasis on it being central to the human condition.[107] It has been advanced, especially in the historical work of German thinkers like Hannah Arendt, who argues that labour, work, and action manifest basic aspects of the human condition.[108] Similar suggestions have been made in the writing of French philosophers, including Charles Fourier,[109] Henri Bergson,[110] Simone de Beauvoir,[111] and Simone Weil.[112]

Supported by these philosophical underpinnings, employment continues to carry substantial value in enabling humans to flourish. Employees, as subjects of the contract of employment, are given not just a sense of purpose in terms of their role as producers of work but also the opportunity to develop good habits or virtues, which are central to their flourishing.[113] It has been recognised judicially that 'a person's employment is usually one of the most important things in his or her life. It gives not only a livelihood but an occupation, an identity and a sense of self-esteem'.[114] Maintaining one's employment encourages 'industriousness, diligence, courage, order, constancy, self-discipline, humility, magnanimity, companionship, and concern for other people'.[115] By extension, these virtues contribute to improved working conditions and results, as well as supporting meaningful work and behaviour.[116] The very state of being employed at all is 'the stuff of meaningful and fulfilling living'.[117] An award of damages for the loss of the chance of maintaining an employment relationship in the event of wrongful termination could therefore be seen as coextensive and correlative of that state.

Assuming an employee could establish that one of the objects or purposes for which their contract of employment was created was to facilitate human flourishing,

[107] *cf*, A Veltman, *Meaningful Work* (Oxford, Oxford University Press, 2016) 35, 55–61, where it is suggested that there are several ways in which work may otherwise detract from a flourishing life, and that engaging in 'meaningful work' is what is truly central to human flourishing.

[108] See, eg, H Arendt, *The Human Condition*, 2nd edn (Chicago, University of Chicago Press, 2018).

[109] Fourier views work as a potentially liberating, creative activity that can gratify deep human needs and express human abilities. See further, J Beecher, *Charles Fourier: The Visionary and His World* (Berkley, California, University of California Press, 1990) ch 14.

[110] Bergson recognises that intelligence is the faculty of manufacturing artificial objects, especially tools to make tools, and of indefinitely varying the manufacture (ie, engaging in 'work'). See further, H Bergson, *Creative Evolution* (A Mitchell trans, New York, Henry Holt, 1911) 139.

[111] In *The Ethics of Ambiguity* and elsewhere, de Beauvoir argues that work that enables transcendence of everyday life permits humanity to achieve a justification for the toil required just to maintain life. See further, A Veltman, 'Simone de Beauvoir and Hannah Arendt on Labor' (Winter 2010) 25(1) *Hypatia* 5578.

[112] See, eg, S Weil, *The Need for Roots* (London, Routledge & Keegan Paul, 1952) 286–7.

[113] See generally, J Fontrodona and A Sison, 'Work, Virtues, and Flourishing: A Special Issue from the EBEN 25th Annual Conference' (2015) 128(4) *Journal of Business Ethics* 701.

[114] *Johnson* (n 84) [35] (Lord Hoffmann).

[115] J Fontrodona and D Melé, 'Thinking About the Future of Work: Promoting Dignity and Human Flourishing' (2022) 7 *Humanistic Management Journal* 181, 183.

[116] See generally, R Beadle and K Knight, 'Virtue and Meaningful Work' (2012) 22(2) *Business Ethics Quarterly* 433.

[117] See, eg, D Gasper, 'Capitalism and Human Flourishing? The Strange Story of the Bias to Activity and the Downgrading of Work' (2009) Institute of Social Studies, Working Paper No. 269, 27, core.ac.uk/download/pdf/18513396.pdf.

a court may be more willing to award damages for the loss of the chance of maintaining that relationship. As was touched on earlier in section IV, the importance of maintaining an employment relationship has already been realised in respect of damages being awarded for the loss of a chance to acquire discretionary benefits. By extension, the chance of maintaining that relationship, in and of itself, could attract compensable value in the event of an employer's wrongful termination, given its links to enabling human flourishing.

As the remaining discussion in this subsection makes clear, establishing a newfound category of damages for loss of a chance of maintaining an employment relationship would by no means be a straightforward task. Perhaps the most persistent concern is that such a lost chance would be particularly challenging to quantify. It would be notoriously difficult for a court to evaluate the worth of an employment relationship in terms of enabling human flourishing. There is no objective measure. Any measure would need to be determined by policy considerations, which the court must endeavour to consistently apply. Such a task may tempt the court into the undesirable province of judicial activism.[118]

Determining the value of the chance of an ongoing and fortuitous employment relationship, which necessitates human flourishing, is clearly an open-ended and speculative exercise.[119] It may 'open the floodgates for highly speculative claims',[120] and it gives rise to many open-ended questions. To what extent would an employee necessarily have 'flourished' as a consequence of their employment? How long would the employment relationship have lasted? How much would the employee have earned during that time? Were there any breaks in the employment in question? How should periods of absence or leave be taken into account? These calculations are even trickier when the relevant employee is young and just starting their career.[121]

It is nonetheless already well-established in case law that just because the calculation of the likelihood of a chance is difficult to quantify, this does not mean that it cannot and should not be. Courts have routinely needed to deal with this potential in assessing the likelihood of other chances and awarding associated damages. Again, as introduced in section II, there is only a need for certainty in respect of the fact of the damages, not the amount.[122] It may therefore be counterintuitive to suggest that allowing damages for loss of a chance in one instance might necessarily give rise to more speculative litigation. Damages for loss of a chance of maintaining an employment relationship could usefully account for the value of an employment relationship insofar as it enables human flourishing, offering a

[118] As to the judicial role in making laws with respect to contracts of employment and the remit of judicial activism, see, eg, Golding (n 13) ch 7.

[119] See, eg, Golding (n 2) 286.

[120] ibid 294.

[121] See, eg, the similar questions put regarding the challenge of assessing 'relational damages' in Golding (n 2) 286.

[122] Chitty (n 27) §1562.

well-balanced and fair solution, which takes the interests of both the employer and employee into account.

An issue of 'reasonable foreseeability' also arises. To return to the well-established rule in *Hadley v Baxendale*,[123] a precondition of liability in damages is the foreseeability of the loss,[124] the existence of which is examined in the time of contracting. However entrenched, it must be acknowledged that such a rule may not be justified in the context of maintaining a contract of employment and the associated value of enabling human flourishing. This suggestion can still be met with the obvious and somewhat circular retort that if the maintenance of an employment relationship is defined and understood as enabling human flourishing, then perhaps it is entirely foreseeable that the wrongful termination of a contract of employment could sound in damages for a loss of the chance of maintaining the associated employment relationship.

The potential for a newfound category of damages to compensate for the loss of the chance of maintaining that relationship could therefore be deemed a suitable adaptation of the common law to suit its contribution to human flourishing. Perhaps then it is entirely appropriate for the law to be implemented with greater flexibility, acknowledging the complexities of contracts of employment and their links to enabling human flourishing, rather than being unduly limited by precepts of judicial activism. After all, endangering human interest in situations in which only a chance is left must not be without suitable legal deterrence.[125]

Normatively speaking, assessing chances of maintaining an employment relationship may be seen to lead to needing to assess the value of all 'employment' in the broadest sense, which is something the law should avoid, as it would destroy the absolute value of what it means to be employed in the first place. Saying that, merely acknowledging a lost chance of an employment relationship being maintained does not necessarily require such an all-encompassing evaluation. Only the chance of maintaining an employment relationship is to be assessed insofar as it relates to human flourishing, so the overarching value of 'employment' can remain untouched.

Overall, despite certain challenges, the position advanced by this chapter is there remains value in an employee's chance to continue in their career and hold a position of employment, since doing so enables them to flourish. Any loss associated with that value is real, tangible, and reasonably foreseeable. It is not just a form of non-pecuniary loss, which is not typically recoverable by wrongfully dismissed employees.[126]

[123] *Hadley* (n 25).
[124] ibid 354.
[125] See, eg, Jansen (n 34) 293.
[126] Golding (n 2) 286.

VI. Conclusion

To conclude, this chapter has looked in detail at the law on damages for loss of a chance where there has been wrongful termination of the contract of employment by the employer. Section II opened with an overarching summary of the law concerning loss of a chance in contract law generally. The doctrinal evaluation in section III was undertaken in the specific context of employment contracting, with a view to better understanding recovery of damages for loss of a chance in the realm of wrongful termination by the employer in both English and Australian law in section IV.

Against that background, in section V it was revealed that there is potential for judges to develop the law concerning damages for loss of chance where there has been a wrongful termination of the contract of employment. To be more specific, there is capacity for an additional category of damages for loss of a chance of maintaining an employment relationship in the event of an employee's wrongful dismissal by their employer. While this exercise may be seen as speculative, potentially luring a court into judicial activism through policy-based reasoning, there remains real and substantial value in the chance of maintaining an employment relationship, given its links to human flourishing. The solution of damages for loss of that chance is preferable to a purely procedural approach.

A category of damages for loss of the chance of maintaining an employment relationship openly addresses the normatively relevant aspects of what it means to be engaged under a contract of employment in the first place, particularly insofar as the value of the relationship between the parties is concerned. It effectively sidesteps an 'all or nothing' solution by allowing the law to deal with the need to not only take chances into account but to recognise the inherent value in remaining engaged under a contract of employment. This value is particularly pronounced in a climate where human flourishing is seen to be supported by the maintenance of the relationship. Whatever this proposed development might achieve, above all else, it is envisaged to provide an approach to assessing damages for loss of a chance in employment contract cases, which acknowledges the value of the chance of remaining employed. It opens the door to allowing a remedial consequence to flow from having entered a contract of employment in the first place.

7

Specific Performance and the Contract of Employment

CATHARINE MACMILLAN

Contracts are formed to allow one or more parties to obtain the performance of defined obligations. Contracts of employment are predicated on this basis. Complications arise in contract law generally when one party fails or refuses to perform their obligations in a way that constitutes a fundamental breach of contract. The usual remedy provided by courts to the injured party is an award of damages, and this monetary sum is to allow, although not compel, the injured party to enter the market to obviate the loss that would otherwise have arisen through breach. As Holmes observed:

> The only universal consequence of a legally binding promise is, that the law makes the promisor pay damages if the promised event does not come to pass. In every case it leaves him free from interference until the time for fulfilment has gone by, and therefore free to break his contract if he chooses.[1]

Holmes' explanation of contract 'as the taking of a risk',[2] was one which Anson was at pains to refute. He argued that 'English Law *does* recognise the contractual obligation as something distinct from the obligation to pay damages in the event of non-performance',[3] and that one could not disregard the reality that the parties to the contract viewed their arrangement as one that would be performed.[4] Both jurists wrote about the common law of contract and largely ignored the equitable remedy of specific performance. It is by the decree of specific performance that a court can compel the party to personally do what he promised, a point which diminishes Holmes' characterisation of contract as the taking of a risk. Although specific performance ensures that the promised obligation is performed, it is, however, rarely granted. This is particularly true in the case of employment

[1] OW Holmes, *The Common Law* (London, Macmillan & Co, 1882) 301.
[2] ibid.
[3] WR Anson, *Principles of the English Law of Contract*, 2nd edn (Oxford, Clarendon Press, 1882) 9.
[4] ibid 10.

contracts, where it is almost invariably refused. This chapter explores why courts are reluctant to order specific performance in the context of an employment contract and considers when such an order might be appropriate. This is primarily considered from the perspective of an employee seeking to remain in their employment, rather than an employer seeking to compel an employee to work. Such an exploration is timely given recent Supreme Court decisions,[5] which relax many of the bars around an order of specific performance and thus open up the subject to reconsideration. The possibility of fundamental change is now present. This exploration is also important to the understanding of both contract law and employment law because the nature of the remedy provided when an obligation is breached is central to the functioning of both areas of law. This chapter also illuminates the interaction of these two bodies of law.

The chapter consists of a number of distinct parts. It begins with a general overview of the employment relationship in England and Wales. It then proceeds to consider the oft-stated proposition or rule that a court will not order the specific performance of a contract of employment. As is argued, there is curiously little explanation or binding precedent to support such a rule. Because of this, an investigation and assessment of possible reasons underpinning this supposed rule are provided. Having examined why a court might not exercise its discretion to make an award of specific performance, an analysis is undertaken as to when a court should exercise its discretion to award specific performance or otherwise compel the continuation of the employment relationship. Conclusions are then drawn from these examinations.

The law applicable to the employment relationship in England and Wales is a combination of the common law and a framework of statutes concerned with different aspects, and sometimes different forms, of employment. The statutory framework is complex and diverse; particular examples can be seen in the Employment Relations Act 1996 and the Trade Union and Labour Relations (Consolidation) Act 1992. The regulatory framework seeks to advance defined social and welfare objectives. The contract of employment, though, provides 'the legal conceptualisation of the employment relationship'.[6] As Kahn-Freund observed, this contract thus provided the 'cornerstone' of labour law.[7] Although contract law forms an important element of employment law, its application to employment situations can be uncertain, and the results can be unsatisfactory for employees. This is apparent in the nature of the remedies available to an employee when their employer breaches the employment contract. Surprisingly, given the importance accorded to remedies in contract studies, there has been little

[5] *Tesco Stores Ltd v Union of Shop, Distributive and Allied Workers* [2024] UKSC 28; *Geys v Société Générale* [2012] UKSC 63.

[6] Z Adams, C Barnard, S Deakin and S Fraser Butlin, *Deakin and Morris' Labour Law*, 7th edn (Oxford, Hart Publishing, 2021) 96.

[7] O Kahn-Freund, 'Legal Framework' in A Flanders and H Clegg (eds), *The System of Industrial Relations in Britain* (Oxford, Basil Blackwell, 1945) 47.

consideration of the remedial consequences of breach in employment studies,[8] until Professor Davies's detailed consideration of the topic in *Valuing Employment Rights*.[9] While these studies emphasise the challenges employees face in obtaining adequate remedies, they also provide reasons for optimism.

Two recent Supreme Court decisions signal a new approach to the remedies available to an employee. *Geys v Société Générale*,[10] provides a substantial reason for optimism in the development of remedies beneficial to employees. The majority resolved what had been considered an 'obstacle',[11] to an employee faced with an employer's repudiatory breach. This was the question of whether the contract was automatically terminated upon such a breach or whether it was only terminated when the employee elected to accept the repudiation and so treat the contract as at an end.[12] The majority rejected a result that would find, uniquely, a contract of employment automatically terminated following an employer's repudiatory breach. In so doing, they firmly situated the contract of employment within the common law of contract: 'we should keep the contract of employment firmly within the harbour which the common law has solidly constructed for the entire fleet of contracts in order to protect the innocent party, as far as practicable, from the consequences of the other's breach'.[13] *Geys'* case opens the door to the possibility that an employee, faced with a repudiatory breach of their contract of employment, is able to seek an order of specific performance keeping them in their position.[14]

The second case, *Tesco v Union of Shop, Distributive and Allied Workers*, decisively establishes the availability of an order of specific performance as an employee's remedy. Tesco restructured its distribution network, closing some existing distribution centres and opening new ones elsewhere. Staff in distribution centres that were closing were offered fairly modest redundancy payments. Tesco needed to retain some of its experienced distribution workers and offered an incentive of 'Retained Pay' for those workers who relocated themselves to work in the new distribution centres. The amount offered was significant, between

[8] Two outstanding exceptions are: D Brodie, 'Specific Performance and Employment Contracts' (1998) 27 *Industrial Law Journal* 37; and KD Ewing, 'Remedies for Breach of the Contract of Employment' (1993) 52 *Cambridge Law Journal* 405.

[9] ACL Davies, *Valuing Employment Rights: A Study of Remedies in Employment Law* (Oxford, Hart Publishing, 2024). See also, G Golding, 'Employment as a Relational Contract and the Impact on Remedies for Breach' (2021) 30 *Griffith Law Review* 270.

[10] *Geys v Société Générale* [2012] UKSC 63. See A Burrows, 'What is the Effect of a Repudiatory Breach of a Contract of Employment?' (2013) 42 *Industrial Law Journal* 281.

[11] Ewing (n 8) 410.

[12] For the differences between the two approaches see A Spowart-Taylor and B Hough, 'Theories of Termination in Contracts of Employment: The Scylla and the Charybdis' (2004) 19 *Journal of Contract Law* 134.

[13] (n 5) [97] (Lord Wilson JSC).

[14] It may be that the action is framed as an injunction restraining the employer from dismissing them. As will be demonstrated below the grant of such an injunction has traditionally been so linked with an order for specific performance that the same legal considerations will arise. See, eg, *Ashworth v The Royal National Theatre* [2014] EWHC 1176 (QB).

32 per cent and 39 per cent of these workers' wages. These workers' employment contracts, incorporating the terms of the collective agreement negotiated by their union, provided that retained pay was 'a permanent feature of an individual's contractual eligibility', which could only be changed by mutual consent or promotion.[15] Tesco was keen to emphasise that retained pay was 'protection for life',[16] 'which remains for as long as you are employed by Tesco in your current role … [it] cannot be negotiated away by either Tesco, USDAW …'.[17] Workers who moved to the new distribution centres, organising their financial affairs around the increase of retained pay, found that 14 years later Tesco sought to remove this higher rate of pay. They were offered an advance payment of 18 months of retained pay to terminate their retained pay arrangements; those who did not accept this offer would be dismissed and rehired on terms not including retained pay. As Tesco explained to its employees, 'Retained Pay arrangements achieved what they were designed to achieve, but we feel it is now the right time to phase those arrangements out.'[18] The claimants, workers with retained pay and their union, issued proceedings against Tesco seeking declaratory relief as to the nature and extent of the workers' contractual rights to retained pay and injunctive relief to restrain Tesco from removing their contractual entitlement to retained pay.[19] Two fundamental issues were before the Supreme Court: first, could a term be implied into the employment contracts that prevented Tesco from dismissing the claimants on notice so as to remove the right to receive permanent retained pay; and second, would an injunction be ordered against Tesco to require them to continue to employ the affected workers where such an injunction amounted to an indirect order of specific performance of an employment contract? The Supreme Court answered both issues in the affirmative. A term was implied in fact that Tesco's power to terminate the employment contracts on notice could not be used as a means to remove the employees' rights to retained pay. To enforce this term, a permanent injunction was granted to restrain Tesco from violating it. Underlying the reasoning in the case, two concerns can be discerned. The first is for employees who were induced to act to their detriment to benefit their employer on the promise, made a contractually binding provision, that they would receive a permanent benefit in exchange. The second is that this permanent promise not be removed once the employer found it no longer to be in their benefit. The decision represents a powerful protection of workers; much will depend in future cases, though, on the precise wording of the particular contract of employment.

[15] (n 5) [17].
[16] ibid [23].
[17] ibid [24].
[18] ibid [12].
[19] The claims were allowed in the High Court, [2022] EWHC 201 (QB) and this decision was overturned by the Court of Appeal, [2022] EWCA Civ 978.

I. The Reluctance to Decree Specific Performance in a Contract of Employment

While these decisions open the possibility of an employee receiving a decree of specific performance in both cases, the Supreme Court was simultaneously concerned to affirm that only in exceptional circumstances would a decree of specific performance be made in a contract of employment. The majority in *Geys v Société Générale* were sympathetic to the situation of an employee wrongfully dismissed by their employer. Although the claim in this instance was for damages, there was a repetition of the proposition that equity would not award an order of specific performance requiring an employer to take back a wrongfully dismissed employee.[20] In *Tesco v USDAW*, the majority judgment reaffirmed that '[a]s regards specific performance against an employer, with which we are concerned, there is certainly a general rule against specific performance which is long-established … [b]ut on this side of the relationship, the courts have recognised exceptions'.[21] Little consideration was given as to the origins, nature or purpose of this 'general rule'.[22] This is unsurprising because it is a proposition widely accepted in the secondary literature concerned with both contract law generally and employment law specifically.[23] Like many accepted propositions of law, though, it is one rarely considered in detail judicially, quite possibly because it is so widely accepted that it is thought to need no further examination.

There are indications that before the nineteenth-century courts of equity would order the specific performance of a contract for services in exceptional circumstances, where damages were an inadequate remedy.[24] As Fry observed in his treatise on specific performance, 'the court now refuses to entertain jurisdiction in regard to [contracts of hiring and service] … [I]n former times this seems to have been otherwise.'[25] It is, therefore, a number of nineteenth-century cases that form

[20] (n 5) [77] (Lord Wilson JSC); [42] (Baroness Hale agreeing).

[21] (n 5) [66] (Lord Burrows and Lady Simler).

[22] Lord Burrows and Lady Simler relied upon three cases for this rule: *Johnson v Shrewsbury and Birmingham Railway Co* (1853) 3 De G M & G 914; 43 ER 358, 926, 363, *Brett v The East India and London Shipping Company (Limited)* (1864) 2 H & M 404; 71 ER 520, and *Rigby v Connol* (1878) 14 Ch D 482.

[23] M Chen-Wishart, 'Action for an Agreed Sum, Specific Performance and Injunction' in H Beale (ed), *Chitty on Contracts*, 35th edn (London, Sweet & Maxwell, 2023) 31-034; E Peel, *Treitel on The Law of Contracts*, 15th edn (London, Sweet & Maxwell, 2020) 21-039; A Burrows, *A Restatement of the English Law of Contract* (Oxford, Oxford University Press, 2016) 26(3(a); *Deakin and Morris* (n 6) 433. The position is the same in texts concerned with equity: see, eg, J O'Sullivan, 'Specific Performance' in J McGhee and S Elliott (eds), *Snell's Equity* 34th edn (London, Sweet and Maxwell, 2020) 17-012; and JD Heydon, MJ Leeming and PG Turner, *Meagher, Gummow & Lehane's Equity Doctrines and Remedies*, 5th edn (Australia, LexisNexis Australia, 2015) [20-055], [21-220].

[24] M Lobban, 'Contract Law' in William Cornish et al. (eds), *The Oxford History of the Laws of England*, vol XII (Oxford, Oxford University Press, 2010) 558. See, also, G Jones and W Goodhart, *Specific Performance* (London, Butterworths, 1986) 135.

[25] E Fry, *A Treatise on the Specific Performance of Contracts* (London, Butterworths, 1858) §§56–57, 22. Fry relied upon *Ball v Coggs* (1710) 1 Bro P C 14; 1 ER 471 in which a servant, employed for life, was

the starting point for the establishment of this proposition that equity will not enforce a contract for personal services. Many of these cases are ones in which the court was concerned not with an application for a decree of specific performance but for an injunction. The age and the procedural context are, in other words, reasons to wonder about the strength of the proposition they are said to expound.

A distinction must be noted here between positive orders and prohibitory orders. An order for specific performance is a positive order and can be further divided into orders to 'give' and orders to 'do'. The former are more easily ordered because they are simple and can be performed more quickly.[26] In contrast, an order to do, into which would fall an order to perform a personal service, is more complicated because of the difficulties attendant upon supervising performance.[27] Courts of equity are, generally, more at ease in granting prohibitory orders: injunctions, whether prohibitory or mandatory. Injunctions are issued to prevent wrongful conduct and order a party to abstain from certain conduct. As Lawson observed, 'an order *not to do*, has on its side the dead weight of inertia; it is easier to obey than to disobey'.[28] A further distinction from a positive order is that there is a greater simplicity in the ascertainment of whether or not there has been compliance with the injunction.

This distinction matters because virtually all of the authorities for the proposition that equity will not perform a contract for personal services have arisen in cases in which an injunction was sought. In a technical sense, the proposition, or rule as it is sometimes referred to, is made in *obiter dicta* and without the binding force of a *ratio decidendi*. It must be admitted, though, that a sufficient accumulation of a proposition made in *obiter dicta* begins to move beyond the persuasive. A second and more substantive importance emerges. Courts are formulating and applying a proposition applicable to a more difficult order (of specific performance) in the context of making a simpler order (an injunction). The result is that the complexities behind an order for specific performance of a contract for services, or involving personal services, are not examined. Nor is there a detailed assessment of the reasons underlying *why* an order for the specific performance of services is not to be granted. This also precludes a consideration of those circumstances in which an order for specific performance would be appropriate. An order for specific performance is equitable and thus exercised at the discretion of the court. We are left in a situation in which the principles governing this exercise of discretion are unclear. And a further result is that we have a proposition, or rule, that an order for specific performance will almost never be granted without a firm explanation of the basis for the rule.

restored to his employment following his wrongful dismissal. See, also, *East India Co v Vincent* (1740) 2 Atk. 83; 26 ER 451.

[26] FH Lawson, *Remedies of English Law* (Middlesex, Penguin Books, 1972) 244 discusses the distinction (emphasis in original).

[27] ibid 249.

[28] ibid 209.

Lumley v Wagner[29] is the leading authority amongst injunction cases for the exposition of the rule that a court will not enforce a contract for the performance of personal services. The managers of rival opera houses, Benjamin Lumley and Frederick Gye, each wanted to engage Johanna Wagner, a rising star of the operatic world. Wagner signed a contract to sing for Lumley in Her Majesty's Theatre only to be later persuaded by his rival, Gye, to sing at the Royal Italian Opera. As Waddams explained, it seems unlikely that Gye realised that an injunction might be issued prohibiting her from singing in his opera house. Lord St Leonards, in upholding the injunction, observed that it was 'beyond all doubt this Court could not interfere to enforce the specific performance of the whole of this contract'.[30] Lord St. Leonards was conscious that the injunction prohibiting Wagner from performing for Gye would have the indirect effect of inducing her to perform her contract with Lumley, although this 'natural effect' was not the object of the court.[31] In the event, Wagner performed at neither opera house, Lumley eventually lost his action against Gye for damages, and 'in the end Lumley, Gye, Wagner, and the opera-going public – everyone in fact except the lawyers – were all losers.'[32]

A similar case, with a contrasting result, is *Warner Brothers Pictures Inc v Nelson*.[33] Warner Brothers obtained an injunction preventing Bette Davis from acting for another in England because she had covenanted with Warner Brothers not to provide acting services for other parties without their agreement. The effect was to drive her back to act for Warner Brothers in California. Branson J emphasised 'the principle that specific performance of a contract of personal service will never be ordered'.[34] While it is explained that an injunction enforcing a negative covenant would not be granted in circumstances where the effect would be to drive the defendant to either starvation or specific performance of the positive covenant, there is no explanation of why specific performance would not be so granted. The repetition of this prohibition against ordering the specific performance for contracts of service is to be found repeated throughout the case law without consideration, sometimes as an absolute prohibition,[35] and other times as a near prohibition, as, for example, 'the general rule … that the courts will not order

[29] *Lumley v Wagner* (1852) 1 De G M & G 604; 42 ER 687. The context of the case, an explanation of the court's reasoning in this and the related case of *Lumley v Gye* (1852) 2 El & Bl 216; 42 ER 687 are found in SM Waddams, 'Johanna Wagner and the Rival Opera Houses' (2001) 117 *LQR* 431.

[30] ibid 618, 693.

[31] The reasoning appears in the fuller, and less referred to, report in 19 *Law Times* 265.

[32] Waddams (n 29) 440.

[33] *Warner Brothers Pictures Inc v Nelson* [1937] 1 KB 209.

[34] ibid 216. Possibly because the injunction drove Davis to perform for Warner Brothers the court in *Page One Records Ltd v Britton* [1968] 1 WLR 157 refused an injunction enforcing the negative covenant on the basis that this would amount to an order for specific performance: [166] (Stamp J).

[35] *Clarke v Price* (1819) 2 Wils Ch 158; 37 ER 270, 164; 273; *Johnson v Shrewsbury and Birmingham Ry Co* (n 22); *Whitwood Chemical Company v Hardman* [1891] 2 Ch 416, 420; *Davis v Foreman* [1894] 3 Ch 654, 657; *William Robinson & Co, Ltd v Heuer* [1898] 2 Ch 451, 456; *Scandinavian Trading Tanker Co AB v Flota Petrolera Ecuatoriana* [1983] 2 AC 694, 700-01.

specific performance of contracts of employment'.[36] The repetition also occurs in cases not concerned with injunctions.[37] The result is a set of authorities explaining the basis for the grant of a prohibitory injunction in a contract for services without any justification as to why specific performance would not be ordered. Equally unanswered is the question of when, if ever, there would be exceptions to this rule.

It is also worth observing that the statement of this proposition is often made in cases where the contract largely does not involve the performance of personal services,[38] or the performance of the services is a component in a contract concerned with other matters.[39] In some instances, the case does not involve a direct action between the employee (or service provider) and the employer (or service receiver) but arises in the context of a dispute between other parties.[40] The dispute often gives rise to judicial concerns regarding matters other than the personal services themselves.[41] It is possible in these cases to discern that the court, in exercising its discretion, is either as concerned about this other feature as it is in the specific performance of the services, or the invocation of a bar in awarding specific performance is a convenient means of addressing this other feature.

Given the paucity and weaknesses of the authorities concerned with an order for specific performance in a contract for services or employment, it is unsurprising that few employees seek the specific performance of their employment contract. Actions tend to be brought to prohibit an employer from implementing a particular decision[42] or a declaration that the employment continues,[43] requiring a particular process surrounding dismissal to be properly implemented.[44] A further, practical factor is that few employees have the financial resources available to afford to bring any legal action to enforce their rights.[45] Trade unions and professional associations have traditionally had a role in such funding, but few bodies will continue to spend their members' dues on causes that are unlikely to succeed. A more cost-effective application, in comparison to an order for specific performance, for an unfairly dismissed employee might appear to lie in a request

[36] *Chappell v Times Newspapers Ltd* [1975] 1 WLR 482, 501 (Lord Denning MR). See, also, *Taylor v National Union of Seamen* [1967] 1 WLR 532, 553; *Wishart v National Association of Citizens Advice Bureaux Ltd* [1990] ICR 794, 807 (the 'normal practice' per Nicholls LJ).

[37] *Vine v National Dock Labour Board* [1957] AC 488, 507; *Gunton v Richmond-upon-Thames LBC* [1980] ICR 755, 763 (in an action for a declaration); *Ridge v Baldwin* AC 40, 65.

[38] *Scandinavian Trading Tanker Co AB v Flota Petrolera Ecuatoriana* (n 26); *Decro-Wall International S.A. v Practitioners in Marketing Ltd* [1971] 1 WLR 361, 369–70.

[39] *Johnson v Shrewsbury and Birmingham Ry Co* (n 22); *Powell Duffryn Steam Coal Company v Taff Vale Railway Co* (1873–74) LR 9 Ch App 331, 335.

[40] *Rigby v Connol* (n 22) at 487; *Ryan v Mutual Tontine Westminster Chambers Association* [1893] 1 Ch 116.

[41] See, eg, the concern as to whether the exemption clause in *Johnson v Shrewsbury and Birmingham Ry Co* (n 22) contravened public policy or the concern for infants in *De Francesco v Barnum* (1890) 45 Ch. D. 430.

[42] *Powell v Brent LBC* [1988] ICR 176; *Wadock v Brent LBC* [1990] IRLR 223.

[43] *Francis v The Municipal Councillors of Kuala Lumpur* [1962] 1 WLR 1511.

[44] *Ridge v Baldwin* [1964] AC 40; *Gryf-Lowczowski v Hinchingbrooke Healthcare NHS Trust* [2005] EWHC 2407 (QB).

[45] Davies (n 9) considers the point in ch 2.

to an employment tribunal for an order of reinstatement under section 114 of the Employment Rights Act 1996 or an order of re-engagement under section 115 of the Act.[46] As Davies details, such orders are largely illusory: less than one per cent of such dismissals result in reinstatement or re-engagement;[47] the considerations involved (such as mutual trust and confidence in the employee, allowing the employer to rely on allegations of misconduct, provided the belief in the allegations is genuine) are weighted in favour of the employer; and the sanctions employed are weaker than those available to a court.[48] The proposition against an award of specific performance in a contract of employment has, seemingly, stymied the development of a potentially enabling order within the legislative framework.

II. Why Equity will not Decree Specific Performance in a Contract of Employment

While courts have not been clear or explicit in their explanation of why an order for specific performance will not be granted in an employment contract, it is possible to discern some of the reasons underlying this refusal. We start from the position that the usual award for a breach of contract, including those of employment, is an award of damages.[49] The underlying rationale behind such an award is that it allows the injured party to enter the market and to make good the loss they have suffered by reason of the other party's breach. The injured party has a duty to mitigate their loss; an employee should seek suitable alternative employment, and any sums so received work to reduce the employer's obligation to pay damages.[50] There is, at times, concern expressed that an employee must not benefit from some sort of holiday: '[h]e cannot sit in the sun for ten years drawing his salary on the basis that he is ready, able and willing to serve … if only the company would allow him to do so.'[51] This is related to another concern, namely, that unlike a claimant seeking damages, a claimant entitled to specific performance is not required to mitigate their loss.[52] Because the usual remedy is an award of damages at common law, the reasons why equity will not decree specific performance need not be compelling, as they serve only to reinforce the existing position. In most cases, an award of

[46] Section 112 provides that the tribunal shall explain to the employee what orders may be made, the circumstances in which they can be made and request if the employee wishes the tribunal to make such an order. Failing such a request, the remedy lies in damages: s 112(4).

[47] (n 9) 142.

[48] ibid 144–45.

[49] *Gunton v Richmond* (n 37) 772; *Decro-Wall International S.A. v Practitioners in Marketing Ltd* [1971] 1 WLR 361, 369–70.

[50] *Shove v Downs Surgical* plc [1984] ICR 532, 542–43.

[51] *Denmark Productions Ltd v Boscobel Productions Ltd* [1969] 1 QB 699, 726 per Salmon LJ.

[52] A Burrows, *Remedies for Torts, Breach of Contract, and Equitable Wrongs*, 4th edn (Oxford University Press, Oxford) 413.

damages is probably a sufficient remedy for an employee who suffers a breach of their employment contract.

It is frequently said that the court will not award an order for specific performance of a contract for services, because such a compulsion is tantamount to slavery. Fry LJ succinctly summed the position up:

> I should be very unwilling to extend decisions the effect of which is to compel persons who are not desirous of maintaining continuous personal relations with one another to continue those personal relations. I have a very strong impression and a strong feeling that it is not in the interest of mankind that the rule of specific performance should be extended to such cases. I think the Courts are bound to be jealous, lest they should turn contracts of service into contracts of slavery.[53]

It is also the case that where an individual is ordered to specifically perform a contract and refuses to do so, the ultimate sanction for such disobedience is imprisonment. This creates the ridiculous position noted by Megarry V-C that 'far from forcing the servant to work for his master, [this] would effectively stop him from doing this'.[54] Krawiec and Oman have raised the practical point that most employment agreements are at-will contracts in which an employee can quit at any time, without giving any reason, without breaching their contracts. The result is that '[f]or most personal service contracts … the question of specific performance simply cannot arise.'[55] While the concern not to enslave is a real one and addresses issues central to individual autonomy, it is misplaced in the instance where an employee seeks an order for specific performance.

Courts cannot, in any event, compel an employee 'to do any work or attend at any place for the doing of any work' by reason of specific performance or otherwise because this is prohibited by section 236 of the Trade Union and Labour Relations (Consolidation) Act 1992. What is a concern when an employee seeks an order for specific performance is mutuality. For a contract to be specifically enforced at the suit of one party, it should also be so enforceable by the other.[56] In recent years, though, exceptions have been admitted to this 'supposed rule' such that the modern approach is to view a want of mutuality as a discretionary rather than an absolute bar to specific performance.[57] Specific performance will be granted in such circumstances where it can be done without injustice to the defendant.[58] Such injustices can be prevented, it is submitted, by the form of the order in any particular case. It would also be perverse that a statutory provision enacted to

[53] *De Francesco v Barnum* (n 41) 438. This statement is *obiter dicta* and was given in circumstances where an injunction was sought by the apprentices' master against a third party (Barnum the circus impresario); it might also be argued in light of *Warner Brothers v Nelson* (n 33) that such an award has been made without concerns of slavery.

[54] *Thomas Marshall (Exports) Ltd v Guinle* [1979] Ch 227, 243.

[55] KD Krawiec and NB Oman, 'The Case for Specific Performance of Personal Service Contracts' (2024) 110 *Iowa Law Review* 1, 3.

[56] *Page One Records v Britton* (n 34) 165, for example.

[57] O'Sullivan (n 23) 17-024.

[58] ibid.

protect employees would act to disadvantage their position in equity. The Supreme Court, in *Tesco v USDAW*, quickly dismissed any 'want of mutuality' obligation to indirect specific performance.[59] In this instance, while an award of damages to the employees would be inadequate, Tesco could be adequately remedied by an award of damages should the employees breach their contracts. A few further observations with regard to mutuality. One is that there is rarely a symmetry of power within an employment context. Employers wield significant power. They usually draft the employment contract. They have the resources to litigate and to enforce by way of injunction, for example, matters such as confidentiality, restrictive covenants and non-compete agreements. A second is that over the years, many exceptions to mutuality have been recognised, and it has been questioned whether this requirement has been supported by any authority.[60] In *Price v Strange*,[61] the Court of Appeal, in considering want of mutuality, held that this was a matter for the court's discretion and exercised in light of the particular case. Where the claimant had performed their obligations, or performance could be ensured, mutuality was not a bar. In the judgment of Buckley LJ, where damages would be an appropriate remedy for the defendant, mutuality would not bar the order.[62] The judgment has led to the observation that where the defendant is assured of a satisfactory remedy against the claimant for any non-performance, it should not be necessary for a defendant to be assured of actual performance: 'the risk of subsequent non-performance is one that the defendant has contractually undertaken'.[63]

A much more forceful argument against an order in favour of an employee that her contract of employment should be the subject of an order for specific performance is the nature of the relationship between employer and employee. Courts have characterised the employment relationship as one of trust and confidence. In *Pickering v The Bishop of Ely*,[64] Knight Bruce VC declined to grant an injunction the effect of which would be to keep the plaintiff in his office as the bishop's receiver because the individual invested with powers of receiver had to be one whom the bishop respected, trusted, and found personally acceptable. 'To force upon him in such characters a person however estimable, however professionally eminent, who is objectionable to him, or in whom he does not happen to confide, would, if legal, be surely hard; and, sitting in a Court of Equity, I do not feel any inclination to do it.'[65] A decade later, in *Johnson v Shrewsbury and Birmingham Railway Co*,[66] Knight Bruce V-C expanded upon this to observe that there must be 'the

[59] (n 5) [82] (Lord Burrows and Lady Simler). *Price v Strange* [1978] Ch 337 was cited as support for the reasoning. It appears that Tesco's counsel only 'faintly mentioned' that want of mutuality would prevents specific performance: [63].

[60] Burrows (n 52) 426.

[61] (n 59).

[62] ibid 367–68.

[63] Burrows (n 52) 427.

[64] *Pickering v The Bishop of Ely* (1843) 2 & & CCC 249; 63 ER 109. See, also, *Brett v The East India Co* (n 22); *Chappell v Times Newspapers* (n 36).

[65] ibid 267, 117 (Knight Bruce V-C).

[66] (n 22).

most entire harmony and spirit of co-operation between the contracting parties' and this could not be achieved by the compulsion of the court, regardless of the competence of the servant in question.[67] From such an order, 'enormous mischief may be done'.[68] This requirement of mutual confidence and trust has remained a constant consideration in the later case law, although there have been cases in which courts have questioned an employer's assertion of a lack of confidence.[69] It is striking that in the few cases in which courts have granted relief which allowed the continuation of an employment relationship, there has been an express finding that there was no want of confidence or trust between the parties.[70] In *Hill v C A Parsons & Co Ltd*,[71] dismissal was brought about by reason of the requirements of the trade union framework then prevailing. In this case, neither the employee nor the employer wanted to end the contract of employment, and there was no impairment to the mutual trust and confidence of the parties. This was, though, as the court recognised, a 'most exceptional case'.[72] There is little detailed consideration of what might constitute trust and confidence. In *Irani v Southampton and South West Hampshire Health Authority*, the implication was that where there was no question of the employee's 'conduct or professional competence', and the problem was incompatibility with a fellow employee, that confidence was not an issue.[73]

In even more exceptional cases, it is said that such a want can be overcome through the retraining of the employee.[74] *Tesco v USDAW* demonstrates that where the employer proposes to fire and rehire employees, it is highly unlikely that there will be a lack of confidence. The requirement cannot, however, be a constant bar to specific performance in all circumstances. In *Robb v Hammersmith and Fulham LBC*,[75] it was suggested that even where there were issues of trust and confidence, these were matters that could be dealt with in the terms of the order. *Robb's* case, however appropriate in an application for an interim injunction, is of less assistance in an order for specific performance. It is also unclear as to whether this lack of confidence is to be measured on a subjective or objective basis. If the former, the effect is to congregate an overwhelming advantage to an employer. The modern employment relationship has changed,[76] both in the increased size and hierarchy of many establishments, the methods of human resource management, and the often-reduced (or limited) ambit in which an employee exercises their own discretion in the performance of their duties. Modern information technology also allows employers to control and monitor the activities of their employees

[67] ibid 363.
[68] ibid (Knight Bruce V-C).
[69] Ewing (n 8) 417–19.
[70] *Hill v C A Parsons & Co Ltd* [1972] Ch 305.
[71] ibid.
[72] ibid 323.
[73] *Irani v Southampton and South West Hampshire Health Authority* [1985] ICR 590, 603.
[74] *Gryf-Lowczowski v Hinchingbrooke Healthcare NHS Trust* (n 44) [70].
[75] *Robb v Hammersmith and Fulham LBC* [1991] ICR 514.
[76] See, eg, *Geys v Société Générale* (n 5) [77] (Lord Wilson).

in ways previously unimaginable. The world no longer operates in a way in which employer and employee may operate in the nature of a partnership. Balanced against this, though, is the very real concern of an employer that an employee's performance is trustworthy and competent. It all depends on the circumstances of the particular case. It seems likely that the greatest single bar to an order for specific performance, even for a definite period, is a lack of trust and confidence in the employee and their performance.

It is important that a court is able to specify with certainty what is to be undertaken through an order for specific performance. Where it is impossible to do so, the order will not be granted. In many circumstances, it may not be possible to delineate the employee's activities, or the employee may occupy a position in which they exercise such discretion that the terms of an appropriate order cannot be drawn. As Megarry V-C observed, there must be a sufficient definition of what has to be done for an order of specific performance.[77] Such a definition can come from the terms of the contract or of the order. This raises, though, the further question of whether or not the terms of the contract sufficiently support, by implication or otherwise, the terms of the proposed order.[78]

A significant barrier to an order for specific performance is the requirement that the order would require the constant supervision of the court. This is particularly true where the order would be of long duration,[79] possibly extending over several years. As Lord Hoffmann has explained, the supervision is not undertaken by the judge or some officer of the court literally but by repeated applications to the court. It is the possibility of these indefinite series of rulings by the court that makes specific performance undesirable.[80] Lord Burrows, writing extra-judicially, has stated that the 'constant supervision objection has little to commend it' as a party will almost always obey the order, and it is hardly sensible to deny a claimant a remedy where problems arise infrequently.[81] The supervision challenge is not an invariable concern of courts. The rule against the specific performance of contracts for personal services or those requiring constant supervision 'is plainly not absolute and without exception, nor do I think that it can be based on any narrow consideration such as difficulties of constant supervision by the court'.[82] However, the problem of how to ensure that the order is carried out can be a very real one in many instances. It also exposes another important consideration in exercising the discretion to award specific performance. The ultimate enforcement for the indefinite series of rulings referred to by Lord Hoffmann is a quasi-criminal punishment for contempt, 'a powerful weapon', which means that the 'heavy-handed nature

[77] *Tito v Waddell (No 2)* [1977] Ch 106, 321–22.
[78] ibid.
[79] *Ryan v Mutual Tontine Westminster Chambers Association* (n 40).
[80] *Co-operative Insurance v Argyll Stores Ltd* [1998] AC 1, 12.
[81] Burrows (n 52) 418.
[82] *C H Giles & Co v Morris* [1972] 1 WLR 307, 318 (Megarry J).

of the enforcement mechanism is a consideration'.[83] Enforcement of the order, in other words, rests on repeated and expensive litigation.

While Lord Hoffmann's concerns are relevant in relation to an order compelling a business to retain an employee or employees, the concern is compelling a business that has decided it is not in their economic interest to undertake a certain activity to continue to do so. Lord Hoffmann referred to this as a business operating with the sword of Damocles (the possible finding of contempt) hanging above their heads.[84] There is a strong disinclination for courts to become involved in the running of a business or, by implication, fettering the managerial discretion of a company in conducting its business. This can be a very real concern in particular contracts of employment;[85] it may also go some way to explaining what Davies has observed as the friendliness of courts towards employers.[86] *Tesco v USDAW* marks a very real turning point, though, in the approach of courts towards this issue of managerial discretion. There was a complete rejection of the argument that an implied term preventing Tesco from dismissing their employees would, in the words of their counsel, 'impose a serious and perpetual constraint on Tesco's ability to manage and operate its business'.[87] Tesco had freely offered the retained pay. It was not the job of the court to identify what the court thought a party should have agreed. Nor was it for the court to relieve a party from the consequences of poor advice or bad judgment.[88] It was open to Tesco to structure their affairs differently or not to make the promise that they did. While the court was keen to stress that the industrial context of the case was far from usual, the determination to enforce a promise given freely to employees is striking.

A question that has not been addressed is whether or not temporal considerations around an order of specific performance are relevant. Mandatory injunctions are more readily granted when limited in time. In relation to an order for the specific performance of a contract of employment, it is unlikely that a court would make such an order for an indefinite time. Much will turn on the terms of the particular employment contract: the issue did not arise in *Tesco v USDAW*, for example, because the employer itself categorised the retained pay as a permanent feature. While this temporal element could be considered a bar to an order for specific performance, it is submitted that it should be a consideration and not a determination of the matter. It is open, for example, to the court to impose a time constraint upon the order. Temporal constraints are a feature in restraint of trade

[83] *Co-operative Insurance v Argyll* (n 80) (Lord Hoffmann).

[84] ibid 13.

[85] It is not insignificant that Cranston J, in *Ashworth v The Royal National Theatre* (n 14) observed that the National Theatre's public subsidy was declining: [4].

[86] Davies (n 9) 139. It is also notable that so many of the cases in which an employee has succeeded in some degree against their employer occurs in the context of a contract with a public body such as a local authority, an NHS trust or a university.

[87] (n 5) [47].

[88] ibid [47] (Lord Burrows and Lady Simler).

cases, and there is no reason why they could not be in an order of specific performance of an employment contract.

Two final restrictions are relevant. First, cases will arise where none of these various reasons is sufficient in itself to prevent an order for specific performance, but, taken cumulatively, two or more are such as to prevent the exercise of such a discretion. Second, the claimant will face the usual equitable restrictions on relief, such as acquiescence, laches, and conduct.

Overall, though, it is suggested that as these various reasons for why an order for specific performance of a contract for the performance of an employment contract are eroded, the less formidable the general 'rule' appears to be.

III. Why Equity should Decree the Specific Performance of a Contract of Employment

The grant of an injunction in *Tesco v USDAW* was, in substance, an order for specific performance, and the court held that the same principles should be applied. The case firmly establishes that the rule against an order for specific performance of an employment contract is not an absolute one. The decision diminishes assertions to the contrary,[89] and reinforces the authority of earlier cases that had the effect of keeping an employee in their employment.[90] An order for indirect specific performance is now, exceptionally, available against an employer where 'it is otherwise just to make the order and … the employer retains sufficient confidence in the employee'.[91] We have considered above the criterion of confidence and consider here the question of when it is otherwise just to order specific performance. In doing so, though, it must be noted that there remains a strong presumption (although not an absolute bar) against such an order: specific performance remains an extraordinary remedy.[92]

An order for specific performance will lie where damages are not an adequate remedy for the employee;[93] this is a substantial restriction on the availability of the order. In those instances in which the contract is only partly for the provision of a service, courts have been more willing to hold that damages were inadequate, and it may be possible to order specific performance of the contract as a whole.[94]

[89] See above (n 35).

[90] *Vine v National Dock Labour Board* [1957] AC 488; *Gryf-Lowczowski v Hinchingbrooke Healthcare NHS Trust* (n 44). Courts have also issued declarations clearing an employee of misconduct: *Taylor v National Union of Seamen* [1967] 1 WLR 532.

[91] (n 5) [70] (Lord Burrows and Lady Simler).

[92] As Megarry J observed in *Giles v Morris* (n 82) in most cases the 'inconvenience and mischief' of decreeing specific performance will outweigh the advantages but that it should not be assumed that any element of personal services or continuous services means that a court, without more, will refuse the order: at 318.

[93] *Giles v Morris* (n 82) 316–17, (Megarry J).

[94] ibid 317–18.

This is likely the reason for Lord Hardwicke's decision in *The East India Company v Vincent*,[95] although the obscurity of the decision makes it unreliable. While it is the basis for *Fortescue v Lostwithiel and Fowey Railway Company*,[96] courts have declined equitable orders in other cases in which the personal services were only a part of the overall contract. In *Ryan v Mutual Tontine Westminster Chambers Association*,[97] only part of the contract was concerned with the services of a porter, a role held by neither party to the suit, but equitable relief was denied. It is possible that the real concern underlying the decision in this instance was the difficulties of supervising the performance of the porter's services over a long time period. Where the services are of critical importance to other parties, such as the public, a concern over the performance of the services may well be sufficient to prevent an order for specific performance. In *Powell Duffryn Steam Coal Company v Taff Vale Railway Company*, James LJ was concerned that the personal services were the manning of points and signals on the railway, 'upon which so much of the safety of mankind now depends'.[98]

In certain circumstances, a court may exercise its discretion to protect an employee from the capricious conduct of their employer. While much of *Ball v Coggs*,[99] is no longer applicable,[100] Cowper LC was clearly trying to protect an employee who, having rescued the employer's business, found himself dismissed in the absence of any default or misbehaviour on his part. The employer sought to resile from the arrangement, taking almost all the benefit and leaving the employee with very little.[101]

Hill v C A Parsons points to a more broadly based situation where damages do not adequately remedy the employee's loss and in which equitable relief is appropriate. In that case, the impending enactment of Part II of the Industrial Relations Act 1971 meant that the employee would then be protected from dismissal. This reasoning is apparent in other cases.[102] In circumstances where an employee needs their employment to further a broader occupational or professional ambition, often where the very continuance of their role within this occupation or profession is dependent upon the particular employment, it may well be thought appropriate to make a decree of specific performance. In such circumstances, the harm to the employee outweighs that to the employer. Damages are unlikely ever to be an adequate remedy to the employee in such a case. As Jenkins LJ observed in *Vine v National Dock Labour Board*,[103] what was at stake was the employee's 'life's

[95] *The East India Company v Vincent* (1740) 2 Atkin 84; 26 ER 451.
[96] *Fortescue v Lostwithiel and Fowey Railway Company* [1894] 3 Ch 621.
[97] (n 32).
[98] (n 39) 335.
[99] (n 25).
[100] It is, eg, fantastical to think that a modern court would restore an employee for the position for life.
[101] This is remarkably similar to the concerns expressed in *Tesco v USDAW*.
[102] *Irani v Southampton and SW Hampshire Health Authority* (n 73); *Vine v National Dock Labour Board* [1957] AC 488.
[103] [*Vine v National Dock Labour Board* 1956] 1 QB 658. Jenkins LJ's decision dissented from the majority, however the majority's decision was overturned on appeal to the House of Lords: ibid.

work', one in which he had been employed since boyhood. The question was therefore, '[w]hy should it not be a consideration, in deciding whether damages is an adequate remedy or not, that a man prefers one way of life to another?'[104]

There is also a much larger sense in which damages are not an adequate remedy for the wrongfully dismissed employee. Employment is a central aspect of the lives of most individuals. It provides people, in greater or lesser degrees, with a sense of self-worth, of independence, and of status. An individual's employment in a particular post may be the culmination of years of training and experience. It is central to the dignity of most individuals.[105] Dismissal, and the manner it is brought about,[106] can often be painful in ways that money cannot repair. The inadequacy of damages was the underlying reason why the House of Lords, in *Beswick v Beswick*,[107] found that an order of specific performance would lie where an award of damages would only be nominal: '[e]quity will grant specific performance when damages are inappropriate to meet the justice of the case'.[108] While later courts have moved away from such a broad view,[109] two further factors often work against such an order. The first is that the common law struggles to measure damages for non-pecuniary losses. Emotional injuries are not, in one sense, a factor a market-based approach to loss and recovery can adapt to easily. *Addis v Gramophone Co Ltd*,[110] works to generally remove compensation 'either for the injured feelings of the servant, or for the loss he may sustain from the fact that his having been dismissed of itself makes it more difficult for him to obtain fresh employment'.[111] By generally ignoring non-pecuniary losses as a head of recoverable damages, the law also removes the injuries and indignities underlying these losses as a reason to grant specific performance of the agreement. *Tesco v USDAW* provides a powerful riposte to such a position. The court recognised that common law damages were unlikely to address non-pecuniary losses such as the loss of job satisfaction and the anxiety and upheaval flowing from dismissal. The very inability of the common law in this regard meant that injunctive relief avoided the problem of inadequate compensation in damages. And if this somewhat side-stepped *Addis v Gramophone Co Ltd* 'so be it'.[112]

The second factor is that the law of damages has already established a mechanism for calculating damages in such situations.[113] This is usually based upon

[104] ibid 676.

[105] A point developed in depth by Davies (n 9).

[106] The manner of the dismissal is unlikely to be compensable in damages: *Johnson v Unisys Ltd* [2001] UKHL 13.

[107] *Beswick v Beswick* [1968] AC 58.

[108] ibid at 102 (Lord UpJohn).

[109] Burrows (n 52) 411.

[110] *Addis v Gramophone Co Ltd* [1909] AC 488.

[111] ibid 491 (Lord Loreburn LC). See, though, *Malik v Bank of Credit and Commerce International SA (In Liquidation)* [1998] AC 20.

[112] (n 5) at [78] (Lord Burrows and Lady Simler.).

[113] It has been argued that the notice rule has, in turn, influenced the way in which the law of personal service contracts conceives of the notion of wrongful dismissal and the remedies available for it: M Freedland, *The Personal Employment Contract* (Oxford, Oxford University Press 2006) ch 6.

the notice period required to be given although different limits exist where an unfair dismissal has occurred.[114] The essential point is, though, that the law has established a mechanism to express the loss in a monetary amount. Once this has been done, it is harder to move away from it on the basis that it is unsatisfactory. What makes *Tesco v USDAW* unique is that the promise of a permanent award of retained pay distinguishes the case from one of notice-based damages.

This takes us to a consideration of more general factors concerned with employment that may indicate that specific performance is a more appropriate remedy than the payment of damages. As the case law indicates, in some instances, career progression or professional accreditation will be harmed in ways that are difficult to assess through damages.[115] Collins has observed that employment is related to status, conferring with it a sense of social belonging and a means of giving purpose to life.[116] The workplace constitutes a significant community in the worker's life. Dismissal is often accompanied by a loss of dignity and reputation. Work is central to individual autonomy. Davies makes a very powerful argument in her recent work that the remedies available in employment law do not always reflect the subject's particular characteristic.[117] While employment rights are needed to uphold the dignity of working people who cannot supply their labour without being present, less attention has been paid to the dignitary considerations arising in relation to remedies. And 'remedies often fail to acknowledge that the consequences of a breach of employment rights are not always purely financial in nature and typically affect working people's social opportunities, standing in the community and life plans'.[118] Adopting Smith's categorisation of rights,[119] Davies observes that replicative remedies, remedies with the potential to secure some form of compliance for the complainant, are rarely awarded to employees. This, she argues, occurs because of a lack of political will to uphold the rights of working people.[120] A central and fundamental issue underpinning her study is the recognition that, in the vast majority of cases, ordinary contract law does not give working people the rights and protections they need in the workplace because of the inequality of bargaining power between the parties. This inequality of treatment is often apparent in the case law. So, for example, in *Warner Brothers v Nelson*, Branson J is utterly unconcerned with how a major motion picture studio tied a young woman to the studio. Indeed, he goes further in castigating Bette Davis for her conduct in coming to England 'for no discoverable reason except that

[114] Employment Rights Act 1996, s 124.
[115] See, eg, *Gryf-Lowczowski v Hinchingbrooke Healthcare NHS Trust* (n 44).
[116] H Collins, *Justice in Dismissal: The Law of Termination of Employment* (Oxford, Oxford University Press 1992) 15–21.
[117] (n 9).
[118] ibid 4.
[119] SA Smith, *Rights, Wrongs, and Injustices: The Structure of Remedial Law* (Oxford, OUP, 2019).
[120] Davies (n 9) ch 6.

she wanted more money'.[121] Presumably, it was also money that brought Warner Brothers to sue Bette Davis, a point unaddressed by the court.

Davies has also observed that employers often do assess the costs and benefits of different actions in relation to the dismissal of their employees.[122] If employers were conscious that they might be required to retain an employee, this could be an important factor in their conduct vis-à-vis employees. Brodie has pointed out that where an employment situation is to continue, the parties are much more likely to resolve their differences.[123] A mutual resolution of differences and a valuing of the employee's contribution make for a better and more productive workplace. As Brodie argued, 'a reform in the law would promote a cultural change'.[124]

It must be emphasised, though, that an order for specific performance is necessarily a discretionary one. Courts will balance those elements in favour of the order against those which militate against it. It seems likely that orders for specific performance will remain rare in the context of an employment contract. The removal of a rule against such orders, though, will enable courts to have greater scope to award prohibitory injunctions amounting to an indirect specific performance.

IV. Conclusions

A number of conclusions arise from this examination. The decision in *Geys*' case and in *Tesco v USDAW* taken together mean that, first, an employee's contract cannot be unilaterally terminated by an employer's repudiatory breach and, second, that courts will hold an employer to their promise by replicating an existing obligation with an injunction. The result is to open the possibility for English courts to order the specific performance of an employment contract in favour of an employee. Such a possibility calls into question the often-stated prohibition on granting specific performance of an employment contract. It is startling that there is so little explanation as to exactly why an order for specific performance is said to be inappropriate in a contract for employment, particularly when it is repeated so often. It is a curious state to have a rule for which there is so little analysis as to why the rule exists and what end it serves. An appraisal of this rule reveals little actual explanation for it and an absence of direct precedent supporting it.

A number of reasons are present that support restrictions upon a decree of specific performance in an employment contract. There is an inherent, yet odd, suspicion that an employee might benefit from some sort of holiday, rather than mitigating her loss. The concern that such an order turns contracts of service into contracts of slavery can be dismissed when the decree is sought by the employee.

[121] (n 33) 213. It seems likely that Bette Davis was also concerned about the wider development of her career as an actor; Warner Brothers had already refused her permission to act in particular films.
[122] (n 9) 153–154.
[123] (n 8) 48.
[124] ibid.

While employees cannot be compelled, by reason of statute, to specifically perform their contracts of employment, this gives rise to the concern that there is no mutuality of remedy between the parties. This, as has been argued above, should not be an absolute bar given the overwhelming power imbalance in the employment relationship in favour of the employer. The employment contract must be such that it is possible for the court to specify with certainty what is to be undertaken pursuant to the decree. Previous concerns regarding the necessity for the constant supervision by the court are, on inspection, unrealistic. An important aspect of *Tesco v USDAW* is that it erodes the apprehension courts have generally exhibited in ordering a business as to how to conduct its affairs. The diminution of each of the elements associated with a prohibition upon specific performance weakens the very nature of the prohibition. The real barrier, though, to specific performance is the nature of the employment relationship; it is one that rests, in varying degrees, on trust and confidence. While concerns about confidence should be measured on an objective basis, where they arise, specific performance is unlikely to be granted.

Specific performance should be granted where damages are an inadequate remedy. The common law struggles to measure the many types of loss, particularly non-pecuniary loss, that can occur to an employee faced with the repudiatory breach of their employer. In certain instances, professional advancement or standing may well depend upon an employee remaining in their employment. In these cases we are left at a loss as to how to value the harm to the employee in a system that serves economic interests and marginalises other considerations. Specific performance can serve to protect these non-economic considerations of employees. There are also indications that employers may also benefit where they are required to invest in their employees. An important factor, rarely addressed, is the temporal element to specific performance: it seems unlikely that there will be few circumstances in which such a decree will be for an indefinite basis. It is also the case that the availability of specific performance is much more likely to increase the possibility of an injunction amounting to indirect specific performance being granted rather than specific performance itself. There is now a new scope to shape specific performance as a remedy available to employees in exceptional circumstances.

8

The Injunction Dilemma

ACL DAVIES

This chapter examines the use of injunctions to enforce obligations in the contract of employment, focusing in particular on cases brought by employees against their employers.[1] Injunctions are a potentially powerful weapon in the hands of the employee, in a context in which powerful weapons tend to be in short supply.[2] In many cases, employees have a strong interest in getting their employer to comply with the terms of their contract, rather than breaching the contract and paying compensation instead. Although there is sometimes a concern that injunctions are onerous for employers, it is important to remember that, while they are backed up by the contempt powers of the court, in substance, they do nothing more than replicate existing obligations: they require the employer to do what it promised to do in the first place.[3] Given the parties' unequal bargaining positions, it seems unlikely that these obligations were not freely undertaken by the employer. However, injunctions present a dilemma because, in practice, they are an effective remedy for a tiny minority of employees: they are relevant only to employees whose contracts of employment contain protective terms that can be enforced by means of an injunction, and there are many practical and financial hurdles to be overcome in order to bring proceedings.

The chapter proceeds in five parts. In the first part, I offer some preliminary thoughts on the importance of getting employers to comply with their obligations. Employment law follows the general pattern of treating compensation as the usual remedy in most cases, but I suggest that a greater use of replicative remedies, such as injunctions, would be desirable. In the second part, I examine the conditions for the grant of an injunction to enforce the contract of employment.

[1] I use the term 'employee' rather than 'worker' in this chapter because most of the cases concern individuals who were clearly employees. As a matter of principle, there is no reason why the same remedial options should not be available to workers too, but in practice, they are much less likely to benefit from elaborate contract terms which the courts could enforce.

[2] For an overview of remedies in employment law, see ACL Davies, *Valuing Employment Rights* (Oxford, Hart Publishing 2024).

[3] For a discussion of 'replicative remedies' in general, see SA Smith, *Rights, Wrongs and Injustices: the Structure of Remedial Law* (Oxford, Oxford University Press 2019) ch 6. For these remedies in employment law, see Davies (n 2) ch 6.

This part of the discussion focuses on key elements of the *American Cyanamid* test, since, in most cases, the injunction sought is an interim injunction pending trial.[4] Two elements of this test as applied in employment cases are of particular interest. First, an injunction will only be granted where damages would not be an adequate remedy if the claimant succeeded at trial. The Supreme Court, in the *Tesco* case, recently acknowledged that this is almost always the case in employment settings.[5] Second, for an injunction to be granted, the employer must have 'trust and confidence' in the employee. I offer a detailed analysis of this requirement and its application in practice, arguing that it should be assessed in the light of the exact terms of the injunction being sought and that it should be an objective test. Overall, I conclude that the *legal* obstacles to obtaining an injunction have become less stringent over time.

I then turn to the *practical* problems that give rise to the injunction dilemma and some possible solutions. Injunctions are only useful where the employee has a protective contractual term to be enforced, which usually occurs when their contract was negotiated through collective bargaining rather than drafted by the employer. One way to broaden the relevance of injunctions across the workforce as a whole would be to use them to restrain threatened breaches of statutory employment rights. In the third part of the chapter, I consider the existing case law on this issue and conclude that it would be quite difficult to persuade the courts to make widespread use of this possibility. In the fourth part, I examine the logistical barriers to obtaining an injunction, particularly the considerable element of financial risk involved in the process. This means that the remedy is unattainable for most ordinary employees who do not have substantial personal wealth, insurance, or support from a trade union. I assess whether there is any mileage in developing some other form of replicative remedy to overcome these difficulties. The fifth part concludes.

I. Employment Law and Compliance

In private law, one of the debates around injunctions and related orders is whether they are or should be the 'primary' remedy for a breach of contract.[6] On one level, this is an empirical question: what do the courts order most often in the event of a breach? But it is usually meant in a different way: are damages seen as the 'norm', so that the claimant has to make some kind of special case to get an injunction instead? Or is it now the case that the courts simply choose from a menu of equally available remedial options? In employment law, this debate does not seem

[4] *American Cyanamid Co v Ethicon Ltd* [1975] AC 396.

[5] *Tesco Stores Ltd v Union of Shop, Distributive and Allied Workers* [2024] UKSC 28.

[6] For an interesting comparative analysis, see S Rowan, *Remedies for Breach of Contract: A Comparative Analysis of the Protection of Performance* (Oxford, Oxford University Press 2012) ch 1.

particularly interesting. Damages for breach of the contract of employment are not usually substantial, and actions for breach are therefore rare. Creative attempts to persuade the courts to increase the level of awards have not, so far at least, succeeded, as I explain further below. So, a lot of breach of contract claims in the employment context are brought with the specific purpose of obtaining an injunction because of the possibility it offers the employee of getting the employer to comply with its original obligations.[7] In this section, I explore some of the special features of employment law which make this compliance function particularly important.

Of course, compliance is a concern of any field of law: we do not want people to commit crimes or torts, and we hope (though the empirical evidence is mixed) that the prospect of legal liability serves some kind of deterrent function. But there is greater scope in employment law for a strong focus on deterrence and compliance. This stems from the fact that, while some employment relationships (particularly nowadays) are of very short duration, many are not. Even in the gig economy, a working person may be signed up to a platform for many years, albeit that their work may be intermittent and their legal status uncertain. And employers are usually in the business of employing people generally (even if not specific individuals) over the longer term. Legal rules can play a different role in long-term relationships and with repeat players.

In a long-term relationship, there are more practical opportunities to use remedies that force the employer to comply with its obligations. In many situations, once a breach has occurred, it cannot be undone: for example, once a negligent driver has caused an injury to another road user, all that the law can do is to require the payment of compensation. Some employment cases have similar characteristics. For example, an angry exchange between a manager and a working person involving a one-off incident of harassment by the manager can only really be dealt with through an order that the employer should pay compensation.[8] However, in other cases, the long-term nature of the relationship means that there is an opportunity to get the employer to do what it was supposed to do in the first place. For example, if the employer fails to give proper consideration to a flexible working request, it could simply be ordered to examine the matter again.[9]

In turn, that practical opportunity to force the employer to comply can be used to generate a more powerful deterrent effect.[10] While the criminal and civil law seek to deter bad driving, for example, it seems unlikely that a person making a poor split-second decision – to look at their phone or to overtake

[7] I consider below whether the injunction is the best route for achieving these objectives.

[8] Equality Act 2010, s 26.

[9] Employment Rights Act 1996, s 80I(1)(a).

[10] For an excellent overview of the complexities of deterrence in the context of 'wage theft', see T Hardy, 'Digging Into Deterrence: An Examination of Deterrence-Based Theories and Evidence in Employment Standards Enforcement' (2021) 37 *International Journal of Comparative Labour Law and Industrial Relations* 133.

on a bend – spends much time considering the legal consequences of their actions.[11] By contrast, many employers contemplating a course of action in relation to their workforce will seek legal advice. In particular, they may engage in a cost-benefit analysis of their options.[12] In many cases, this is a simple comparison of the cost of compliance with the likely award of damages if the matter ends up before a court or tribunal, with some assessment of the likelihood of a challenge being brought at all. The availability of an injunction to force the employer to comply with its obligations changes the calculation from a purely financial one into one in which there is a potentially significant element of delay, hassle and embarrassment associated with breach. While the impact of this on employers' decision-making is an empirical question, it seems fair to assume that, in many cases, it will serve as a stronger encouragement to compliance than the prospect of a financial award, which can simply be treated as one of the many costs of doing business.

Just because the law could do more to encourage compliance does not mean that it should. But in employment law, there are some good arguments to be made in favour of making use of this possibility. One promising way to do this is to focus on the harms suffered (or potentially suffered) by a working person when their employment rights are breached. These harms are different in some important respects from the harm suffered when, for example, a commercial contract is breached. I do not suggest that employment cases are unique in this regard – other types of claim might share some of these characteristics – nor do I suggest that every employment case involves all the harms I am about to identify, but they are a significant and distinguishing feature of many employment cases. These harms are usually present in addition to pecuniary losses.

First, in many employment cases, the working person's fundamental rights are infringed by the employer's breach, resulting in a hard-to-quantify but important loss of dignity.[13] For example, a job applicant who is unsuccessful will often be disappointed, sometimes greatly so, but the situation is altogether different if it becomes clear that they were rejected because of their race or religion, or their trade union membership. The prospective employer has taken into account an irrelevant consideration in a way that is shocking, distressing, and likely to make the person feel that they have not been treated with appropriate respect. This loss of dignity may be exacerbated where it takes place in a long-term relationship, where there can often be a great sense of betrayal. For example, an employee who is unfairly dismissed as a result of false allegations without having an opportunity to

[11] For examples of behavioural critiques of the classic law and economics account, see C Jolls, C Sunstein and R Thaler, 'A Behavioral Approach to Law and Economics' (1998) 50 *Stanford Law Review* 1471; P Robinson and J Darley, 'Does Criminal Law Deter? A Behavioural Science Investigation' (2004) 24 *Oxford Journal of Legal Studies* 173.

[12] Though the empirical reality is highly complex: see T Hardy and J Howe, 'Creating Ripples, Making Waves? Assessing the General Deterrence Effects of Enforcement Activities of the Fair Work Ombudsman' (2017) 39 *Sydney Law Review* 471.

[13] See H Collins, *Justice in Dismissal* (Oxford, Oxford University Press, 1992) ch 1.

be heard is likely to feel particularly harshly treated if they have not been listened to or believed after many years of loyal service.

Second, it is widely accepted that the benefits of having a job often extend well beyond the wages earned by the working person.[14] The workplace can provide significant opportunities for social interaction: work colleagues may become friends and socialise together, for example, or simply enjoy each other's company during the working day. In many cases, work itself can be a source of personal satisfaction, as the working person exercises existing skills or learns new ones or helps other people to solve problems. For many people, there is also significant satisfaction in being able to support themselves or their family financially. A person's reputation or standing in the community often depends on their job: 'what do you do?' is a common enquiry on social occasions, and many people want to be able to answer this question with a degree of pride. Conversely, problems at work – such as allegations of wrongdoing – may lead to adverse comment and isolation both in the workplace and in the wider local community. Finally, many working people view their job as one element in a wider 'career', a trajectory in which they move to positions with more responsibility and reward as they gain experience or, perhaps more commonly nowadays, transfer their skills from one sector to another in a way that brings either financial reward or personal satisfaction. A problem with one job may jeopardise a person's wider life plan.

Third, there is a sense in which the harms suffered in employment cases often take the form of lost opportunities, not just in the career-building sense. For example, many employment rights seek to protect the individual or collective rights of working people to have their say on workplace issues that affect them, such as disciplinary matters or potential redundancies.[15] Where these rights are breached, working people lose both the right to participate in itself and the opportunity to persuade the employer to change its mind or act in a particular way.

Of course, some of these losses are too remote for the law to address in any form. Others might be compensated through an award for injury to feelings. In employment law, this is available in a discrimination claim (which is compensated as if it were a tort)[16] but not in a claim for breach of contract or unfair dismissal.[17] Part of the test for the award of an injunction is that damages would not be an adequate remedy for the claimant, so to some extent, a consideration of the employee's non-financial losses is already built into the legal framework. However, my point here is a broader one. Even if the award for injury to feelings were to be available in any employment case, a small sum of money is a poor recompense for the harms just outlined and would do little to deter breaches. Injunctions have the potential to reduce and perhaps even eliminate the non-tangible and hard-to-compensate

[14] ibid, and see *Tesco* (n 5) [78].

[15] Eg, Trade Union and Labour Relations (Consolidation) Act 1992 (TULRCA), s 188.

[16] Equality Act 2010, s 119(4).

[17] *Addis v Gramophone Co Ltd* [1909] AC 488; *Norton Tool Co Ltd v Tewson* [1972] ICR 501; *Dunnachie v Kingston upon Hull City Council* [2004] UKHL 36, [2005] 1 AC 226.

losses suffered by the employee and to give the employer a stronger incentive to comply with the law in the first place.

II. Conditions for the Grant of an Injunction

In this section, I argue that the courts have not always struck the right balance between employers and employees in cases in which employees have sought injunctions, either by failing to acknowledge their interests as outlined above or by placing other hurdles in the way of their claims. But there are some promising signs of a more employee-friendly approach in recent cases, most notably in *Tesco*.[18] It is important to be clear at the outset that there are very considerable practical barriers facing an employee who wants to obtain an injunction, but my focus here is on the legal requirements. I return to the practical problems towards the end of the chapter.

Most of the cases to be considered in this section involve seeking an interim injunction, pending trial, under the rules laid down in the well-known *American Cyanamid* case.[19] The claimant must show that their case discloses a serious issue to be tried, and that the 'balance of convenience' favours the grant of an injunction. The 'balance of convenience' is assessed in what Burrows describes as a 'sequential' approach, looking first at whether damages would be an adequate remedy for the claimant employee if they succeeded at trial.[20] This involves some consideration of what the employee's likely losses will be and what compensation they could recover under the applicable rules, bearing in mind that damages for breach of the contract of employment are rarely substantial.

If damages would not be an adequate remedy for the claimant employee, the court should then consider what losses, if any, the defendant employer would suffer if they were required to comply with an injunction but ultimately won at trial. The person seeking an interim injunction is usually expected to give an undertaking to pay damages if they lose. In employment settings, this requirement is problematic. Breaching the undertaking amounts to contempt of court, so employees may be reluctant to give the undertaking where the employer's damages claim might exceed their means. But if the judge grants the injunction without any undertaking to pay damages on the part of the employee, there is a greater risk of unfairness to the employer and greater pressure on the judge to make the 'right' decision at the interim stage.

Where damages would be an inadequate remedy on both sides (which, for the reasons just given, is highly likely in an employment case), the court can consider the balance of convenience in more general terms, looking at the hardship to each

[18] (n 5).
[19] (n 4).
[20] A Burrows, *Remedies for Torts, Breach of Contract, and Equitable Wrongs* (Oxford, Oxford University Press, 2019) 469–474.

party and the strength of their respective arguments. One very important part of the 'hardship' enquiry in an employment case is whether the employer continues to have 'trust and confidence' in the employee seeking the injunction. It is regarded as oppressive to force the employer to remain in a contract with an employee if the relationship between them has broken down. More broadly, the courts are also wary of granting injunctions where they would not be workable in practice or would require constant judicial supervision, something which is more likely if the parties' relationship is poor. However, the extent of these potential problems depends, in turn, on the exact terms of the injunction.

I will focus on the courts' approach to the two main elements of the *American Cyanamid* test of particular salience in employment cases: the adequacy of damages for the claimant and the relationship of trust and confidence between the parties. Given that any particular case requires the court to exercise discretion after balancing the various factors, it is obviously somewhat artificial to examine the factors individually, but it is difficult to work out what is going on without adopting this approach.

A. Adequacy of Damages for the Claimant

The adequacy of damages obviously falls to be assessed on a case-by-case basis. However, it is possible to identify some general themes in the courts' discussion of this question. There are two broad issues to explore. First, awards of damages for breach of the contract of employment have historically been low because they are usually limited to the employee's earnings during the notice period. In *Tesco*, where the employer's power to dismiss with notice was qualified, the Supreme Court found that a more substantial award would be difficult to quantify.[21] Second, there is no possibility of an award for injury to feelings. This means that any non-financial losses suffered by the employee will not be compensated. Both of these factors point strongly in favour of the grant of an injunction.

i. Calculating Financial Loss

This is clearly not the place for a detailed discussion of the complex body of rules governing compensatory damages for breach of the contract of employment. But some background is necessary, because the Supreme Court has itself acknowledged, in *Chhabra* and, more recently, in *Tesco*, that the limited availability of damages in this context is a factor pointing strongly in favour of the grant of an injunction.[22]

[21] (n 5) [77].

[22] *Chhabra v West London Mental Health NHS Trust* [2013] UKSC 80, [2014] ICR 194, [39]; *Tesco* (n 5).

The starting point is the assumption of 'minimum performance': that the employer (or, indeed, any other contracting party) will do the minimum necessary to fulfil its legal obligations.[23] This means that, in a 'standard' wrongful dismissal case in which the employee is dismissed without the contractual notice to which they were entitled, the courts assume that, had the wrongful dismissal not occurred, a lawful dismissal would have occurred in which the employee was given due notice.[24] Thus, all the employee can usually expect – and can therefore obtain in contract damages – is payment for the notice period itself. No consideration is given to the possibility that the employee might, in practice, have expected to continue working for the employer for a much longer period of time.

In the *Tesco* case, the employees had been promised extra pay 'for life' to incentivise them to relocate to another depot.[25] When the employer later wanted to withdraw the extra pay, it threatened to 'fire and rehire' the employees on different terms, relying on its contractual right to dismiss with notice. However, the Supreme Court held that a term should be implied into the contract to the effect that the right to dismiss with notice could not be used for the purpose of removing the extra pay.[26] This meant that, in principle, the employees could claim damages for lost future earnings up to the point at which the employer could lawfully have dismissed them on some other ground. While these damages could have been substantial, the Supreme Court noted that they would be difficult to assess:

> To work out the quantum of damages would require speculation as to how long the employees would have otherwise remained employed by Tesco and, if they were to be lawfully dismissed, what their prospects would be of mitigating their loss by finding alternative employment. In short, the assessment of damages would be very difficult and prone to error.[27]

Granting the injunction avoided these difficulties. There is some irony here, in the sense that tribunals routinely carry out these kinds of complex assessments in unfair dismissal and discrimination claims, but of course, they have no other remedial options, a point to which I return below.[28]

The *Tesco* case casts an interesting light on some of the older cases in which employees have sought injunctions in termination cases (other than those involving disciplinary procedures, to which I return below). For example, in *Anderson*, the employer had agreed to a 'last in, first out' (LIFO) redundancy selection procedure but then sought to make employees redundant on a different basis.[29] An injunction was granted to hold the employer to its original promise, on the ground that the claimant employees would have retained their jobs under LIFO, and would

[23] L Barmes, 'The Contract of Employment and the Remedial Dimension' in M Freedland et al. (eds), *The Contract of Employment* (Oxford, Oxford University Press 2016) 184.
[24] Minimum notice periods are set out in Employment Rights Act 1996 (ERA), s 86.
[25] (n 5).
[26] ibid [57].
[27] ibid [77].
[28] See Davies (n 2) ch 7.
[29] *Anderson v Pringle of Scotland Ltd* 1998 SLT 754, [1998] IRLR 64.

only have received compensation for loss of earnings during the notice period at common law, which was clearly inadequate. In another LIFO case, *Alexander*, the judge refused to grant an injunction on the basis that an employee wrongfully dismissed in breach of LIFO would be able to get (adequate) damages until the retirement age.[30] Neither case was discussed in *Tesco*. It seems that the judge in *Alexander* might have been right about the measure of damages, but not the difficulty of assessing them, but that the judge in *Anderson* reached the right answer by granting the injunction.

Tesco also has interesting implications for contracts of employment incorporating disciplinary procedures. On a commonsense construction, along the lines adopted in *Tesco*, one might expect to find an implied term that the employer could not use the power to dismiss with notice to override a contractual disciplinary process. An employee dismissed in breach of that term would be able to claim substantial damages for lost future earnings where they could demonstrate that the process would have exonerated them and they would have continued to work for the employer. Alternatively, they might be able to frame the claim as one for loss of a chance of remaining in their employment, though this principle, which is widely recognised in the law of contract more generally,[31] has not been applied in employment cases.[32] However, the problem of calculating the employee's loss of earnings – seen as an obstacle in *Tesco* itself – would remain, and for now, at least, the legal position continues to be that set out in the *Edwards* case.[33] The employee, in that case, alleged that the employer's flawed disciplinary process had negatively affected their ability to get another job, giving rise to a substantial claim for future loss of earnings. The Supreme Court held, for a variety of unconvincing reasons, that damages for wrongful dismissal were for wages during the notice period only and that claims for lost future earnings could not be made.[34]

A number of cases in which employees have successfully obtained an injunction to force the employer to complete a contractual disciplinary process have focused on the *Edwards*-type situation: where the employee's future job prospects will be damaged by the dismissal and associated implication of wrongdoing. Indeed, this is true of one of the earliest cases in which an injunction was granted to an employee, *Irani*.[35] The claimant was an ophthalmologist who had fallen out

[30] *Alexander v Standard Telephones & Cables Ltd (No 1)*, [1990] ICR 291, 308.

[31] *Chaplin v Hicks* [1911] 2 KB 786.

[32] *Janciuk v Winerite Ltd* [1998] IRLR 63.

[33] *Edwards v Chesterfield Royal Hospital NHS Foundation Trust* [2011] UKSC 58, [2012] 2 AC 22. The courts have sometimes allowed damages claims for the time it would have taken to go through the process, in addition to the notice period: *Gunton v Richmond-upon-Thames London Borough Council* [1980] ICR 755.

[34] For critique, see, eg, L Barmes, 'Judicial Influence and *Edwards v Chesterfield Royal Hospital NHS Foundation Trust* and *Botham v Ministry of Defence*' (2013) 42 *Industrial Law Journal* 192; A Bogg, 'Express Disciplinary Procedures in the Contract of Employment: Parliamentary Intention and the Supreme Court' (2015) 131 *Law Quarterly Review* 15; H Collins, 'Compensation for Dismissal: in Search of Principle' (2012) 41 *Industrial Law Journal* 208.

[35] *Irani v Southampton and South West Hampshire HA* [1985] ICR 590.

with the consultant in charge of the department. Although there was no criticism of his work, the employer, an NHS hospital, wanted to dismiss him because of the breakdown in relationships. He was granted an injunction to force the employer to go through the disciplinary process before dismissing him. One of the factors that persuaded the judge to grant the injunction was that the claimant would not be able to secure another job in the NHS if his record showed that he had been summarily dismissed.[36] In *Gryf-Lowczowski*, a more complex case in which the claimant had been ordered to undergo a period of retraining, the judge granted the injunction after noting the following:

> If Mr Gryf-Lowczowski is dismissed, he will be deprived of the disciplinary procedures which would provide him with the opportunity to justify and vindicate himself in that context. What is more, Mr Gryf-Lowczowski would lose the congenial (albeit stressful) employment he has had with the trust and might well find himself unable to find alternative employment at least within the NHS.[37]

While some of these points relate to non-financial losses, to be discussed further below, the impact on the claimant's job prospects was clearly a significant consideration for the judge in this case.

Finally, it is worth noting that employees often have a particularly strong argument that damages would be an inadequate remedy where the employer's breach of contract is not related to termination. Where the employee is wrongfully demoted, the traditional contractual analysis is that the employee is dismissed and re-engaged on new terms.[38] For example, in *Smith v Trafford Housing Trust*, the claimant was demoted because the employer took exception to his activity on Facebook.[39] This was found to be a breach of contract. But, the claimant was only able to secure compensation for the difference in pay between his old and new salaries for the notice period, because the employer could lawfully have fired and rehired him with notice. This limitation gives rise to a strong claim for an injunction, as was the case in *Powell v Brent LBC* (discussed in detail below), where the employee got an injunction to stop the employer withdrawing a promotion.[40] In other non-termination cases, the employee's financial losses may be small or non-existent on the facts. For example, suspending an employee on full pay in breach of contract is unlikely to give rise to any significant economic loss. And redeploying an employee in breach of contract to a different type of work also causes no financial harm unless there is also a change in pay. Again, there should be a strong case for an injunction to restrain the employer's actions in these situations, as exemplified by the *Hughes* case.[41]

[36] ibid 597.
[37] *Gryf-Lowczowski v Hinchingbrooke Healthcare NHS Trust* [2005] EWHC 2407 (QB), [2006] ICR 425, [76].
[38] This limitation may not apply where it is clear that the employer had no intention of dismissing the employee: *Rigby v Ferodo Ltd* [1988] ICR 2.
[39] *Smith v Trafford Housing Trust* [2012] EWHC 3221 (Ch), [2013] IRLR 86.
[40] *Powell v Brent LBC* [1988] ICR 176.
[41] *Hughes v Southwark LBC* [1988] IRLR 55.

All of this is not to say that, in *every* case in which the employer threatens a breach of the contract of employment, damages will be an inadequate remedy. Each case falls to be assessed on its facts. But breaches of the contract of employment do not generally give rise to substantial damages claims, and this factor points strongly in favour of the grant of an injunction. Even where they might, as in *Tesco*, the Supreme Court's concern about the speculative nature of the assessment of damages also suggests that an injunction should be the preferred course.

ii. Non-financial Loss

A second factor pointing strongly in favour of the grant of an injunction in employment cases is that working people often suffer significant non-financial losses when their contract of employment is breached. The (questionable) decision in *Addis* is treated as authority for the proposition that no award for injury to feelings may be made in respect of a breach of the contract of employment.[42] Even if such an award were to be available, it might still be argued that the payment of a token sum of money does not adequately redress some or all of these losses.

The courts have shown themselves to be alert to these non-financial considerations in a variety of different situations. In *Gryf-Lowczowksi*, quoted above, the claimant's opportunity to vindicate himself by making his case at a hearing was a significant factor pointing towards the grant of an injunction requiring the employer to complete a contractual disciplinary procedure.[43] Equally, there seems to be an implicit acknowledgement that forcing an employee to go through a disciplinary process where there is no sufficient basis for the charges against them will cause harms, which are not likely to be compensated by means of an award of damages. This is apparent from the Supreme Court's decision in *Chhabra*.[44] The courts are particularly sensitive to the reputational and social consequences of being suspended from work or forced to work under restrictions. In *Mezey*, the court granted an injunction to restrain an unlawful suspension on full pay,[45] and in *Al-Obaidi*, the court granted an injunction to lift what it described as 'demeaning and humiliating' limitations on the claimant doctor's practice.[46]

Non-financial considerations may also arise even where cases do not involve disciplinary issues. For example, in *Powell v Brent LBC*, the claimant successfully applied for a promotion and began work in her new job, but was then told to return to her old job because a grievance from one of the unsuccessful candidates had exposed flaws in the appointment process (largely to do with a failure to keep

[42] (n 17).
[43] (n 37).
[44] (n 22).
[45] *Mezey v South West London and St George's Mental Health NHS Trust* [2007] EWCA Civ 106, [2007] IRLR 244.
[46] *Al-Obaidi v Frimley Health NHS Foundation Trust* [2018] EWHC 2494 (QB).

proper records).[47] She argued that she had been properly appointed to the new post, so the council could not simply withdraw the offer and would instead have to pursue disciplinary or dismissal proceedings. The Court of Appeal granted the injunction on the basis that damages would not compensate for the disappointment and embarrassment involved in having the promotion withdrawn. Similarly, in *Hughes v Southwark LBC*, the council sought to redeploy the claimant hospital social workers to work in its community teams because of a funding crisis.[48] The judge held that there was a serious issue to be tried as to whether the instruction was lawful, because the claimants had not been consulted or given an opportunity to raise a grievance about it in accordance with contractual procedures, and because the instruction itself was arguably unreasonable in that it would damage the social work provision in the hospital without necessarily resolving the council's wider staffing problems. Damages would not have been an adequate remedy because money would not compensate for the distress and loss of job satisfaction that would result from the redeployment.

While many of the older cases have involved 'high status' employees who can make strong claims about their professional reputation and identity,[49] the *Tesco* case offers the important clarification that non-pecuniary losses are potentially relevant in *all* work situations. The majority noted that:

> [D]amages for wrongful dismissal have not traditionally reflected the non-pecuniary loss – for example, the loss of job satisfaction, the anxiety and upheaval – caused by losing one's job.[50]

In *Tesco* itself, the employees had moved to a new area and taken on financial commitments on the strength of the original promise of additional pay, so losing their jobs would have generated considerable anxiety about making ends meet and finding another job, alongside a strong sense that their trust had been betrayed. But implicit in the majority's comment is that these losses may occur whenever a person loses a job, of whatever kind, and regardless of the circumstances.

iii. Conclusion

It should be relatively easy for an employee to prove that damages would not be an adequate remedy for their losses if they succeeded at trial. In termination cases, the weight of authority still indicates that damages for breach of the contract of employment are confined to wages during the notice period only. Although the Supreme Court in *Tesco* was willing to limit the employer's power to dismiss with notice in the particular circumstances of the case, so that substantial damages for

[47] (n 40).
[48] (n 41). See also *Wadcock v Brent LBC* [1990] IRLR 223.
[49] See the discussion in Z Adams, C Barnard, S Deakin, and S Fraser Butlin, *Deakin and Morris' Labour Law*, 7th edn (Oxford, Hart Publishing, 2021) para 4.61, which of course pre-dates *Tesco*.
[50] (n 5) [78].

lost future earnings were potentially available, it noted the difficulties of quantifying the award in this situation, a factor that also pointed in favour of the grant of an injunction. In cases not involving termination, the employee's financial losses may be limited or non-existent on the facts. A further factor in the employee's favour is that there is no possibility of obtaining an award for injury to feelings, despite the obvious non-pecuniary harms suffered by someone who loses their job or experiences some other breach of contract by their employer. *Tesco* demonstrates that this factor is not confined to employment in 'high status' roles.

B. Mutual Trust and Confidence

Another element in the test for the grant of an injunction is the requirement that there be 'trust and confidence' between the parties.[51] This reflects the law's understanding of the contract of employment as a personal relationship. As noted above, in the *American Cyanamid* test, the requirement can be seen as relevant to determining whether the grant of the injunction would cause hardship to the employer and, more generally, as a factor going to the 'workability' of the injunction.[52] It is regarded as unduly onerous to force one party (using the threat of contempt proceedings) to remain in a relationship in which they no longer have trust and confidence in the other party.

Before examining the cases in detail, it is worth noting that although the cases often refer to 'mutual' trust and confidence, the courts are, in fact, concerned with the employer's trust in the employee. The employee's confidence in the employer is unlikely to be very high under the circumstances, but presumably, their willingness to remain in the relationship with the court's protection is evidenced by their decision to seek an injunction. When the courts are considering trust from the employer's perspective, two factors should be taken into account: the precise nature of the injunction being sought and the reasons for the employer's assertion that it no longer has confidence in the employee. I examine each of these in turn.

The extent to which it is, in fact, oppressive to force the employer to remain in a relationship with the employee depends on the terms of the injunction. Some cases raise no issue of trust and confidence at all. For example, in *Keir*, the claimants sought an injunction to stop their local authority employer from withdrawing a car allowance in breach of contract.[53] There was no issue about their work or their relationship with colleagues or the employer. The employer was simply trying to save money by cutting their pay without changing their duties. Questions about trust and confidence tend to arise where the employee is seeking the protection

[51] An obligation to maintain mutual trust and confidence is an implied term of the contract of employment. For detailed discussion, see MR Freedland, *The Personal Employment Contract* (Oxford, Oxford University Press, 2005) ch 3.

[52] (n 4).

[53] *Keir v Hereford and Worcester CC* [1985] IRLR 505.

of a contractual disciplinary procedure, since *ex hypothesi* there is some criticism of the employee's work. However, even in these cases, most employees are only seeking an order that the employer carry out the contractual process and are often willing to accept a suspension from work while the process takes place. This was the case in *Irani*, for example.[54] As it happened, there was no criticism of Irani's work – the problem had arisen because he had fallen out with a superior – but it did not matter because he was not seeking to work at all. This is not a situation in which a great deal of trust is required. Similarly, in *Robb*, the council's relationship with its finance director had completely broken down after the interest rate swaps litigation,[55] but an injunction was nevertheless granted to force it to complete the disciplinary process to which he was entitled under his contract.[56] He agreed to stay away from the office and to refrain from carrying out any of his duties while the process took place.

Employer trust is – or should be – more of an issue where the injunction is likely to have a long-term effect, either because the court orders the continuation of the employment or (arguably) because the practical effect of going through the disciplinary process may be a finding that there are no grounds for dismissal. Many commentators have pointed out that the trust argument loses a lot of its force in workplaces where the employer is a large firm or public body rather than an individual human being.[57] However, in any workplace, it is important that the employer has some faith in the worker's ability to carry out their job satisfactorily.

The crucial factor is whether the presence or absence of trust and confidence on the part of the employer is a subjective or objective question. Brodie points out that if mutual trust and confidence are treated as subjective requirements the employer can simply assert that it does not have confidence in the employee, based on unsubstantiated allegations.[58] This would allow the employer to bypass the contractual requirement to conduct disciplinary proceedings and to undermine the protection supposedly being afforded to the employee. Unfortunately, there are examples of cases in which this approach has been adopted. One such is *Lakshmi*, in which the claimant doctor was accused of signing cremation forms without seeing the deceased's body on multiple occasions.[59] Her employer, a hospital, refused to adjourn a disciplinary hearing for a short period of time while the police conducted further enquiries and the CPS decided whether to prosecute. She had been advised by her lawyer to offer no comment while the police investigation was ongoing.[60] The judge held that an injunction could not be granted because the

[54] (n 35) 603.

[55] See *Hazell v Hammersmith and Fulham LBC* [1992] 2 AC 1.

[56] *Robb v Hammersmith and Fulham LBC* [1991] ICR 514.

[57] For an excellent critique of traditional arguments against granting injunctions see D Brodie, 'Specific Performance and Employment Contracts' (1998) 27 *Industrial Law Journal* 37.

[58] ibid 40.

[59] *Lakshmi v Mid Cheshire Hospitals NHS Trust* [2008] EWHC 878 (QB), [2008] IRLR 956.

[60] The judge criticised this legal advice (ibid [34]) but recognised that it would have been difficult for the claimant to disregard her own lawyer's opinion.

relationship between the parties had broken down, even though the claimant had not had an opportunity to explain her conduct because of the employer's refusal to delay the disciplinary process.[61]

In other cases, the courts have been more willing to accept that the disciplinary process should play a part in determining whether or not the employer has grounds for its lack of trust and confidence in the employee. For example, in *Barros D'Sa*, the employer received an investigator's report into allegations of misconduct that did not recommend dismissal but decided to dismiss anyway on the basis of its own view that its relationship with the employee had broken down.[62] This argument was rejected on the basis that it would wholly undermine the safeguards intended to be put in place by the disciplinary process. The Court of Appeal upheld the judge's order prohibiting the employer from considering any matters during the disciplinary process other than the investigator's report. Although *Barros D'Sa* was a procedural decision about the evidence to be considered at a disciplinary hearing, it also reveals a more robust approach to trust and confidence: the judges were not impressed by the employer's claim that it no longer had (subjective) trust and confidence in the employee when this was not supported by the investigator's (objective) report.[63]

Perhaps the strongest decision on this point is that in *Jones*.[64] The claimant in that case, a college lecturer, had been cleared of an allegation of gross misconduct at a disciplinary hearing, but the college governors did not want her to return to her old job because they believed that a breakdown in relationships would occur. They conducted a further disciplinary process, which the claimant refused to attend, and persuaded the local council (technically her employer) to dismiss her. The judge granted a permanent injunction prohibiting the council from acting on its dismissal letter and an interim injunction 'restraining the defendant council from dismissing her unless proper grounds exist and after carrying out a proper procedure in accordance with her contract of employment'.[65]

This objective approach is to be welcomed. The employer should not simply be able to assert that it no longer trusts the employee, particularly not where its own procedures have exonerated the employee or where it has failed to conduct its own procedures in a proper way.[66] A requirement to conduct a disciplinary procedure does not prevent the employer from dismissing the employee if proper grounds exist and that procedure is duly followed. Nor does it preclude termination on other grounds, such as redundancy.

[61] ibid [51].
[62] *Barros D'Sa v University Hospital Coventry and Warwickshire NHS Trust* [2001] EWCA Civ 983, [2001] IRLR 691.
[63] ibid [28]–[29], [35].
[64] *Jones v Gwent CC* [1992] IRLR 521.
[65] ibid [55].
[66] Brodie (n 57).

C. Conclusion

Injunctions are a useful means of forcing employers to comply with the contractual commitments they have made. Employees can typically make a strong case that damages would not be an adequate remedy for them were they to succeed at trial, given the various common law restrictions on what can be claimed. The requirement that the employer should still have trust and confidence in the employee can be more of a challenge, but there are signs that the courts are increasingly willing to take a context-dependent and objective approach to this requirement.

III. Injunctions to Enforce Statutory Rights

One obvious issue arising out of the discussion so far is that although the injunction is a valuable remedy, its worth to the employee depends on the precise terms of their contract of employment. The employees in the *Tesco* case had a very clear contractual term incorporated from a collective agreement stating that their additional pay entitlement was permanent. The various doctors challenging their disciplinary procedures, discussed above, benefitted from a contractual entitlement to the Maintaining High Professional Standards (MHPS) framework in the NHS.[67] But for most ordinary employees, particularly those in the private sector who are less likely to be covered by collective bargaining, employee-protective terms and conditions may be few and far between. Employers may specify that disciplinary processes have no contractual effect or grant themselves express power to change key terms and conditions.[68] This means that however effective an injunction is as a remedy, there may be nothing in the employee's contract on which it could bite.

A development of potentially much greater significance to the ordinary working person would be the possibility of using an injunction to restrain a threatened breach of *statutory* employment rights.[69] This would not depend on the contents of the contract of employment. In most cases, an injunction would be a significant improvement on the statutory remedy on offer: typically a modest award of compensation for the breach.

There is some (admittedly limited) precedent for the use of common law remedies to reinforce a statutory scheme in the context of the Working Time Regulations 1998. In *Barber*, the claimants were asked by their employer to sign an opt-out when the Regulations came into force because they routinely worked more

[67] Department of Health and Social Care, *Maintaining High Professional Standards in the Modern NHS* (2003) HCS 2003/012.

[68] See, eg, *Bateman v Asda Stores Ltd* [2010] IRLR 370.

[69] Of course, another option would be to make greater use of implied terms to qualify the express power to dismiss with notice. There is an interesting discussion of this in Lord Leggatt's judgment in *Tesco* (n 5), though it attracted an immediate rebuke from Lord Reed in the same case. Space precludes a full discussion of this point here.

than 48 hours per week.[70] They refused to sign (in the context of ongoing negotiations with the employer on pay) and sought a declaration that, having already worked in excess of 48 hours per week on average in the reference period, they could refuse to work any more hours until their average fell within the limit. The judge held that reg 4(1) could be treated as a standalone contractual obligation on the employer not to require its workers to work more than 48 hours per week.[71] Although reg 4(2) provided for a duty on the employer to take reasonable steps to ensure compliance, which was enforceable via the criminal law, this did not preclude other routes to enforcement of the clear-cut duty in reg 4(1). However, while the judge was content to confirm the workers' rights by means of a declaration, he refused to grant the injunction because to stop the employer insisting (even in breach of contract) that the workers continued to work would have had serious consequences for the employer's ability to carry on its business.[72] A declaration was also granted in the *Fire Brigades' Union* case that a shift system in operation in some fire stations in South Yorkshire was in breach of reg 10 WTR, providing an entitlement to 11 hours' rest in every 24-hour-period.[73] Although there were exceptions to reg 10, these did not apply in the case because the authority had not sought to provide the workers with the equivalent periods of rest they would require. Under the Regulations, a remedy of individual complaint to the tribunal was provided for breach of reg 10, but the court held that it could also grant the union (which would not be able to bring a claim in the tribunal) a declaration that the shift system was unlawful.[74] The court was particularly unsympathetic to the authority's position that firefighters at the relevant stations had accepted the unlawful arrangements (in return for a pay rise) and that it was simply too expensive to comply with the law.[75]

This approach could be extended to other statutory duties where a breach can be anticipated and potentially restrained. For example, there are several statutory provisions requiring the employer to give a working person time off: to attend ante-natal appointments,[76] carry out public duties,[77] serve as a trade union representative,[78] and so on. The remedy for an infringement of these rights is typically a modest monetary award. Sometimes, the courts may even decline to make an award, because the statutory wording often indicates that the award is compensatory, but it is unlikely that the claimant will have suffered any recognisable loss. If the employer refuses time off, the claimant will have worked and been

[70] *Barber v RJB Mining (UK) Ltd* [1999] ICR 679.
[71] ibid 690.
[72] ibid 692–3.
[73] *R (Fire Brigades Union) v South Yorkshire Fire and Rescue Authority* [2018] EWHC 1229 (Admin), [2018] IRLR 717.
[74] ibid [132]–[150].
[75] ibid [147].
[76] ERA, s 55.
[77] ERA, s 50.
[78] TULRCA, s 168.

paid during the relevant time. An injunction requiring the employer to grant the time off when required would be a much more relevant and appropriate remedy. Even more radically, injunctions could be used to restrain a threatened unfair dismissal. There is no generally applicable statutory mechanism to do this. There is a possibility of seeking interim relief from the tribunal where it is alleged that the potentially unfair dismissal is taking place on trade union grounds, though even this is limited in scope and effect.[79] In all other cases, the claimant must accept the dismissal and seek redress, usually compensation, in the tribunal. While reinstatement or re-engagement are the primary remedies in the statute, they are rarely sought or awarded. One major reason for this is that re-employment months or years after an unfair dismissal has taken place and the claimant has been away from the workplace is hardly an attractive remedy. Restraining the employer from going through with the dismissal, at least until a proper reason has been given and a fair procedure followed, would be much more likely to enable some claimants to keep their jobs.

So why do we not see many more attempts to use injunctions in these circumstances? The obvious answer, I think, is that they would not succeed because the courts would be concerned to avoid 'subverting' the statutory scheme. This is one of the arguments that was influential in *Johnson v Unisys*, in which the claimant sought substantial damages for wrongful dismissal in breach of the implied term of mutual trust and confidence.[80] The claimant in that case had already obtained damages for unfair dismissal up to the statutory maximum applicable at the time, and was seeking to use the common law action to obtain compensation for the additional losses he claimed to have incurred. The concern was that to allow this claim to proceed would undermine Parliament's intention to limit the compensation obtainable in the event of a dismissal. This reasoning has proved highly controversial among labour law scholars.[81] But even if one accepts its validity on the facts of *Johnson*, does it apply to preclude the wider use of injunctions?

The decision in *Mackenzie* suggests that it does.[82] The claimant in that case had won an unfair dismissal claim and obtained a re-engagement order against the employer. The employer refused to comply with the order and paid compensation under the statute instead.[83] The claimant sought an order quashing the employer's decision not to comply. The Court of Appeal declined to grant the order on two grounds. First, the statutory right to re-engagement was found not to 'impose an absolute and indefeasible obligation on the employer to re-engage the employee'.[84]

[79] ERA, s 128. I discuss this in more detail below.

[80] *Johnson v Unisys Ltd* [2001] UKHL 13, [2003] 1 AC 518.

[81] (n 34).

[82] *R (Mackenzie) v University of Cambridge* [2019] EWCA Civ 1060, [2019] ICR 1477.

[83] ERA, s 117.

[84] (n 82) [20].

Instead, it imposed an obligation to re-engage or to pay additional compensation. Second, to grant the order sought would subvert the statutory scheme:

> The statutory scheme of employment protection is intended to be entirely self-contained and fall under the exclusive jurisdiction of the employment tribunal.[85]

Underhill LJ distinguished the (routine) enforcement of tribunal awards through the courts, noting that an injunction could not simply replicate the tribunal's order and would require fresh consideration by the court of what the employer was being asked to do.

There is an element of circularity in this reasoning. The fact that Parliament has not provided for injunctive relief is treated as a reason for regarding the employer's statutory obligation as a limited one, to comply or pay compensation, but of course it is the availability of injunctive relief that the court is being asked to consider. Nonetheless, the decision does not bode well for the wider use of injunctions to enforce statutory rights, though each 'statutory scheme' should be considered on its own merits.

This may help to explain why the cases we do have on this issue have involved the WTR. A distinguishing feature of the WTR is that it has a significant gap in enforcement. The entitlements it contains are divided into two groups: rights enforceable by the worker in the Employment Tribunal and limits enforceable by public authorities (usually HSE or a local authority, depending on the sector) through regulatory means and, ultimately, the criminal law.[86] Working people affected by a breach of limits (as in the two cases just described) have no individual right to redress as a matter of law. In practice, public enforcement is also highly unlikely in a working time case, given the resource constraints on the enforcement bodies and the low priority they give to enforcement in cases not involving death or serious injury.[87] Although the point was not very apparent in the two cases discussed above, it is arguable that this set of arrangements breaches workers' rights of access to the courts and to an effective remedy. There is very little 'subversion' of the statutory scheme when it grants no redress at all.

However, this point is less easy to make in relation to the other two examples discussed above: time off rights and unfair dismissal (both generally and in respect of non-compliance with a re-employment order). Here, the working person does have a remedy in the form of a claim for compensation. It is not a very effective or helpful remedy, but it is a remedy nonetheless. There may be an important difference for the courts between providing a remedy where none exists, and providing a better remedy than the one in the statute. A further complication in unfair dismissal cases is the availability of interim relief where the employee alleges that

[85] ibid [22].
[86] C Barnard, 'The Working Time Regulations 1998' (1999) 28 *Industrial Law Journal* 61.
[87] See ACL Davies and L Rodgers, 'Towards a More Effective Health and Safety Regime for UK Workplaces post COVID-19' (2023) 52 *Industrial Law Journal* 665.

they have been dismissed on trade union and related grounds.[88] This does not have the same effect as an injunction because it is not backed by the contempt powers of the courts, but the fact that Parliament has put in place an analogous remedy in a subset of cases may make the courts even more reluctant to step in.

IV. Practicalities

Of course, the main problem with injunctions – and the reason why we do not see more of them in employment settings – is that they are expensive and difficult to obtain on purely practical grounds. I reflect here on some of the access to justice issues they raise, before considering whether any steps could be taken to mitigate these problems.

A first point to note is that it is important to act promptly to obtain an injunction when a breach is threatened, without accepting the employer's breach and bringing the contract to an end.[89] This means that the employee will need rapid access to legal advice as soon as a potential problem arises. The application will usually be made in the High Court, so there are fees to pay, and there is a costs risk if the employee loses. Moreover, as noted above, the employee seeking an injunction is normally expected to give an undertaking to pay damages to the employer if they lose at trial. This introduces a further element of risk and uncertainty, unless the court is willing to dispense with the requirement. Taken together, these elements help to explain a feature that most of the cases discussed above have in common: the employee either has a well-paid job and insurance, or is a member of a trade union, or both.

There has been a long-running debate in employment law about the status of employment tribunals (now, realistically, employment judges) in the legal system. A decision was taken early on that they should not have the contempt powers of the courts and should operate within a less legalistic framework.[90] Although they have become much more court-like over time, the Law Commission relatively recently rejected a suggestion that they should be able to grant injunctions.[91] There are some practical obstacles: the tribunals do not have the same infrastructure that the High Court does to list and hear cases quickly. Unless they were also given contempt powers, tribunals would not be able to enforce any injunctions that they issued, with the result that the claimant would have to pursue separate court proceedings for that purpose. And there still seems to be a strongly held

[88] ERA, s 128.

[89] *Rigby v Ferodo Ltd* [1988] ICR 2. If the contract is brought to an end by acceptance, a claim lies in damages instead: *Gunton v Richmond-upon-Thames London Borough Council* [1980] ICR 755. On acceptance, see *Geys v Societe Generale* [2012] UKSC 63, [2013] 1 AC 523.

[90] P Davies and M Freedland, *Labour Legislation and Public Policy: A Contemporary History* (Oxford, Clarendon Press 1993) ch 5.

[91] Law Commission, *Employment Law Hearing Structures* (Law Com No 390, 2020).

view among many practitioners that only a High Court judge is suitably qualified to issue an injunction, given the serious consequences of breach.

There are obviously a number of different possible solutions to this set of problems, at varying levels of plausibility. One route – well beyond the scope of this chapter – would be to improve the accessibility of the civil courts, for example, by reinvigorating legal aid or capping costs. Another would be to provide tribunals with the training and infrastructure to support an injunctions jurisdiction. Another would be to come up with some alternative to the injunction that shares its characteristics as a 'replicative' remedy – its ability to get the employer to comply with whatever obligation it is threatening to infringe – without being so expensive and difficult to obtain. I offer some brief reflections on this third option – the 'injunction-lite' – here.

For accessibility reasons, it would be important that the 'injunction-lite' was available in the tribunal rather than in the courts, with no fees or costs risk (though there are still plenty of practical barriers to access even at this level).[92] This means that we are confined to implementing something that the tribunal can order. The closest parallel is with interim relief in certain unfair dismissal cases. At present, this is only available in a small group of cases listed in section 128 ERA where the reason for dismissal is related to whistleblowing, trade union activities, or serving as a worker representative.[93] An application for interim relief must be made within seven days and heard promptly by the tribunal.[94] If the tribunal finds that one of the listed reasons is 'likely' to be found to be the reason for dismissal, it must ask the employer whether it is willing to reinstate or re-engage the employee.[95] If the employer fails to attend or refuses to re-employ the dismissed employee, the tribunal must make an order to continue the employee's contract of employment.[96] This order applies for the purposes of pay, other benefits, and continuity of employment. If an order is made but the employer does not comply, the tribunal must order the continuation of the contract instead and the payment of compensation to the employee.[97] In theory at least, interim relief should help by maintaining the employment relationship until the time of trial, making it more likely that the employee can keep their job over the longer term.

However, there are a number of flaws in the scheme as it stands. First, the employer can simply refuse to take the employee back either by not turning up to the hearing or by stating that it is 'unwilling' to do so. There is no opportunity for the tribunal to scrutinise the employer's decision or to require it to do anything against its wishes. Second, while the employee's objective in seeking interim relief

[92] For an overview, see Davies (n 2) ch 2.

[93] An attempt to use human rights law to argue that interim relief should be available in discrimination cases was unsuccessful in *Steer v Stormsure Ltd* [2021] EWCA Civ 887, [2021] ICR 1671.

[94] ERA, s 128(2) and (3).

[95] ERA, s 129.

[96] ERA, s 129(9).

[97] ERA, s 132.

in a trade union dismissal case will be to get their job back, the provisions are more focused on keeping the contract alive. This has financial benefits for the employee but is much less effective as a remedy. Third, any consequences of non-compliance for the employer are purely financial, so the employer can simply pay its way out of difficulty.

Obviously, in developing an 'injunction-lite' model for employment tribunals, one could avoid giving it some of the worst characteristics of the current regime of interim relief, such as the employer's right to refuse. The tribunal could be empowered to order compliance with a particular obligation against the employer's wishes, provided that it was reasonable to do so. This would probably involve many of the same considerations underlying the 'balance of convenience' test. The main problem with any sort of 'injunction-lite' is that the penalty for breach is likely to be financial: the payment of additional compensation to the affected employee, or perhaps an actual penalty to the Secretary of State.[98] Unless the financial consequences are very severe, many employers will treat this as a 'tax' on doing business and pay up rather than complying with the law. The threat of being found in contempt of court where an injunction has been granted casts a very different light on non-compliance and is much more likely to result in respect for the employee's rights.

V. Conclusion

This chapter has mapped out the dilemma presented by injunctions in employment law. The injunction is a powerful remedy for the aggrieved employee. The legal barriers to obtaining an injunction to restrain the employer's threatened breach of contract have reduced over time, as the courts have recognised the inadequacy of damages as a remedy for the employee and the need to take an objective approach to trust and confidence. However, the injunction is also something of a niche remedy for employees who are well-paid or have trade union backing or both. This is because only employees in these categories are likely to have collectively-bargained contracts with protective terms and conditions, plus the financial resources to seek an injunction with all the attendant risks. The option of using injunctions to restrain threatened breaches of statutory rights – which would apply much more widely – does not seem particularly promising. And there are also difficulties in improving access to justice: injunctions work because they are backed up by contempt powers, but it is (unsurprisingly) difficult to come up with a lesser equivalent that would work equally well.

More broadly, injunctions offer an interesting insight into an important problem in employment law: working people enjoy a wide range of statutory rights (albeit with various well-documented weaknesses), but the associated remedy is

[98] See Davies (n 2) ch 5, for a discussion of penalties in employment law.

typically a (small) compensatory award. This often fails to deter employers from breaches or to provide claimants with effective redress. The law is capable of delivering much better remedial options – like injunctions – but there seems to be a longstanding consensus among policy makers that working people do not 'deserve' these forms of protection. Given the reasons outlined above for thinking that compliance is a particularly important interest in employment law, this consensus ought to be challenged.

9

The Impact of the Law of Tort

DOUGLAS BRODIE*

I. Introduction

This chapter focuses on the law of vicarious liability, but it would seem appropriate to begin by commenting upon the relationship between tort and labour law more generally. Historically, the operation of the law of tort, from an employee's perspective, has often had an unwelcome impact in the workplace. For many years, the doctrine of common employment acted as a barrier to recovery for personal injury. Where collective relations were concerned, the constantly evolving economic torts would often diminish the protection afforded by the statutory immunities should industrial action arise. The contemporary picture is a very different one. The common law of employer's liability has, to a considerable extent, ameliorated the impact of the Enterprise and Regulatory Reform Act 2013.[1] Developments in the law of the economic torts have not posed a threat to collective interests for quite some time, but that may be explained by the remarkable extent of hostile legislative activity and, as a corollary, the absence of any need for employer creativity (far less ingenuity) in framing common law arguments.[2]

II. The Function of Tort Law

Tort law allows for the espousal of collective goals and has the capacity to vindicate social policy. The extent to which this happens varies considerably depending on

* I would like to express my gratitude to all who attended the conference at UCL for some very helpful feedback. I am particularly grateful to the editors and Charles Wynn-Evans who was a particularly supportive and insightful discussant. The usual disclaimer applies.

[1] Decisions such as *Cockerill v CXK Ltd* [2018] EWHC 1155 view statutory obligations as an exposition of the common law position.

[2] See D Brodie, 'The Irrepressible Common Law: The Economic Torts and the Right to Strike' in A Bogg, J Rowbottom, and A Young (eds), *The Constitution of Social Democracy* (Oxford, Hart Publishing, 2020) ch 15.

the outlook of the courts concerned. In the US, it has been said judicially, with reference to wrongful discharge cases, that

> the theoretical reason for labelling the discharge wrongful in such cases is not based on the terms and conditions of the contract, but rather arises out of a duty implied in law on the part of the employer to conduct its affairs in compliance with public policy, expressed judicially or by statute.[3]

In the UK, implied terms provide the conduit through which judicial views on the behavioural standards expected of an employer take effect. A tortious solution may, though, offer more to claimants than a contractual approach. Recourse to tort law may allow the common law to bring a collective dimension to bear by condemning particularly egregious behaviour: 'the courts awarded the employee a remedy as much to vindicate the board policy at stake as to redress the private wrong'.[4] It also may provide more effective protection for employees by improving the position on remedies. This can be illustrated by the way in which, in some US jurisdictions, tort has been used to fashion exceptions to the doctrine of employment at will. Tortious discharge in violation of public policy occurs 'when an employer's discharge of an employee violates fundamental principles of public policy'.[5] A claimant who succeeds on this basis may be awarded punitive damages.[6] Decisions in some states have been much more willing than courts in the UK to develop the law on the basis that a wrongful act committed in the course of a contractual relationship may afford both tortious and contractual relief.

Against that backdrop, this chapter looks at a number of developments in the law of vicarious liability. In particular, it examines how the law of tort has been concerned to ensure that its scope is not circumvented by employers resorting to contractual arrangements that do not give rise to a contract of employment. The 'akin to employment' test has emerged to combat this issue and has had a powerful impact. The chapter explores whether this development will be mirrored in the law of the employment contract. It also reviews changes to the way in which the scope of employment is determined. In both cases, it asks whether the policy considerations that underpin the facilitation of recovery by third parties are more cogent than those concerned with employee protection and whether the courts might be persuaded that greater coherence is called for.

[3] *Cleary v American Airlines* 111 Cal App 3d 443 with reference to *Tameny v Atlantic Richfield Co* 27 Cal 3d 167.

[4] BF Berger, 'Defining Public Policy Torts in At-Will Dismissals' (1981) 34 *Stanford Law Review* 153, 155.

[5] *Tameny* (n 3).

[6] *Cleary* (n 3).

III. The Modern Law of Vicarious Liability

The law in this area has changed dramatically in the last 25 years, and cases concerned with child abuse have been the primary catalyst. The jurisprudence of the Canadian Supreme Court has been hugely influential. The challenges thrown up have compelled the courts to interrogate the underlying policy reasons underpinning vicarious liability. With the passage of time, it has become increasingly clear that enterprise liability is viewed as the dominant explanatory factor; to borrow from the language of the Canadian courts in contractual settings, it may be seen as an 'organising norm'.[7] In *Trustees of the Barry Congregation* v *BXB* Lord Burrows observed, with reference to *Armes v Nottinghamshire CC*, that:

> In looking at the justification for vicarious liability, Lord Reed … referred to what has been termed in the academic literature as 'enterprise risk' or 'enterprise liability' … in the following passage at para 67: 'The most influential idea in modern times has been that it is just that an enterprise which takes the benefit of activities carried on by a person integrated into its organisation should also bear the cost of harm wrongfully caused by that person in the course of those activities'.[8]

It is now trite law that consideration of any claim involving vicarious liability requires the application of a two-stage approach:

> The first is a relationship between the two persons which makes it proper for the law to make the one pay for the fault of the other. Historically … that was limited to the relationship between employer and employee, but that has now been somewhat broadened … The second is the connection between that relationship and the tortfeasor's wrongdoing. Historically, the tort had to be committed in the course or within the scope of the tortfeasor's employment, but that too has now been somewhat broadened.[9]

At both stages, policy considerations have led to judicial reform to the benefit of third parties, but what of employees?

IV. Stage One and Scope of Employment

Where the interests of third parties are in issue, the approach has been increasingly expansive. The 2016 case of *Mohamud v Morrison Supermarkets* represents

[7] In *Bhasin v Hrynew* [2014] 3 SCR 494, the Canadian Supreme Court explained that good faith was an 'organising norm' where contractual relations are concerned.

[8] *Trustees of the Barry Congregation* v *BXB* [2023] UKSC 15 [47] referring to *Armes v Nottinghamshire CC* [2018] AC 355 [67]. For further discussion of the implications of judicial endorsement of enterprise liability see D Brodie, 'Enterprise liability: the consequences of a "single accepted truth"' [2025] *Jur. Rev.* (forthcoming).

[9] *Barclays Bank v Various Claimants* [2020] UKSC 13 [1].

the peak of a trend of taking a much broader view of the scope of employment.[10] This is much less evident where responsibility for the employee is concerned. The approach is more conservative, and *Reynolds v Strutt & Parker*, which arose in the context of an accident occurring during an away day, illustrates this very well.[11] The conclusion was reached that an employee who was injured while cycling in a race as part of the day's activities was not within the scope of his employment. *Reynolds* is in line with the view that the courts have traditionally taken over 'voluntary' activities. Two Court of Appeal decisions, dealing with broadly analogous circumstances to *Reynolds*, illustrate this: *R v National Insurance Co Ex Parte Michael*,[12] and *Faulkner v Chief Adjudication Officer*.[13] Both dealt with claims for industrial injuries benefits brought by police officers who had been injured whilst playing football for a police force team. In both cases, the claimants were not required to play but were expected and encouraged to do so. Indeed, refusing to participate may have been imprudent: 'a young man looking for promotion ought to play for the force when he can. If he goes off and does other things, it would do him no good'.[14] Similarly, whilst attendance at an away day will not always be required by the terms of the contract, employees will generally feel compelled to take part.

Michael and *Faulkner* held that the claimants were not in the course of employment, and their claims failed. The outcomes in both cases lend support to the decision in *Reynolds* and might be thought to supply the more detailed reasoning that the latter lacks. It should be said that both adopt a narrow conception of the kind of activities that can arise in the course of employment. In *Michael*, the key question was whether playing football should be viewed as reasonably incidental to the job the claimant was employed to do. A restrictive view of that test was taken: the words 'reasonably incidental to the employment' were seen as merely a 'judicial gloss' on the statutory provisions and were not to be applied expansively.[15] It may be doubted whether limiting the scope of the test in this way is correct. In the subsequent decision of the House of Lords in *Smith v Stages*, no such limitation was apparent.[16] It was clear, though, that the court in *Michael* saw the activity as entirely recreational and not sufficiently related to the work the claimant was employed to do. However, employment relationships are not conducted solely on the basis of what employees can be contractually compelled to do but also on the basis of what the employer's expectations are known to be. This was recognised by the Court of Appeal in *Nancollas v Insurance Officer*: 'In a changed social matrix, the foundation of the employment relationship is no longer so much based on orders and instructions as on requests and information, and contractual rights

[10] *Mohamud v Morrison Supermarkets* [2016] UKSC 11, [2016] AC 677.
[11] *Reynolds v Strutt & Parker* [2011] EWHC 2263.
[12] *R v National Insurance Co Ex Parte Michael* [1977] ICR 121.
[13] *Faulkner v Chief Adjudication Officer* [1994] PIQR P244.
[14] *Michael* (n 12) 125.
[15] ibid 130.
[16] *Smith v Stages* [1989] AC 928.

and duties are supplemented by mutual expectations of co-operation.'[17] As a consequence, *Nancollas* accepted that the lack of a contractual obligation does not and should not preclude a finding that the employee was acting in the course of employment.

The analysis in *Nancollas* has much to commend; the employer, given his control of the enterprise and accompanying authority, can bring about his bidding by making requests and suggestions rather than issuing orders. Particularly, in a culture where defiance of the employer's will is known to be unwise and likely to lead to adverse consequences, the distinction between orders and requests evaporates.

The decision in *Nancollas* was alert to the realities of working life, whereas in *Reynolds* it was 'impossible to say that having a fun day out is an ordinary incident of normal employment. On the contrary, by its very nature, it is an extraordinary incident'.[18] Is this correct? There is nothing extraordinary about either attending an away day or that day including a 'bonding' activity. The reality is that away days are now part and parcel of working life, and employees often have no real choice but to attend. Any activities that give rise to risks of harm are set up by the employer for the benefit of the business. In my opinion, those activities should be viewed as falling within the course of employment.

I would suggest that recourse to enterprise liability would have pointed to a different outcome in *Reynolds*. In order to capture the full extent of risks created by the enterprise, it is important to look beyond what employees are contractually obliged to do. Thus, as *Smith* makes clear, in determining whether an act falls within the course of employment, one must have regard to things that are reasonably incidental to the employment. The reasonably incidental test is concerned to hold the employer responsible for behaviour that naturally and predictably occurs in the course of running the business rather than narrowly focussing on the particularity of what an individual employee may be required to do. Against that backdrop, holding an employer responsible when the employee is injured participating in a competition intended to foster an esprit de corps to the employer's benefit would seem a more than legitimate conclusion. The employer generated the risk and should therefore bear the loss.

V. Stage Two and the Akin to Employment Test

As the scope of the law of vicarious liability has expanded over the last 25 years, the courts have had to consider the position of wrongdoers who are not employees far more than previously. In abuse cases, one of the difficulties in the path of claimants has often been the fact that defenders have not been in mainstream employment

[17] *Nancollas v Insurance Officer* [1985] 1 All ER 833, 835.
[18] *Reynolds* (n 11) [37].

(or employment at all) but have been members of religious orders and the like. The need for reform went beyond that required to address cases of intentional harm, as the homely example given in *JGE v English Province of our Lady of Charity* (*JGE*) illustrates very well:

> [The priest] … jumps on his battered old bicycle and pedals furiously down the hill to attend his ailing parishioner. Alas he does so negligently, fails to observe another of his flock on a controlled pedestrian crossing. She is knocked down and suffers injury. The priest was clearly in the course of doing what he was appointed to do. There is no problem about applying stage 2 of the test. But he has taken a vow of poverty. He is not himself insured. But the parish is. Are we really having to conclude that his bishop and/or the diocesan trust are not vicariously liable because he is not employed or in a relationship akin to employment? Are we to say he is simply an office holder personally responsible for the manner in which he conducts his office. I think not.[19]

At this juncture we find that another decision of the Canadian Supreme Court has been very influential: *John Doe v Bennett*.[20] The Court held that the defendant was responsible for the behaviour of a priest who had sexually assaulted boys in his parishes on the basis that the relationship was akin to employment: 'The bishop exercises extensive control over the priest, including the power of assignment, the power to remove the priest from his post and the power to discipline him.'[21] However, the judgment(s) are somewhat brief, and the Supreme Court chose not to provide guidance on how the concept might be applied in future cases or to explain the significance of policy. There is a marked contrast with *Bazley* in these respects. It may be that there was felt to be no need to explore policy justifications as they had been examined in some depth by the Supreme Court only a few years previously.[22] Moreover, in *Jacobi v Griffiths* (handed down with *Bazley*), it had been said that:

> this Court endorses the "enterprise risk" approach to vicarious liability … McLachlin J. explains, "[t]he employer puts in the community an enterprise which carries with it certain risks. When those risks materialize and cause injury to a member of the public despite the employer's reasonable efforts, it is fair that the person or organization that creates the enterprise and hence the risk should bear the loss."[23]

This, though, does not explain why more in the way of guidance on the application of the concept was not forthcoming. As a result, whilst the employer's responsibility was now extended to relationships 'akin to employment', it is much less clear when the Canadian Supreme Court believed that description would be merited.

Cases against religious bodies may be relatively straightforward as, on occasion, the extent of control may be considerable. Wrongdoers may not be employees

[19] *JGE v English Province of our Lady of Charity* [2012] EWCA Civ 938, [2013] 1 QB 722 [83].
[20] *John Doe v Bennett* [2004] 1 SCR 436.
[21] ibid [27].
[22] See also *Ontario Ltd v Sagaz Industries Canada* [2001] 2 SCR 983.
[23] *Jacobi v Griffiths* [1999] 2 SCR 570 [42].

because, for example, of the spiritual dimension, but an analogy with employment may still be readily drawn. The Australian case of *Bird v DP* illustrates that those holding office within religious organisations may be subject to a far greater degree of control than would often be found in a modern employment situation.[24] The hierarchical system in *Bird* was very relevant to this conclusion, and wrongdoers in the position of the one in the case are often more like traditional employees than current ones. Organisational structures vary a great deal, and consideration of the question of control may not provide an easy solution. The challenge then becomes one of giving meaning to the concept of akin to employment.

A. Akin to Employment in the UK

In a highly influential decision in *JGE*, the Court of Appeal followed *John Doe* and chose to take a broad view of the scope of 'akin to employment' by not restricting it to roles outwith mainstream employment. It can also be said that the Court elected to adopt what might be termed a 'labour law' approach to the question.[25] *JGE* concerned the responsibility of the Church for a parish priest whose appointment did not give rise to a contractual relationship; the priest holding nothing other than ecclesiastical office. The Court of Appeal had to determine, by way of a preliminary question, whether vicarious liability could still arise. The conventional response would have been no. However, a majority of the Court held that the relationship was so close in character to one of employer/employee that it was just and fair to hold the employer vicariously liable. It is said that one should seek to establish 'the broad characteristics of the employer/employee relationship' and ask whether the contract in issue 'bears a sufficiently close resemblance and affinity in character' to one of employment.[26] This might be said to be a labour law test because the process of identifying such a relationship would be almost indistinguishable from that used to identify the existence of an employment contract. However, the traditional goals of vicarious liability (compensation and deterrence) would be furthered as 'near misses' would be captured. It should be said that it would have been possible to decide *JGE* through an approach that was confined to religious and similar organisations.

It was immediately apparent that the approach would prove troublesome.[27] In particular, it should be appreciated that many contracts for services could be said to be akin to those of employment, as the similarities will often be greater than the differences. For instance, it is probably not possible to identify terms whose

[24] *Bird v DP* [2023] VSCA 66.
[25] *JGE* (n 19).
[26] See also *BXB* (n 8) [58].
[27] Lord Hope of Craighead, 'Tailoring the Law on Vicarious Liability' (2013) 129 *Law Quarterly Review* 514.

presence is consistent with the latter form of contract but not the former.[28] Nor is greater clarity necessarily forthcoming if one looks to the extent to which the individual concerned functions as part of the defendant's organisation. *Mei Fields Designs v Saffron Cards* points out that many independent contractors 'are fully integrated into the businesses in which they work and will for many purposes be indistinguishable from employees'.[29]

The current tests deployed by the courts to establish the existence of an employment contract are rather blunt instruments should adjudication require (as it often will) a highly ambiguous situation to be addressed. It will often be the case that the relationship in issue will be revealed to be just as analogous to a contract for services as one of employment. An employment or labour law approach to the akin to employment test is likely to suffer from the same challenges of classification where there are close affinities with more than one type of contractual relation.

B. Retrenchment

The creation of an expansionist framework driven by policy concerns gave rise to the possibility of further common law reform consistent with those considerations. The prospects of such development were fuelled by the judgment of Lord Phillips in *Various Claimants v Catholic Child Welfare Society* (*Christian Bros*), where he highlighted a number of policy reasons that are said to explain why an employer is liable for the acts of employees.[30] It was said that the presence of these considerations would 'usually make it fair, just and reasonable to impose vicarious liability on the employer'.[31] Lord Philips's approach can be said to be in line with an enterprise liability theory of vicarious liability. The judgment in *Christian Bros* had the potential to increase the range of relevant relationships far more extensively. It could have led, if allowed to flow to its logical conclusion, to a radically different position at common law, as a number of the policy reasons set out by Lord Phillips are very much applicable where a wide range of working relationships are concerned.

C. Countervailing Factors

Such an expansionist framework offered great encouragement to claimants and reached its zenith in the decision of the Court of Appeal in *Various Claimants v Barclays Bank*, which called into question the entire future (at least so far as the law

[28] D Brodie, *The Employment Contract* (Oxford, Oxford University Press, 2005) ch 6.
[29] *Mei Fields Designs v Saffron Cards* [2018] FSR 33 [43].
[30] *Various Claimants v Catholic Child Welfare Society* [2013] 2 AC 1 [35].
[31] ibid.

of negligence was concerned) of the employment/self-employment dichotomy.[32] The case concerned responsibility for a Dr Bates who practised as a general practitioner but also undertook medical examinations on behalf of commercial clients, including the defendants. Litigation arose following allegations that he abused employees and prospective employees in the course of carrying out medical examinations for the defendants. The response to the claim was, in effect, that the status of independent contractor conferred a 'defence'. This was rejected, and the Court found for the claimants. The leading judgment of Irwin LJ in the Court of Appeal placed explicit reliance upon the policy considerations contained in *Christian Bros* in justifying the imposition of liability.

The latter decision was several steps too far for the Supreme Court which allowed the defendant's appeal.[33] The Supreme Court, in a single relatively short speech delivered by Lady Hale, which contains a limited discussion of the key policy factors, rejected the claim that the relationship between the defendants was one that attracted the doctrine of vicarious liability. The divide between employment and self-employment was regarded as a fundamental one that the courts should not set aside. Why did the Supreme Court elect to reaffirm? After all, changes in the labour market might have pointed to a different outcome, and Lady Hale herself had previously acknowledged that 'large organisations may well outsource their responsibilities to much poorer and un- or under-insured contractors'.[34]

Lady Hale's approach, by way of explanation, was to point to recent judicial endorsements of the dichotomy (such as *Woodland v Essex CC*) and to suggest that there was no question of going beyond this position.[35] However, while she acknowledges the increasing influence of enterprise liability, she does not feel the need to explain why vicarious liability did not arise even though, on occasion, an independent contractor might be regarded as constituting part of the enterprise. This strikes me as amounting to a significant gap in the reasoning in the case. Denying vicarious liability for the acts of an independent contractor will often be at odds with enterprise liability, which provides the contemporary justification for this area of law. The explanation for this inherent tension is perhaps to be found in Lady Hale's judgment in *Woodhall;* viz the change being seen as too big a leap for the common law, which 'must proceed with caution, incrementally by analogy with existing categories, and consistently with some underlying principle'.[36] Collapsing the traditional dichotomy was no doubt viewed as a change of such a magnitude that it should be left to the legislature.

At the same time, it would be wrong to view the approach of the Court of Appeal as being idiosyncratic. After all, the courts have held, in a related context,

[32] *Various Claimants v Barclays Bank* [2018] EWCA Civ 1670.

[33] *Barclays* (n 9) discussed by P Giliker, 'Can the Supreme Court Halt the Ongoing Expansion of Vicarious Liability?' (2021) 37 *Journal of Professional Negligence* 55.

[34] ibid [42].

[35] *Woodland v Essex CC* [2013] UKSC 66, [2014] 1 AC 537.

[36] ibid [28].

that an independent contractor may be part of the employer's enterprise; a more inclusive approach being found in the judicial application of the statutory provisions that are contained in part one of the Health and Safety at Work Act 1974. In the House of Lords decision in *R v Associated Octel*, a chemicals company engaged a firm of independent contractors, RGP, to repair the lining of a tank, in the course of which RGP's employee suffered severe injury.[37] The company was prosecuted under section 3(1) for failure to conduct its undertaking so that, as far as practicable, persons not in its employment were not exposed to health and safety risks. The judge in *Associated Octel* found that repair of the tank, whether by the company's employees or by contractors, was part of their undertaking as a chemicals producer. Where an employer engaged contractors to carry out work that was part of the employer's undertaking, such as routine maintenance, the employer must take whatever steps were reasonably practicable to avoid risks to those contractors. The House of Lords went on to observe that

> [section 3] of the Act of 1974 is not concerned with vicarious liability. It imposes a duty upon the employer himself. That duty is defined by reference to a certain kind of activity, namely, the conduct by the employer of his undertaking. It is indifferent to the nature of the contractual relationships by which the employer chooses to conduct it.[38]

It is possible that the statutory position where criminal liability is concerned has offered a measure of encouragement to common law reform.

Retrenchment in *Barclays Bank* required a downplaying of *Christian Bros* and its emphasis on the significance of policy. There appears to have been an acceptance of the part played by the latter decision in fundamental demarcation lines being imperilled, and it was observed that there had been a

> tendency to elide the policy reasons for the doctrine of the employer's liability for the acts of his employee, set out … *Christian Bros*, with the principles which should guide the development of that liability into relationships which are not employment but which are sufficiently akin to employment to make it fair and just to impose such liability.[39]

D. Endorsement

Barclays Bank sought to achieve retrenchment, but that should not blind us to the fact that it also confirms that the law has 'broadened' as is evidenced by the fact that *JGE* is viewed as correctly decided. This is likely to result in more borderline cases being determined in favour of employment where the context of the proceedings is reparation. The Supreme Court accepted that the law has evolved

[37] *R v Associated Octel* [1996] ICR 972.
[38] ibid 977.
[39] *Barclays Bank* (n 9) [16].

beyond a singular approach to the identification of an employment contract and is now more cognisant of context: it had been

> largely assumed that a person would be an employee for all purposes – employment law, tax, social security and vicarious liability. Recent developments have broken that link, which may be of benefit to people harmed by the torts of those working in the 'gig' economy.[40]

The 'akin to employment' approach will undoubtedly continue to be more inclusive than before, but it is, at root, one based on analogy and, as a corollary, inherently limited in its scope. It may be expected that relationships that are very similar to employment will be treated as if they were one and the same. The stance adopted can be said to be in keeping with the incremental approach to law reform favoured by the common law.

The akin to employment test not only survives *Barclay's Bank* but can be regarded as gaining added strength through reappraisal by the Supreme Court. It is thought to be applied in a manner less closely informed by policy reasons. This will ensure that those who are clearly independent contractors will not be caught, but some individuals who are regarded as self-employed in other contexts will be. It would seem very likely that the akin to employment test will continue to serve to protect victims of abuse where the wrongdoer was not an employee. The very significant residual question that remains unanswered is whether vicarious liability has kept pace with changes in the labour market. This is very much open to doubt. In the Court of Appeal, it had been observed that:

> Changes in the structures of employment, and of contracts for the provisions of services, are widespread. Operations intrinsic to a business enterprise are routinely performed by independent contractors, over long periods, accompanied by precise obligations and high levels of control. Such patterns are evident in widely different fields of enterprise, from construction, to manufacture, to the services sector.

E. Private Law Coherence

To what extent can we expect the foregoing developments in the law of tort to impact the classification of relationships in a contractual context? Might a concern with coherence advance the cause of worker protection? As we shall see, I take the view that the impact is likely to be limited. I do not expect the akin to employment test to be adopted as such, but that is not to say that the underpinning driver of enterprise liability may not have some effect. I will also consider whether a broader approach to the course of employment is likely to be taken where employer's liability is in issue.

[40] ibid [29].

F. The Integration Test: An Alternative Route?

The akin to employment test is unlikely to be adopted in contractual disputes, but the underpinning notions of enterprise liability may nevertheless prompt changes in approach where classification of a relationship is at stake. The concept has the capacity to find expression through the integration test.[41] The use of the latter test (hitherto underutilised) as a means to identify the existence of an employment contract may now be more likely to be favoured. In *Stevenson Jordan v Harrison*, Denning LJ had said that:

> One feature which seems to run through the instances is that, under a contract of service, a man is employed as part of the business, and his work is done as an integral part of the business; whereas, under a contract for services, his work, although done for the business, is not integrated into it but is only accessory to it.[42]

Some such recent cases are to be found in the law of vicarious liability and may spark wider utilisation.[43] The greater the degree of integration, the easier it is to say that the enterprise should be responsible. In *JGE*, it was observed that

> the role of the parish priest is wholly integrated into the organisational structure of the Church's enterprise. He is, in Denning LJ's terms … part and parcel of the organisation, not only accessory to it. This picks up on the test applied by Rix LJ at [79] of *Viasystems*.[44]

Again, in language reminiscent of the test, the Supreme Court has held that an employer bears responsibility where the wrongdoer is 'effectively part and parcel of the employer's business'. *Grubb v Shannon* provides a recent Scottish instance of the test's application where it was accepted that the correct contractual classification for general purposes was one of self-employment, but the extent of integration into the business was sufficient to allow the conclusion that the relationship was akin to employment and that therefore the employer was vicariously liable.[45] Integration has also proved to be a factor of some importance in determining

[41] It is not surprising to find that statutory versions of the test in Australia deploy the language of integration. For example, in New South Wales, s 6G of the Civil Liability Act 2002 now contains the following definition: 'An *individual* is '*akin to an employee*' of an organisation if the *individual* carries out activities as an integral part of the activities carried on by the organisation and does so for the benefit of the organisation. However, an *individual* is not '*akin to an employee*' if-- (a) the activities are carried out for a recognisably independent business of the *individual* or of another person or organisation' (emphasis added).

[42] *Stevenson Jordan v Harrison* [1952] 1 TLR 101, 111.

[43] *Rees v Abertawe Bro Morgannwg* [2013] 8 WLUK 41.

[44] *JGE* (n 19) [78].

[45] *Grubb v Shannon* [2018] ScotSC 13. It was found at [13] 'that at the material time, Ms Higgins carried on activities (namely, the provision of beauty therapy treatments … assigned to her by the defender as an integral part of the defender's business, for the defender's benefit and subject to the defender's control, and not as part of a recognisably independent business of her own'. This approach can also be seen in the earlier Scottish case of *United Wholescale Grocers v Sher* 1993 SLT 284, where it was said that that an important consideration is whether the work carried out by these workmen fell to be regarded as part and parcel of a business carried out by the defender.

whether a claimant is a section 230(3)(b) worker.[46] Fraser Butlin and Allen have persuasively argued that worker status and a relationship akin to employment can be readily aligned.[47] Resort to the latter test may also accord with a purposive approach to the interpretation of worker rights.[48]

Such thinking would be relevant to contractual disputes as well as ones in tort and the need to avoid claimants being excluded from employment protection. The test can readily be seen as an expression of enterprise liability:

> There are some similarities between the expression of this test ('part and parcel of the organisation') and other attempts to explain vicarious liability by reference to an analysis of 'enterprise risk' (for example, as considered by the Supreme Court of Canada.[49]

A development of this sort would be very much in line with traditional incremental development.

The application of the integration test may also involve an element of presumption: 'if the question is whether the activity or worker is integral to the employer's business, this question can usually be answered affirmatively'.[50] This might be thought to be helpful as it would ease the challenges of adjudication in borderline cases. There would also be nothing new in the formulation of a test for the existence of the employment contract having such a feature. Many years ago, Davies and Freedland pointed out that the question 'are the arrangements in a given case consistent with a contract of service or a contract for services, can easily suggest its own answer depending upon which way round the question is put'.[51] Hepple and O'Higgins also state that 'the form of the question will dictate the answer given'.[52]

G. The Significance of Holding Out

A further way that the law of tort looks to be more inclusive is through interaction with (or perhaps under the influence of) the law of estoppel. As a result, in a tortious context, an employer who leads the public to believe that workers are his employees may be found to be vicariously liable. Holding out has already

[46] *Cotswold Developments Construction Ltd v Williams* [2006] IRLR 181 [53]; *Hospital Medical Group Limited v Westwood* [2013] ICR 415.

[47] S Fraser Butlin, and R Allen, 'Worker Status and Vicarious Liability: The Need for Coherence' (2018) University of Cambridge Faculty of Law Research Paper No 21/2018, 11: papers.ssrn.com/sol3/papers.cfm?abstract_id=3123061.

[48] A Bogg, 'The Death of Contract in Determining Employment Status' (2021) 137 *Law Quarterly Review* 392.

[49] *Sweeney v Boylan* [2006] HCA 19, (2006) 226 CLR 16; *Love v North Goonyella Coal Mining* [2017] QSC 140.

[50] *Sagaz* (n 22).

[51] P Davies and M Freedland, *Labour Law Text and Materials*, 2nd edn (London, Weidenfeld and Nicolson, 1984) 87.

[52] BA Hepple, *Hepple & O'Higgins: Employment Law*, 4th edn (London, Sweet and Maxwell, 1981) 67.

been found to be relevant in both the law of partnership and agency in determining who can be held responsible for a wrongdoer. *Hawley v Luminar Leisure Ltd* extended such reasoning to an employment situation.[53] The case dealt with a company (Luminar) that ran nightclubs and had contracted with ASE to provide them with bouncers. An employee of ASE assaulted a customer, and the court had to consider whether Luminar were vicariously liable on the basis that they were the temporary employer. The extent of factual control pointed towards a conclusion that vicarious liability arose and, in addition, the outer manifestations of the relationship between Luminar and the worker supported this position. In *Hawley*, third parties would have been unable to differentiate between borrowed workers and employees of Luminar:

> [T]here can be no doubt that any customer, passer-by or police officer seeing the doormen decked out in Luminar uniforms would have assumed they were Luminar staff. In effect, this is what they were held out to be. The doormen were not recognisable physically as the employees of ASE.[54]

It does not seem unreasonable to suggest that the court viewed Luminar as being prohibited by a form of estoppel from denying that they were in an employment relationship with the wrongdoer. *Hawley* involves an incremental change in the law by rendering representation of significance in situations other than partnership and agency.

The decision in *Hawley* was in line with an earlier decision of the High Court of Australia in *Hollis v Vabu*: 'the facts show that couriers were presented to the public and to those using the courier service as emanations of *Vabu*. They were to wear uniforms bearing *Vabu's* logo'.[55] It was observed that: 'in general the conduct of an enterprise in which persons are identified as representing that enterprise should carry an obligation to third persons to bear the cost of injury or damage'.[56] *Hollis* was, of course, a decision in tort where the interest of the injured third party may weigh heavily.[57]

How is this approach to be explained in doctrinal terms? Estoppel is not mentioned as such in *Hawley* but may nevertheless have been influential. In the alternative, might it be said that there has been an assumption of responsibility for the conduct of the wrongdoers given the way in which they were presented to the general public? A concern with doctrinal purity should not become too much of a

[53] *Hawley v Luminar Leisure Ltd* [2006] EWCA Civ 18.
[54] ibid [80].
[55] *Hollis v Vabu* [2001] HCA 44 [50].
[56] ibid [42].
[57] The Full Court examined the importance of the fact that the company 'ostensibly required, or at least expected' drivers to display the company logo on their trucks and clothing. It was found that 'although there may not have been a prescriptive policy or any express directions regarding clothing, the evidence "support[ed] the inference of an expectation" that the respondents would ordinarily wear company-branded clothing'.

focal point given the established role of representation in other areas of the law of vicarious liability.[58] In a contractual situation, any relevant statements can be seen as taking effect through the factual matrix.

Notions of holding out have not come to the fore to the same extent in employment cases, though there are some signs this is changing. In the UK, courts have found, in disputes involving platform workers, that the employer's business model may well lead to them communicating with the public in terms that suggest that those concerned are employees. Unsurprisingly, the Uber litigation confirms that those using an Uber would have assumed that the driver was an employee from the way that the business was operated; for example, passenger complaints, including those about the driver, were to be made to Uber.[59] In *Aslam v Uber* the employment tribunal had found that a number of public statements made by Uber suggested that the company itself considered the drivers employees.[60] The Court of Appeal highlighted that the:

> ET were also right to attach significance to what they described as 'the many things said and written in the name of Uber in unguarded moments which reinforce the Claimants' simple case that the organisation runs a transportation business and employs the drivers to that end'.[61]

The language used was 'incompatible' with any other conclusion.[62] This was seen as supporting a conclusion favourable to the claimant.

Addison Lee Ltd v Gascoigne offers another useful illustration in a situation where the employer sought to deny entitlement to holiday pay to a cycle courier on the basis that he was self-employed. The employment tribunal held that the written contract between the parties, which described the worker as an independent contractor, did not reflect the reality of the situation.[63] The latter conclusion was supported by scrutiny of the recruitment material on the company's website, which was

> at odds with the arms-length relationship emphasised by the contract. The website material was seeking to attract people to work for a company and to be directed by it. It rejected the company's contention that the website language should be distinguished as mere advertising puff.[64]

[58] S Deakin and Z Adams, *Markesinis and Deakin's Tort Law*, 8th edn (Oxford, Oxford University Press, 2019) point out at 551 that 'clerical and religious officers are generally held out to third parties as acting on behalf of the church or order to which they are affiliated.'

[59] *Uber v Aslam* [2021] UKSC 5. The claimants did not argue that they were employees but sought to establish with success that they were workers within the meaning of s 230(3) of the Employment Rights Act 1996.

[60] *Aslam v Uber* [2017] IRLR 4.

[61] *Uber BV v Aslam* [2018] EWCA Civ 2748; [2019] IRLR 257 [94].

[62] ibid.

[63] *Addison Lee Ltd v Gascoigne* [2018] ICR 1826.

[64] ibid [16].

Moreover:

> This was a working arrangement which did not lend itself to the interpretation which the armies of lawyers tried to promote. The claimant was part of a homogenous fleet and a homogenous operation which promoted Addison Lee to customers and looked after its own. There is nothing wrong or bad about that, it simply does not fit with the employment status for which the respondent contends.[65]

The Full Court of the Federal Court of Australia in *Jamsek v ZG Operations* took a similar approach.[66] However, on appeal, a much narrower view was taken by the High Court in deciding upon the type of material that was relevant despite the inherently inclusive nature of the contemporary factual matrix approach to interpretation.[67] The significance of this becomes apparent when the judgments of the Full Court and High Court are compared; a markedly different view was taken of the significance of public statements by the employer (or on its behalf), which related to the contractual status of workers.

The Full Court examined the importance of the fact that the company 'ostensibly required, or at least expected' drivers to display the company logo on their trucks and clothing. It was found that 'although there may not have been a prescriptive policy or any express directions regarding clothing, the evidence "support[ed] the inference of an expectation" that the respondents would ordinarily wear company-branded clothing'.[68] It was considered that, as a result, third parties would have identified 'the respondents as part of the company's staff, which may have limited the opportunity for the respondents to obtain work from others'.[69] This assessment of public understanding supported the conclusion of the Full Court that a relationship of employment existed.

This conclusion on external perception seems eminently plausible; a member of the public would almost certainly have assumed that those wearing company-branded clothing were employees. It is also the case that, in law, statements made by a party to a contract that are communicated to a wider audience may be relevant to interpretation. *Cherry Tree Investments v Landmain* dealt with the significance of documents placed on a public register. It was said that 'The reasonable reader's background knowledge would, of course, include the knowledge that the charge would be registered in a publicly accessible register upon which third parties might be expected to rely.'[70] The Court was also astute to emphasise that 'The reasonable reader would also understand that the parties had a choice about what they put into the public domain and what they kept private'.[71] A decision to communicate information to a third party is likely to be made with a specific aim

[65] ibid [22].
[66] *Jamsek v ZG Operations* [2020] FC AFC 119.
[67] *Jamsek v ZG Operations* [2022] HCA 2.
[68] *Jamsek* (n 66) [224].
[69] ibid [225].
[70] *Cherry Tree Investments v Landmain* [2013] Ch 305 [130].
[71] ibid.

in mind. I would suggest that where the contractual status of workers is concerned, it will tend to be to offer reassurance to consumers over matters such as reliability and safety. Consumers may well take the view that the degree of organisational integration associated with employment so provides.

The High Court in *Jamsek* took a different view and, in so doing, put up an alternative explanation for the display of the company's branding. It was seen as 'quite consistent with a sensible, self-interested response of an independent contractor to legitimate commercial pressure from its best customer'.[72] However, I would have thought that the Full Court's view that a true entrepreneur would not have wished to indicate a preference to trade with one customer only was much more realistic. Indeed, 'it would be impossible for the drivers to work for any other customer, or to engage in any type of entrepreneurial or profit-making activity'.[73] In any event, from the perspective of contractual interpretation, if public utterances are to be taken into account, it is surely the case that the relevant question becomes what was the likely impact on public perception. As I have already indicated, I believe that such branding would lead members of the public to assume that the activity in question was being carried out by employees. It may also be noted that the basis of overrule was not on account of any perceived doctoral misunderstanding.

H. Judicial Discretion

The innovative nature of the akin-to employment test notwithstanding, it lends itself to conservative application should the court concerned be so minded; like many common law concepts, it is highly malleable. The extent of control may be pointed to should a finding that a defendant was not responsible be favoured; it is not just employment relationships where this element may be fairly nominal.

X v Lord Advocate raised the question of whether the Crown may be vicariously liable for the delicts of a sheriff committed when not exercising his judicial functions.[74] This required the Inner House to consider whether the relationship between the Crown and a sheriff is 'akin to employment'. It was held that the Crown is not vicariously liable: 'The lack of control by the Scottish Government over the judiciary, individually and institutionally, is marked, and, we think, telling.' At one level, the decision deals with a very narrow point. However, it also flags that if more emphasis is put on the question of control, it may be more difficult to satisfy the akin to employment test. It should, of course, be borne in mind that even where employment is concerned, the degree of control possessed may be very limited.

[72] *Jamsek* (n 66) [53].

[73] C Sutherland, 'Judging the Employment Status of Workers: An Analysis of Commonsense Reasoning' (2022) 46 *Melbourne University Law Review* 281, 311.

[74] *X v Lord Advocate* [2024] CSIH 6.

Ultimately, the question is one of policy. The recognition in recent years that employers may be jointly liable where vicarious liability is concerned has not led to a similarly bold departure in employment law.[75] Tort developments may not be viewed as appropriate for transplant should the policy concerns be different.[76] However, I would maintain that changes in the labour market point towards a need for a more inclusive approach where both third party and worker rights are concerned. Contractual arrangements should not be a means to deny recovery in either case.

I. The Consequences for Employment Law

As I have indicated, I do not believe that a radical change in the common law approach is likely. There is an apparent absence of judicial enthusiasm for the creation of any new test. This may be in part because of the inherent difficulty in devising one that is better than what we already have. The increasing range of arrangements for work makes the creative challenge even harder. A more significant factor may be the increasing role that the legislature has assumed. Parliament has taken a number of decisions to expand the range of workers who attract protection to varying degrees. The courts are much more conscious of the need to respect the nuances of schemes of this sort.

The utility of the integration test was highlighted in *Sagaz*, and this may point the way towards a more likely means of connecting developments in tort with the law of the employment contract. Where the latter is concerned, the integration test is long established, though, historically, it appears to have been applied in a limited number of cases. This is perhaps because the judges have failed to elaborate upon what must be shown to demonstrate that integration has taken place. Lord Reed's speech in *Cox* v *Ministry of Justice* shows the difficulties where he concluded that

> a relationship other than one of employment is in principle capable of giving rise to vicarious liability where harm is wrongfully done by an individual who carries on activities as an integral part of the business activities carried on by a defendant and for its benefit (rather than his activities being entirely attributable to the conduct of a recognisably independent business of his own or of a third party).[77]

This might be thought to restate the problem rather than to advance a superior analytical tool.

Where labour law and the law of tort meet, the aims of the latter are likely to prevail. A finding that an employment relationship exists is more likely in the

[75] See also C Wynn-Evans, 'One Man, two Guvnors: Revisiting the Principle against two Employers' (2024) 53 *Industrial Law Journal* 94.
[76] *Cairns v Visteon* [2007] ICR 616.
[77] *Cox* v *Ministry of Justice* [2016] UKSC 10, [2016] AC 660 [24].

personal injuries context than, for instance, in an unfair dismissal claim.[78] This was apparent before *Barclays Bank* but has now been made explicit at the highest level. In the face of the shadowy boundary line between employment and self-employment, the most likely resolution, in a difficult case, will be one that furthers the aims of the law of tort. After all, as Sedley LJ pointed out in *Dacas v Brook Street Bureau*:

> [A] great deal more hangs on the legal status of a worker than the worker's own rights, though they are important enough. An employer is vicariously liable for injury to others caused by an employee's carelessness, and is required by statute to insure against it; but an enterprise will have no such liability for harm done by somebody working for it who is not an employee.[79]

Those concerns might be thought to be particularly acute where personal injury is in issue. Nevertheless, the question remains whether the akin-to employment test should or will have purchase outside of the law of tort. Were it to do so, the consequences for both employers and workers would be considerable. It is, though, far from certain that any degree of judicial boldness will be displayed in the case of the employment relationship.

One reason for doubting that this will be the way forward lies in the fact that statute has already spoken.[80] In particular, a number of statutory employment rights have been extended to workers who meet the definition set out in legislation. The limited extent of the increased protection has been quite deliberate. Legislative intervention indicates a recognition that the common law tests for the existence of a contract of employment have made it too easy for employers to construct working relationships in a way that denies the benefit of core employment protection rights. The creation of the section 230 (3)(b) worker can be seen as a response to the use of contractual arrangements to avoid employment protection. Given the creation (relatively recently) of that carefully calibrated scheme, it is arguable that the courts should not go beyond this. Similar arguments over the impact of statutory intervention prevailed in *Johnson v Unisys*.[81] It is worth noting that the legislature has been content to acquiesce in modest changes to the judicial position.[82] The common law tests have evolved over the years, and that appears to be without controversy and does not lead to suggestions that legislative intervention is called for to constrain, control, or direct. It should also be said that common law invention is invited on occasion. The statutory definition of employee

[78] *Lane v Shire Roofing* [1995] IRLR 495.

[79] *Dacas v Brook Street Bureau* [2004] IRLR 358, 368.

[80] In his dissenting speech in *Uber* (n 61) [166], Underhill LJ said that 'Even if it were open to the Courts to seek to fashion a common law route to affording protection to Uber drivers and others in the same position, I would be cautious about going down that road. The whole question of whether and how to adapt existing employment law protections to the development of the so-called gig economy, and in particular to the use of service-provision platforms such as Uber, is under active review by the Government at present'.

[81] *Johnson v Unisys* [2001] UKHL 13, [2003] 1 AC 513.

[82] *Dacas* (n 79) 368.

in section 230 of the Employment Rights Act 1996, by its utterly minimalist nature, is dependent for its successful operation upon judicial elaboration. The courts, in turn, have evolved their approach in the light of developments in working arrangements and practices, and this process continues to this day. The significance, for example, placed on the employer's right of control has changed a great deal over the years, and, in *Cox*, Lord Reed commented as follows: control 'is a factor which is unlikely to be of independent significance in most cases'.[83] It seems unlikely that the common law tests have become set in stone, and further evolution may be anticipated. Had Parliament wished otherwise, then it would have been obliged to set out a much more detailed scheme in the 1996 Act.

Incremental change is one thing, but importing the 'akin to employment' test into the law of contract might be seen as an altogether different matter. Hitherto, judicial changes, where categorisation is concerned, have been made with a view to the provision of greater clarity and precision when the identification of the contract of employment is in issue. The changes in tort law are not of that ilk. The law of vicarious liability accepts that the categories of relevant relationships are not closed and that it is legitimate to extend an employer's responsibility to relationships beyond the existing categories that further the same policy factors. I would suggest that it is much more likely that the courts will not adopt the akin to employment test out with cases of vicarious liability. The context of tort actions is very different; it will often be the case that the harm suffered is personal injury, and facilitating recovery goes to the very core of the aims of the law. The legislature has been much more content to leave matters of reparation to the courts.

VI. Conclusions

It appears that enterprise liability is much less likely to be a consideration where the interests of employees are at stake. This is not inevitable. The decision of the Supreme Court in *Dryden v Johnson Matthey*, which took an expansive view of actionable physical injury, can be seen as an example.[84] In *Dryden*, it was alleged that the claimants had suffered financially as a result of sensitisation to platinum salts, being unable to take work in any environment where further exposure might occur. The employer's behaviour gave rise to a breach of a duty in negligence at common law, but, by way of defence to the claim, it was denied that sensitisation constituted damage for the purposes of a personal injury action.[85] This was the key point of contention in *Dryden*, as physical symptoms do not result from platinum

[83] *Cox* (n 77) [21].
[84] *Dryden v Johnson Matthey* [2018] UKSC 18, [2019] AC 403.
[85] *Rothwell v Chemical & Insulating Co* [2006] EWCA Civ 27 confirmed that a successful claim requires demonstrable physical injury.

sensitisation in the absence of further exposure. The Court of Appeal had denied recovery on the basis that there had been no physical injury.

In allowing the appeal, the Supreme Court took the view that sensitisation involved a physiological change to the body that was more than negligible and indeed actionable. There is surprisingly little judicial guidance on what constitutes personal injury, and the approach of the Supreme Court is to be welcomed; a condition that was asymptomatic and would only lead to physical symptoms in a very restricted and avoidable set of circumstances sufficed.

A more conservative court may well have taken a different view.[86] In *Barber v Somerset CC*, in the context of judicial elaboration of a restrictive set of rules on occupational stress claims, risks arising from the 'reasonable pressures' of working life were not to be borne by the employer.[87] It would not have been surprising if 'mere physiological changes which happen to have financial consequences' (to adopt the language of Sales LJ in the Court of Appeal) had been viewed in a similar light. The Court of Appeal was of the view that personal injury had not occurred because sensitisation did not lead to 'detrimental physical effects in the course of ordinary life'. *Dryden* constitutes a laudable common law reform to ensure that protection against the risk of physical harm is comprehensive and requires that the employer bear the risk of physiological changes that impair bodily capacity. In so doing, the decision is consistent with the law of employers' liability being driven by notions of enterprise liability.

An important feature of the employer's common law obligations to employees is that the duty to take reasonable care in respect of health and safety is non-delegable.[88] In my view, enterprise liability is just as capable of providing a contemporary rationalisation as it is where vicarious liability is concerned. In any event, it is more than arguable that the employer's duty extends beyond employees to those in a relationship akin to employment. The employer is responsible for those individuals when third parties are harmed on the basis that they are integral to the enterprise. Logically, the position must surely be the same when the worker is injured. This would be consistent with the way in which the law of employer's liability is evolving. Munkman states that

> under the general law of negligence, duties perhaps similar to those owed to employees have in certain circumstances been found to be owed by an undertaking to persons not in its employment. The cases have often been viewed as exceptions. Yet they increasingly illustrate the readiness of the law to award damages where one person has assumed a responsibility for another whether through contract or through the factual nature of their relationship … But much uncertainty remains.[89]

[86] For further discussion see C Wynn-Evans, 'The Vicissitudes of (Working) Life: Employee Economic Well-being, Risk Allocation and Indemnification' (2023) 52 *Industrial Law Journal* 776.

[87] *Barber v Somerset CC* [2004] UKHL 13.

[88] *McDermid v Nash Dredging and Reclamation Co Ltd* [1987] AC 906.

[89] B Cotter, and D Bennet (eds), *Munkman on Employer's Liability*, 17th edn (London, LexisNexis Butterworths, 2019) 4.78 and referred to by Lord Sandison in *Rose v WNL Investments* [2023] CSOH 49 [24].

More generally, though, enterprise liability has driven reform for the benefit of third parties rather than the enterprise's workers. The element of disparate treatment is readily apparent. Where the scope of employment is concerned, this would seem particularly difficult to justify. It is hard to imagine that, should a member of the public have been injured in *Reynolds*, they would not have been able to recover on the basis of vicarious responsibility. Categorising something done at the employer's instigation as voluntary may, in some circumstances, be nothing more than a form of contracting-out of the employer's responsibilities for health and safety. The employer should not be able to escape responsibility for the consequences of personal injury arising should a risk of the enterprise materialise.

Hesitancy over the akin to employment test is somewhat easier to understand; deference to the legislature looms large. More could readily be done, though, by greater creativity over the application of existing concepts. Holding-out could also play a bigger part and readier recourse to the integration test could be significant.

10

Is There a Right to Work?

ROBERT STEVENS

I. Introduction

Our topic in this chapter is the common law, our judge-made law. The claim is that it neither does nor should recognise any 'right to work'.[1] By 'right to work' is meant a claim-right against others that they do not (unreasonably or otherwise) impede our ability to work or trade. The judicial statements from time-to-time,[2] that such a right exists involve a confusion, whether negligent or deliberate, of the liberty to work, the special immunities from enforcement of contractual restrictions on working or trading, with the quite different question of whether there is a claim-right to work, with correlative duties on others.

This claim involves bringing together three areas of law usually examined separately: the so-called economic torts; the doctrine of restraint of trade; and the availability of injunctive relief to restrain employees from working for others.

I shall (largely) leave unexamined the extent to which the UK's international obligations, in particular in human rights instruments, give rise to a duty on the state to secure work for citizens. Also uncovered will be the question of when and why a contract of employment will require an employer to provide a worker with work to do (as where someone is employed on piece rates, or, in the modern era, on a 'zero hours' contract).

II. Damages

A. The Economic Torts (sic)

I first studied the economic torts more than 30 years ago. I had chosen to study 'Labour Law' as one of my options on the Oxford Jurisprudence BA. In order to

[1] For an earlier more wide-ranging study, see B Hepple, 'A Right to Work?' (1981) 10 *Industrial Law Journal* 65.

[2] Eg, *Keeble v Hickeringill* (1708) 11 East 574, 103 ER 1172 (Holt CJ).

understand the various statutory immunities that trade unions enjoy from civil action in trade disputes (and the withdrawal of those immunities where the union has failed to take various procedural steps such as ballots) it is first necessary to understand the economic torts. My regular tutor in 'Tort Law' (*sic*) did not teach the area, and so I was sent to a different tutor at another college who did. I was then presented with reading lists of staggering length and expected to learn by rote the various formulas for relief that there were (and are).

These formulas seemed to have no rhyme nor reason to them. Some 'torts' required intent, whilst others did not, and what needed to be intended varied. Some required 'unlawfulness', but what that meant was obscure and seemed to differ from one rule to the next. Some, inexplicably, required an agreement with a third party, whilst some did not. In this apparent randomness, these 'torts' resembled other areas of law that I had been taught, such as equitable estoppel and constructive trusts, where the student was expected to take a leap of faith, accept that the rules existed, and then, through a feat of memory, remember the case names that stood for each element of each separate magic spell of liability. Back then, being less world-weary, more deferential to authority, and with a better memory than now, I happily complied with the task expected of me. Around two weeks after the exams had taken place, however, most of what I had forced into my skull through an effort of will had disappeared.

This approach was, and sadly still is, characteristic of the pragmatic or realist approach to the law of torts that was and is so prevalent. If we try to understand private law in general, and the law of torts in particular, as a series of liability spells, with formulas constructed on the basis of the more or less arbitrary choices of here today gone tomorrow judges, we have no basis for either understanding or assessing it. Worse, the law itself will have no stability, as any decision by any court, regardless of its priority in the legal pecking order, may always potentially be overturned. Perhaps judges and practitioners may sometimes be forgiven for ignoring even the most basic theorising about private law. There is no such excuse for academics.

Torts are civil wrongs. Civil wrongs are the breach of a duty owed to another. The breach of a duty owed to another is, synonymously, the infringement of the right of another. Where such a wrong occurs, a secondary obligation, to pay damages, arises. This secondary obligation takes the form of seeking to achieve the result, so far as money can do so, of placing the party wronged in the position they would have been in if the wrong had not occurred. This secondary duty of next best compliance is best understood as based upon the same reasons that justified the primary right that has been infringed. The reasons for the primary entitlement do not disappear but continue, now justifying an entitlement to damages that are their monetarised form.[3]

[3] For authors from different perspective making versions of the above argument, see N MacCormick, *Legal Right and Social Democracy: Essays in Legal and Political Philosophy* (Oxford, Oxford University Press, 1982) 212; E Weinrib, *The Idea of Private Law* (Oxford, Oxford University Press,1995) 135; J Raz,

As will be explained, most of the 'economic torts' cannot be justified by reference to reasoning of this form. The belief that they are 'torts' seems to be a product of the invalid syllogism: (1) torts allow for the recovery of loss suffered; (2) rule X allows for the recovery of loss suffered; (3) therefore rule X is a tort.[4] Perhaps, even less charitably, it is no more than the assumption that the rules that have traditionally appeared in standard textbooks on the law of torts must be torts, without further reflection.

B. Rights and Loss

It is vital to distinguish between *rights* and *loss*.[5] Put in Latin, we must distinguish between *iniuria* and *damnum*. So, to take a simple example:

> A driver negligently crashes his lorry into a bridge, damaging it and rendering it unsafe. The bridge has been leased by a railway company. The railway company is forced to cease operations while the bridge is repaired. As a result, it suffers £10m of loss.

Can the railway company claim for its losses from the lorry driver (or his employer)? As we all know, a lease gives the owner a right *in rem*. A right *in rem* is a right to a thing good against the rest of the world. The rest of the world includes the lorry driver. The lorry driver, through his negligence, violated this (property) right to the bridge. (At one time, as the damage was directly inflicted, the tort would have been called trespass in England, and still would be in some jurisdictions such as Australia). A claim for damages is therefore possible by the lessee.

What if the railway company merely had a contractual licence for trains to cross the bridge from time to time? A contractual licence, unlike a lease, merely gives rise to a right *in personam* against the owner of the bridge. Certainly, the owner of the bridge has a claim against the negligent lorry driver, but does the railway company? In principle, the answer is no. A licence, as the word states, merely confers a privilege. The licensee commits no wrong, as against the bridge owner, by making use of the bridge. Such a licence does not, however, give rise to a right *in rem*, exigible against the rest of the world. The railway company has suffered *damnum sine iniuria:* loss without the violation of a right.

'Personal Practical Conflicts' in P Baumann and M Betzler (eds), *Practical Conflicts: New Philosophical Essays* (Cambridge, Cambridge University Press, 2004) 172; R Stevens, *Torts and Rights* (Oxford, Oxford University Press, 2007) 59; A Ripstein, 'As if it Never Happened' (2007) 48 *William and Mary Law Review* 1968. The best long treatment of the idea is J Gardner 'What Is Tort Law For? Part 1: The Place of Corrective Justice' (2011) 30 *Law and Philosophy* 1.

[4] It is perhaps unfair to single out any particular author, but J Murphy, *The Province and Politics of the Economic Torts* (Oxford, Hart Publishing, 2022) reflects that widespread line of thought.

[5] See *Rogers v Dutt* (1860) 13 Moo PC 209, 241; 15 ER 78 (PC), 90: 'it is essential to an action in tort that the action complained of should, under the circumstances, be legally wrongful as regards the party complaining: that is, it must prejudicially affect the plaintiff in some legal right; merely that it will however directly do him harm in his interests is not enough'. (Dr Lushington).

At least as a claim framed as a tort, such loss is not actionable, not because of the operation of any exclusionary rule in relation to economic loss, but because no tort has in fact occurred with respect to the railway company. Of course, the railway company may have a claim for breach of contract against the bridge owner if the bridge is inaccessible, and the bridge owner certainly has a claim against the lorry driver, but *damnum sine iniuria*, loss without the violation of a right, is not, without more, actionable.

C. Abuse of Rights (sic)

Hohfeld,[6] building on the work of others,[7] stipulated that clarity of thought was assisted by distinguishing between different senses in which we use rights: claim-rights, liberties,[8] powers, and immunities. Hohfeld's distinctions are based upon our usage in ordinary language (if they were not, he might as well have distinguished blue-rights from green-rights). However, he was also stipulative: the distinctions he drew were logical ones and could not be 'incorrect' even if many others used these words in different senses. In Hohfeld's world, powers cannot correlate with duties, and that is the end of the matter. All Hohfeldian relations involve two persons and an action or state of affairs.[9]

For our purposes, the important distinction is between claim-rights and liberties. I have a claim-right that you do not walk on my land without permission. You have a liberty with respect to me to walk down the highway. Where my claim-rights with respect to you end, your liberties with respect to me begin.

With these strictures in mind, we can see that it makes no sense to talk of a doctrine of 'abuse of claim-rights'. If I have a claim right against you, you are under a duty to me to do or not do an action. I cannot by *my* action abuse that right.

Technically, the only form of Hohfeldian right that is ever exercised is a power. And so the terminology of 'abuse of rights' should in principle only apply to the abuse of powers (eg, arbitrary dismissal of an employee). If I take a walk in the park, I have a liberty to do so, but that effects no legal change. The only thing exercised by walking is me.[10]

Some civilian legal systems recognise liability for loss where the defendant intentionally acts in a way that the law stipulates that the action was one the

[6] WN Hohfeld, 'Some Fundamental Legal Conceptions as Applied in Judicial Reasoning' (1913) 23 *Yale Law Journal* 16.

[7] See especially J Salmond, *The First Principles of Jurisprudence* (London, Stevens and Haynes, 1893).

[8] Called by Hohfeld 'privileges'. A privilege is a special liberty that is not possessed by persons generally. See also immunities, which are exceptional situations where another has no power with respect to us. We have no word in English for 'immunities possessed by persons generally'.

[9] E Eldridge, 'Rights That' (2024) 44 *Oxford Journal of Legal Studies* 808.

[10] See E Eldrige, 'Rights and Their Exercise' (forthcoming).

defendant had liberty to do if this is done with the intention of inflicting harm on another. This is also, if inelegantly, often described as an 'abuse of rights'.

A classic example of the kind of fact scenario caught by this doctrine would be that of *Tuttle v Buck*.[11] Ned Tuttle was the only barber in the village of Howard Lake, Missouri. He made profits of $800 per annum. Cassius Buck ('Mega Buck'),[12] a rich man who allegedly held a grudge against Tuttle, opened premises that he leased at a nominal rent to barbers whom he paid a wage in return for their work. Tuttle claimed that this was done maliciously with the sole purpose of driving him out of business. The court accepted as a matter of principle that if this malice could be established, this was actionable.

If a legal system does recognise liability in such a case, it would be better described as an 'abuse of liberty' rule. Such a rule is premised upon there being no general right that others do not harm us through trade, so that no tort is committed. What makes the loss actionable is the intention with which the loss is inflicted, not the nature of the act. This may be contrasted with torts properly so-called, where a *mens rea* element (ie, a state of mind) is never a requirement for actionability.

Both inside and outside the law, duties arise because of reasons for action that exist independently of our being aware of them. Legal obligations owed to other people, our entitlements one against another, are a sub-set of our duties. They, too, are legitimately based upon objective reasons that apply to each of us equally. My entitlements against you, to my person, my things, and my reputation, do not depend upon, or vary according to, your state of mind. We are familiar with this from the objective standard of care applied in the law of negligence,[13] that a defendant may be liable for false imprisonment even if they honestly and reasonably believed that they had authority to deter the claimant,[14] and that a defamatory statement is wrongful regardless of whether the speaker honestly and reasonably believed it to be true. Similarly, parties can change the default set of rights they have one against another, primarily through the law of contract, but this is done through their actions together in the world that have an objective meaning, not through their subjective wills, even when they fortuitously coincide.[15]

Crimes often have, as part of their definition, a *mens rea* requirement. Torts properly so-called, which are the infringement of rights, never turn upon what is happening in the defendant's head.[16]

[11] *Tuttle v Buck* 119 NW 946 (Minn 1909). But see *Eldridge v Johndrow* 345 P 3d 553 (Utah 2015) where the Utah Supreme Court refused to follow *Tuttle v Buck*.

[12] The joke is Tony Weir's.

[13] *Vaughan v Menlove* (1837) 3 Bing NC 468, 132 ER 490 (CP).

[14] *Governor of Brockhill Prison, ex p Evans (No 2)* [2001] 2 AC 19 (HL).

[15] See further R Stevens, 'What is an Agreement?' (2020) 136 *Law Quarterly Review* 599.

[16] In some extreme cases the movements of our bodies cease to be our responsibility, as in cases of automatism. As in the criminal law, that is a matter of *actus reus* not *mens rea*. On deceit, see below p 213.

D. *Allen v Flood*

The 'great case' of *Allen v Flood*,[17] has a far stronger claim to be the most important decision in the law of torts than the trivial, but more famous, *Donoghue v Stevenson*.[18] It stands for two foundational principles in the common law: first, that the intentional infliction of economic loss is not prima facie actionable,[19] and second, that we have no (general) right to work or trade.

The claimants were shipwrights, engaged each day to work on their employer's ship. The defendant was the secretary of a union who informed his employer that if the claimants continued to be re-engaged, the union members would not work. The employer consequently refused to re-engage the claimants, who claimed for their consequent economic loss from the defendant. The claim failed. A 6-3 majority concluded that the intentional infliction of economic harm is not, without more, actionable, and that we have no general right that others do not inhibit our ability to trade. (The eight judges who had been asked to assist the House by giving advice split 6-2 in favour of the action succeeding).

Is *Allen v Flood* defensible? Should the intentional infliction of economic harm be actionable?

Regardless of the merits in the abstract of such a starting point, the judges of the 1890s were wise to reject any such general judge-made rule.

No doubt someone who acts with the intention of inflicting harm on another without good motive where no compelling countervailing reason applies is lacking in virtue. This is, as a matter of morality, a very bad way to behave. Where the harm occurs, we can identify a victim of the appalling behaviour. However, we cannot justify using the force of the state to enforce virtuous behaviour where no right violation occurs. Those who deliberately do not pick up babies drowning in an inch of water may be appalling and disgusting individuals, but it should not be the job of the law to make us be good. The mere fact that Mega Buck's behaviour was wanting in virtue, and that another is worse off as a result, cannot be sufficient to bring it within the province of the law.

However, it might be said that the central purpose of law is to give each of us the ability to live our lives independently of the choices of others. If rights afford us the space within which we may pursue our own ends, equally with others, abusing the freedom that the law accords us with the intention of harming others (and thereby inhibiting their freedom) may be thought to be contrary to a system of rights.[20] Although making such intentional infliction of harm actionable may be

[17] *Allen v Flood* [1898] AC 1; Hohfeld (n 6) 40. See also R Heuston, 'Judicial Prosopography' (1986) 102 *Law Quarterly Review* 90, 97.

[18] *Donoghue v Stevenson* [1932] AC 562.

[19] See also *Mogul Steamship Co v McGregor Gow & Co* [1892] AC 25 (HL); *Bradford v Pickles* [1895] AC 587 (HL).

[20] See E Weinrib, 'Private Law and Public Right' (2011) 61 *University of Toronto Law Journal* 191 discussed in JW Neyers, 'Explaining the Inexplicable? Four Manifestations of Abuse of Rights in

justifiable, it could not be because such behaviour constitutes a tort, in the sense of the violation of a specific claim-right. The entire point of such a rule is that no tort, or claim-right infringement, is in play.

That there are good reasons for the common law of England not having adopted a doctrine that the *intentional* infliction of loss is actionable is well illustrated by *Tuttle v Buck* and *Allen v Flood*. In the former case, the defendant's behaviour enhanced the competition in the area for the provision of haircuts. The price fell, benefiting everyone other than Tuttle. What kind of competitive practice should and should not be actionable is a matter of public policy, largely driven by economic concerns. Judges are peculiarly ill-suited to judge these matters, lacking both the political legitimacy and technical competence to engage in the line-drawing exercise that is required. Similarly, a general doctrine of liability for the intentional infliction of loss would seem to render actionable all forms of industrial action by trade unions. What should and should not be permitted (eg, secondary action) and the procedural hurdles that such unions should have to take (eg balloting) are questions for a democratic legislature, not a judge. There seem, therefore, to be good prudential reasons why the common law refused to recognise any general rule that the intentional infliction of loss is actionable, as this would have forced judges into answering policy questions as to the scope of justifiable exceptions to actionability that they are not equipped to answer.

Some authors claim that the judges do have the practical competence and political legitimacy to answer questions of this kind.[21] However, although judges do sometimes rely upon 'policy' arguments in reaching decisions, how and why this may be legitimate needs careful treatment. If, for example, a statute lays down a rule reflecting a certain policy choice, this may legitimately be relied upon by the judges in determining other related rules. An example of this form of reasoning is the use by the House of Lords of the scope of the statutory rules for trade union immunities in the law of torts to determine the separate issue of what constitutes 'illegitimate pressure' for purposes of the law of duress.[22] Sometimes, a policy decision may properly lie with the government, so that judicial decisions should take into account that policy and seek not to impede it. For example, in *Denis v Ministry of Defence*,[23] an injunction restraining the take-off of Harrier jump jets from an airbase in the Cotswolds, which constituted a private nuisance, was refused because of the public interest in the defence of the realm. Under our constitutional order, what is required for the defence of the UK is a matter for the government, specifically, the Secretary of State for Defence, and the courts should

English Law' in D Nolan and A Robertson (eds), *Rights and Private Law* (Oxford, Hart Publishing, 2011).

[21] C Purshouse, 'Tort Theory and the Interpretive Sleight of Hand' (2024) 140 *Law Quarterly Review* 318.

[22] *Universal Tankships of Monrovia v International Transport Workers Federation* [1983] 1 AC 366.

[23] *Denis v Ministry of Defence* [2003] EWHC 793 (QB).

not stultify the policy adopted. This does not entail, however, that no wrong was being committed, and damages should be, and were, available.

However, these legitimate uses of policy reasoning are quite different from requiring a judge to exercise their *personal* judgement as to when and why industrial action or competition is legitimate. Such questions are a matter for the legislature, not them, and the judges should not create rules that require them to give answers to questions that they have neither the technical nor political competence to give.

It may be thought unjust for judges to hold back from correcting injustice based upon prudential reasons such as these. However, there is a chasm of difference between using state force, especially if only sourced in a judge-made rule, to compel individuals to behave in a particular way based upon prudential policy reasons unrelated to the parties before the court and refusing to use state power, especially where only sanctioned by judicial decision, to correct an injustice where there may be powerful policy reasons, which a court is unable to assess, not to do so.

But we can identify specific examples of the 'abuse of rights' doctrine within the common law, where these problems of legitimacy do not arise. The familiar comparative pattern of the common law eschewing the sweeping general rule of civilian systems while accepting specifically defined examples is discernible. None of these amount to a 'right to work' doctrine, however.

E. Causing Loss by Unlawful Means

If, in a modern-day English equivalent of *Tuttle v Buck*, the disgruntled Buck had achieved his ends not through an act of competition but through threats of violence to Tuttle's customers, there is no doubt that a claim by Tuttle would succeed. It has long been accepted,[24] that if unlawful means are used to inflict the loss, this may be actionable, even though vis-à-vis the claimant, the means do not constitute a wrong done to them.

However, we still need to articulate the basis for this rule if we are to properly formulate what its boundaries ought to be. The claim is *not* based upon the violation of any right of the claimant, and as a result, cannot be justified as a tort, or the continuity of the reasons for the rights that the claimant had *ex ante*.[25]

One view, which I confess I have expressed but which I would now reject, is that it is an exception to the doctrine of privity of right.[26] Privity is normally associated with the law of contract, but it is a general feature of private law, necessitated

[24] *Garret v Taylor* (1620) Cro Jac 567; *Tarleton v M'Gawley* (1793) 1 Peake NPC 270; *Allen v Flood* [1898] AC 1, 96 (Lord Watson).

[25] JW Neyers, 'Rights-Based Justifications for the Tort of Unlawful Interference with Economic Relations' (2008) 28 *Legal Studies* 215.

[26] Stevens (n 3) 188–190.

by its logic. Unfortunately, it is sometimes thought of as an exclusionary rule, when in reality, the reason why others cannot sue when I am punched on the nose is that their rights are not violated. The only person who can enforce a right is the right-holder, and persons who suffer loss as a result of the infringement of the right of another have no standing to complain against the wrongdoer. We have seen an example of this principle already. No doubt, the damage to the bridge by the lorry driver infringed a right of the owner, but others who suffered loss but had no right to it cannot sue. If a husband is worse off because of the defamation of his wife that resulted in her losing her job, he has no standing to sue. If a nuisance is created so as to interfere with the quiet enjoyment of land, licensees cannot claim for their loss. If I am injured by the careless driving of a taxi driver, and so unable to work, my dependent children have no right of action. A third party who suffers loss because of the failure to satisfy an assumption of responsibility made to someone else has no right upon which to found a claim.[27]

There are exceptions to the doctrine of privity, but they are mainly statutory in origin. For example, the Fatal Accidents Act 1976 and the Congenital Disabilities (Civil Liability) Act 1976 both create such exceptions. These have clear (if controversial) policy bases.[28] These statutes are not, and should not be thought of as creating torts. Rather, dependants and children unborn at the time of a tort are allowed to sue for the loss they suffer as a result of a tort suffered by someone else.

One possibility, therefore, is that causing loss by unlawful means is similarly an exception to privity. If this were correct, then 'unlawfulness' should not include crimes and other public wrongs that do not also constitute private wrongs. Proof of loss by the person used should not be required, but a wrong to them should be. This restriction on what could constitute 'unlawfulness' to torts was accepted by four of the members of the House of Lords in what is now our leading case, *OBG v Allan*.[29]

Such an exception to privity can be criticised as ad hoc.[30] It seems to lack the policy rationales of the statutory exceptions. Further, it is difficult to articulate why, as a matter of principle, any such exception should be made merely because the defendant intended to cause the claimant loss.[31] If no claim by anybody at all is allowed, this would mean that the hypothetical Buck has used the potential customers as a means to his own ends, but this would indicate that they should have a claim, not Tuttle.

[27] This is the best explanation for *Paul v Royal Wolverhampton NHS Trust* [2024] UKSC 1.

[28] See Stevens (n 3) 176, 185–186; T Liau, *Standing in Private Law* (Oxford, Oxford University Press, 2023) 201–214, 228–236.

[29] *OBG v Allan* [2007] UKHL 21 [49] (Lord Hoffmann), [270] (Lord Walker), [306] (Baroness Hale), [320] (Lord Brown), but see Lord Nicholls in dissent [150]–[155].

[30] P Davies and P Sales, 'Intentional Harm, Accessories and Conspiracies' (2018) 134 *Law Quarterly Review* 69, 75.

[31] For a valiant attempt, see J Neyers, 'Causing Loss by Unlawful Means: Should the High Court of Australia follow *OBG Ltd v Allan*?' in S Degeling, J Edelman and J Goudkamp (eds), *Torts in Commercial Law* (Pyrmont, NSW, Thomas Reuters, 2012), 117, 125–131.

A better rationale would be to see the doctrine as a species of 'abuse of rights'. If the objection to the recognition of a *general* principle against the intentional infliction of loss is the incompatibility with the necessary policy restrictions upon it with the judicial function, this disappears as a problem where the means used are themselves independently unlawful. Once the law has already said 'this should not be done' no further policy question as to whether it should be permitted arises. If this is the rationale for this species of claim, then it would indicate that *any* kind of unlawfulness should suffice.

It can be argued that the 'unlawfulness' restriction is irrelevant to what is just as between claimant and defendant. If the defendant intentionally inflicts loss on the claimant, why should it matter, as between them, if the conduct used to do so also constitutes a traffic offence, insider trading, or a wrong to an unrelated third party?[32] What has that got to do with the claimant? This objection has force, but the reason for the restriction on actionability is unrelated to the justice as between the parties; rather, it relates to systemic concerns that would arise if judge-made law started from the proposition that intentionally inflicting loss is actionable without more ado.[33] The 'unlawful means' restriction removes an objection to this kind of claim; it is not part of its positive justification.

Two further arguments may be made in favour of the narrow approach to unlawfulness of the majority of the House of Lords. First, it may be said that, in practice, the 'economic torts' most commonly arise in a competition or industrial action dispute. These areas are now largely regulated by legislation. It is unacceptable for judges to take an expansive approach and thereby upset the balance struck by the legislature, as the House of Lords arguably did by recognising a 'tort' of intimidation in *Rookes v Barnard*[34] that, because of its novelty, was not covered by the various statutory immunities applicable to trade unions.[35] This is certainly an important reason for adopting a conservative approach, but it does not explain why this particular restriction is the one preferred (save that it is consistent with case law up until now). Further, it does not fit happily with the House of Lords' apparent expansion of what can constitute an intention to cause loss in this context,[36] nor, as we shall see, with the subsequent expansionist approach to other 'economic torts.'

Second English law, like other common law jurisdictions, has not traditionally drawn any distinction between offences that are *malum in se* and those that are *malum prohibitum*. As a matter of history, the latter are the province of the legislature, but some offences that are without doubt *malum in se* (such as malicious

[32] For this thought see *OBG v Allen* [146] *per* Lord Nicholls.

[33] See also T Weir, *Economic Torts* (Oxford, Oxford University Press, 1997).

[34] *Rookes v Barnard* [1964] AC 1129.

[35] See *OBG* [306] (Baroness Hale); Leonard Hoffmann 'The Rise and Fall of the Economic Torts' in S Degeling, J Edelman and J Goudkamp (eds), *Torts in Commercial Law* (Pyrmont, NSW, Thomas Reuters, 2012) 105.

[36] *OBG* [62], criticised by H Carty, *An Analysis of the Economic Torts*, 2nd edn (Oxford, Oxford University Press, 2010) 80–84.

wounding) are now also put into statutory form. It may be that it would go beyond the regulatory purpose of some statutory offences that are merely *malum prohibitum* (eg, speeding offences) if they also sufficed for the private law action of causing loss by unlawful means. However, this possible vice could be dealt with through construction of the statute to assess whether it was intended to provide a comprehensive scheme.

If the suggested more expansive approach to unlawfulness had been taken, it would have been possible to amalgamate this principle of recovery with that adopted in relation to the 'tort' of misfeasance in a public office. This, again, is a liability rule that does not require that 'the defendant has invaded a legally protected right'.[37] The classic example of such liability is the deliberate and unjustified withholding of a licence by an official that the plaintiff requires to trade, causing consequential loss.[38] Here again, we have independent unlawfulness, albeit of a public, not private, kind. The mental element required is an intention to harm or knowledge of both the unlawfulness and that this would probably cause harm to the plaintiff.[39] This claim too should not be seen as a tort in the sense of private wrong, a violation of a specific right. Rather, it too is a species of liability for the intentional infliction of loss, kept within bounds by the requirement of independent unlawfulness. There can be no question as to whether behaviour of this kind is something we wish to hold back from inhibiting (see also deceit). We fail to see these connections between these different 'torts' in part because of our conceiving of the 'economic torts' as formulas for the recovery of loss, whose rules have no logic, save a policy choice.

F. Conspiracy

First, the position in principle.

Where two or more persons conspire together, how in principle can this agreement impact upon their respective liabilities?

If the actions of one of them carried out under the agreement constitute a tort, a violation of a right of the claimant, it is possible to say that because of the conspiracy, the actions of each party to the agreement are attributed to all other parties. Where the actions by one conspirator have been agreed to and constitute a tort, each commits the same tort. Similarly, if the actions of one conspirator constitute a crime, it is possible for the law to say that all parties to the agreement commit this crime because of the effect of their conspiring together. Because the criminal law, unlike the law of torts, contains inchoate offences, it should not necessarily be required that the criminal action is carried out for the offence to be made out.

[37] *Three Rivers District Council v Bank of England (No 3)* [2003] 2 AC 1, 239 (Lord Hobhouse).
[38] Eg, *Roncarelli v Duplessis* [1959] SCR 121 (SCC).
[39] *Three Rivers District Council v Bank of England (No 3)* [2003] 2 AC 1, 191 (Lord Steyn).

For conspirators to be criminals, what they must conspire to do must be a crime, and for conspirators to be tortfeasors, what they must conspire to do must be a tort. Where the actions do not constitute a tort, the agreement alone cannot, as a matter of principle, transform it into one. Synonymously, where the actions agreed to be carried out do not constitute the violation of any right, the agreement cannot create any right violation. A conspiracy to commit a tort is not necessarily a crime, and a conspiracy to commit a crime is not necessarily a tort.

Put another way, if D doing a specific action does not constitute the violation of any right of C, can D doing the same action pursuant to an agreement with X, constitute the violation of any right of C? No. It should not matter whether the action is lawful or a crime. If it does not constitute a violation of any right of C, it is not a tort.

A criminal law wrong is a breach of a public duty, in the sense of a duty that is undirected and not owed to any specific person or group. If I possess heroin, or park on double yellow lines, or trade using insider information, my crime may have no identifiable victim. Even where a victim may be identified, as in murder or theft, the duty that is breached is not owed to the victim but to society. Not all crimes are torts, and not all torts are crimes.

The distinction between torts and crimes is not, therefore, based upon the gravity of the wrongdoing. Some crimes are trivial, some torts are extremely serious. Indeed, most of the most serious crimes are simultaneously torts. It is, therefore, an error to think that because 'unlawfulness' for a particular purpose includes private wrongs, it should follow a fortiori that it should include public wrongs, such as crimes.

Again, not only should there not be any separate 'tort' of conspiracy, if by a tort we mean the invasion of an identifiable right, it is difficult to conceive how there could be. Instead, the doctrine of conspiracy attributes the action of one person to that of another. It forms part of the same sequence as authorisation, ratification, and procurement.[40] Its only resemblance to recovery for losses intentionally caused by unlawful means is that neither are torts. The justifications for these two sets of rules are completely different.

A classic example of 'unlawful means conspiracy' is *Brooke v Bool.*[41] The defendant let a shop next door to the claimant's shop. By arrangement, he entered the shop to check that everything was secure. A lodger told the defendant that he could smell gas, and the two of them went to investigate. Unfortunately, they each chose to investigate the suspected gas pipe leak using a naked flame. An explosion occurred as a result of the lodger examining the pipe. The defendant was held liable even though it was not his flame that had caused the explosion. Because the two of them were acting under a 'common design', the actions of each were attributed to the other, and both were jointly liable.

[40] See *The Koursk* (1924) P 140 (CA), 155 (Scrutton LJ).
[41] *Brooke v Bool* (1864) 2 H&C 822.

Three features of this rule may be noted. First, there is no requirement of an intention to cause harm.[42] The agreement alone is sufficient for the attribution of acts carried out under it. Second, there is no requirement to show that the defendant caused or contributed to the harm. As with cases of authorisation and ratification, it does not matter that the other party or parties to the agreement would have behaved in precisely the same way. Third, the parties to the agreement are jointly liable for the same tort. None is liable for a separate 'tort' of conspiracy.

Unfortunately, the above statement of principle does not represent the law as it currently stands, at least in England. On the criminal law side, the recognition by the House of Lords (Lord Reid dissenting) in *Shaw v DPP* of an offence of 'conspiracy to corrupt public morals', when there is no offence of corrupting public morals, was a low point in English jurisprudence.[43]

On the private law side, the root of the problem is the decision of the House of Lords in *Quinn v Leathem*,[44] where a differently constituted court refused to follow *Allen v Flood*.[45] Trade union officials in the Belfast Journeymen Butchers' and Assistants' Association objected to the plaintiff, a butcher, employing men, none of whom were members of the union. The plaintiff offered to make his employees members of the union, an offer that was rejected. The officials insisted that the claimant dismiss his employees and employ existing union members. The plaintiff refused, and in retaliation, the union officials threatened the plaintiff's chief customer that if he continued to purchase meat from the claimant, his workers, who were members of the union would leave his employ. The customer acceded to this demand, and the claimant lost custom. It was found that the conspiracy to injure the claimant was not done in order to further any legitimate interest of the union, but rather in retaliation for the plaintiff's behaviour. The House of Lords accepted that the defendant was liable.

In response to counsel's objection that the defendants had not infringed any right of the plaintiff, Lord Lindley stated:

> The plaintiff had the ordinary rights of the British subject. He was at liberty to earn his living in his own way, provided he did not violate some special law prohibiting him from so doing, and provided he did not infringe the rights of other people. This liberty involved the liberty to deal with other persons who were willing to deal with him. This liberty is a right recognised by law; its correlative is the general duty of every one not to prevent the free exercise of this liberty except so far as his own liberty of action may justify him in so doing. But a person's liberty or right to deal with others is nugatory unless they are at liberty to deal with him if they choose to do so. Any interference with their liberty to deal with him affects him.

[42] *cf Lonrho v Fayed* [1992] 1 AC 448.
[43] *Shaw v DPP* [1962] AC 220. Followed in *Knuller v DPP* [1973] AC 435.
[44] *Quinn v Leathem* [1901] AC 496.
[45] For discussion of the composition of the two panels, and how they changed over the four years, see R Heuston, 'Judicial Prosopography' (1986) 102 *Law Quarterly Review* 90.

This appears to be a statement that we have a 'right to work'. Hohfeld's devastating criticism of this reasoning is as valid today as it was more than a century ago:

> In the middle of the above passage … there is a sudden and question-begging shift in the use of terms. First, the 'liberty' in question is transmuted into a 'right'; and then, possibly under the seductive influence of the latter word, it is assumed that the 'correlative' must be 'the general duty of every one not to prevent' etc.[46]

Quinn v Leathem was and is a very suspect decision, at least as reasoned. One way in which it can be formally distinguished from *Allen v Flood* is on the basis that there was an agreement between multiple parties. However, few commentators today are prepared to accept that in a world where multinational conglomerates forming single legal entities can inflict losses on weaker parties, this is a distinction that makes much sense.[47] Although I am not usually cynical about judicial decision-making, *Quinn v Leathem* gives off the distinct odour of motivated reasoning. The Conservative Lord Chancellor, Lord Halsbury, who had dissented in *Allen v Flood*, came close to disclaiming common law reasoning when he stated: 'a case is only an authority for what it actually decides. I entirely deny that it can be quoted for a proposition that may seem to follow logically from it'.[48]

The 'unlawful' variant of conspiracy had, for many years, no existence wider than that justified by the rules for attributing one conspirator's actions to the other parties to an agreement. If, as was generally thought,[49] 'unlawful means' meant 'tort', there was no liability beyond that justified in principle, and no room at all for any freestanding anomalous conspiracy' tort'.[50]

Unfortunately, this was changed by the decision of the House of Lords in *Total Network SL v HMRC*.[51] The defendants were very undeserving. They conspired to defraud the revenue through a carousel scheme that enabled the claiming back of Value Added Tax from the revenue. The Revenue sued, pleading the relevant unlawfulness as the common law offence of cheating the Revenue and fraudulent misrepresentation of entitlement to the VAT credit. The Revenue sought to rely on the former in argument because the evidence for the latter may have been weaker. Once counsel for the defendants had astonishingly conceded that there existed a freestanding 'tort' of unlawful means conspiracy, separate from the rules for the

[46] Hohfeld (n 6) 37.

[47] See, eg, *Lonrho v Shell (No 2)* [1982] AC 173, 189 (Lord Diplock).

[48] [1901] AC 495, 506.

[49] *Rookes v Barnard* [1964] AC 1129, 1204 (Lord Diplock); *Powell v Boladz* [1998] 1 Lloyds' Rep Med 116 (CA) 126. See also *Crédit Lyonnais v ECGD* [1998] 1 Lloyds' Rep 19 (CA) 32 (Stuart-Smith LJ); *Yukong Line Ltd v Rendsburg Investments Corp (No 2)* [1998] 1 WLR 294 at 314 (Toulson J); *Michaels v Taylor Woodrow Developments Limited* [2001] CH 493 at [32]–[34] (Laddie J); *Mahonia Limited v J P Morgan Chase Bank*[2004] EWHC 1938 (Comm) at [356]–[371] (Cook J) *Lonrho v Shell* [1982] AC 173 (HL) 188–89 (Lord Diplock); *Lonrho v Fayed* [1992] 1 AC 448 (HL) 463 (Lord Bridge). But not universally, see *Kuwait Oil Tanker Co SAK v Al Bader* [2000] 2 All ER (Comm) 271 (CA) (Nourse LJ).

[50] The idea of there being such a 'tort' is extremely recent, see Lord Denning MR *Midland Bank v Green* [1982] Ch 529, 539.

[51] *Total Network SL v HMRC* [2008] UKHL 19.

attribution of action for joint tortfeasors, the case was inevitably lost. If there is such an independent 'tort', then it must encompass cases of unlawfulness beyond torts, otherwise, it is otiose.[52] There is little analysis in *Total Network* as to how the presence of a crime could transform the conspirators' actions into a tort, beyond assertions that it is obvious.[53] Confusion was increased by the suggestion of Lord Mance that only some, but not all, crimes should count,[54] and by Lord Neuberger's somewhat alarming suggestion that as an alternative *Quinn v Leathem* be brought back from the near dead and relied upon more generally.[55] On the facts, there seems to have been little need for the decision save for the curious litigation tactics of the Revenue, as the defendants had had to commit the wrong of deceit in order to induce the Revenue to pay.

Total Network Solutions was followed in its wide analysis of 'unlawful' by the decision of the Supreme Court in *JSC BTA Bank v Khrapunov*,[56] where contempt of court was held to suffice for the purposes of 'unlawful means conspiracy'. The court's justification for the expanded conspiracy rule is worth quoting in full.

> A person has a right to advance his own interests by lawful means even if the foreseeable consequence is to damage the interests of others. The existence of that right affords a just cause or excuse. Where, on the other hand, he seeks to advance his interests by unlawful means he has no such right. The position is the same where the means used are lawful but the predominant intention of the defendant was to injure the claimant rather than to further some legitimate interest of his own. This is because in that case it cannot be an answer to say that he was simply exercising a legal right. He had no interest recognised by the law in exercising his legal right for the predominant purpose not of advancing his own interests but of injuring the claimant. In either case, there is no just cause or excuse *for the combination*.[57]

Much the same confusion that Hohfeld identified as problematic in Lord Lindley's speech is evident here. Taken literally, the first proposition would lead to the abolition of most of the law of torts: it is lawful to drive my car for my own interests, so am I not liable if a foreseeable consequence is the injury of others? Rather, more accurately, we each have a *liberty* to advance our own interests, even if it leaves others worse off, so long as we do not violate another's right. There is nothing thereby to excuse as there is no prima facie wrong. Again, taken literally, this passage would mean that *any* unlawful action leaving another worse off would be actionable, regardless of the intent with which it was carried out. Further, if it were the case, as stated, that the intent to harm were enough to justify actionability,

[52] ibid [94] (Lord Walker). See *Sorrell v Smith* [1925] AC 700, 716: 'mere surplusage' Lord Dunedin, accepting that there is no such freestanding tort.

[53] See, eg, *Total Network* [43] (Lord Hope): 'Why not?' – the proper question was 'Why?'; [120] (Lord Scott) 'evident lacuna'.

[54] ibid [119].

[55] ibid [228]. See also JW Neyers, 'The Economic Torts as Corrective Justice' (2009) 17 *Torts Law Journal* 162.

[56] *JSC BTA Bank v Khrapunov* [2018] UKSC 19.

[57] ibid [10] (emphasis in original).

then *Allen v Flood* would not be good law. In England, it is indeed a perfectly good answer to a complaint that you have intentionally made me worse off, that you were simply exercising a liberty the law conferred upon you. How any of the court's analysis above is relevant to whether the action is carried out under an agreement with a third party, or not, is mysterious. What the relevance of the combination might be, that pops up from nowhere in italics at the end of this analysis, is completely obscure.

Looking at the rules as they currently stand, the end result is that English law has got back to front what can constitute 'unlawfulness' for the purposes of causing loss by unlawful means, and liability for conspiracy. If we see the former as a species of the 'abuse of rights' doctrine, then any action contrary to law, whether tortious or criminal, should suffice to ground liability. If we see the latter as part of our general rules for the attribution of action from one party to an agreement to another, then only tortious conduct should suffice for liability in tort, not breaches of criminal (or contractual) duties. It is only by (re-)confining 'conspiracy' to being part of our rules for attribution of action that the relevance of there being a combination at all becomes explicable. The former rule should require there to be an intent to harm; conspiracy should not.

The two mistakes are, as a matter of history, related. The expansion of 'unlawful means conspiracy' would not have been thought necessary if 'causing loss by unlawful means' had not been unduly restricted.

Even if I am wrong, and the law has not got itself into a terrible mess, *Allen v Flood* is the law and should remain so.

G. Sole Purpose: *Quinn v Leathem* Revisited

Although distinguishing *Quinn v Leathem* from *Allen v Flood* on the basis of the existence of an agreement to cause loss is unsatisfactory, it may be that another ground for distinction is possible.

The dispute in *Quinn* had concerned the employment of non-union labour. However, the plaintiff employer had already offered to ensure that all of his employees joined the union. The union had already won the dispute, and the union's action was a reprisal for the earlier employment. In *Allen v Flood*, by contrast, the union's purpose was to maintain a closed shop, not merely to inflict loss.

Although not overruled, because at the time it could not be as before the Practice Statement, *Quinn v Leathem* was confined by the subsequent decision of the House of Lords in *Crofter Hand Woven Harris Tweed Co Ltd v Veitch*.[58] There, it was held that 'lawful means' conspiracy is only actionable where the loss is inflicted for no good reason and that self-interest counts as sufficient justification. If the *sole purpose* of the defendants' action in *Quinn v Leathem* was to inflict loss

[58] *Crofter Hand Woven Harris Tweed Co Ltd v Veitch* [1942] AC 435.

as a form of revenge, and not in pursuit of any remaining interest of the union in maintenance of a closed shop, the decision may be justifiable. Here, there was no dispute between employer and union left to resolve. This was not a party whose self-interested purpose was legitimate, who knew that pursuing their goal would inevitably inflict loss on another. Rather, it was the unusual case of a party whose *sole* purpose was to inflict harm on another. The difficult policy question of when industrial action may be justified in pursuance of a dispute did not, therefore, arise. *Tuttle v Buck* may similarly be justifiable on the same basis as an unusual case where the sole purpose was to inflict harm.

Quinn v Leathem is, as far as I am aware, the only case where 'lawful means conspiracy' has ever sufficed to hold the defendant liable. It would be better to reconceive this decision as independent of the conspiracy, and to quietly forget this 'tort'.

III. Declarations and Injunctions

A. Enforceability

Although we do not have a (claim-)right against others that they do not inhibit our ability to work, our interest in being able to work (or more loosely, our interest in our 'autonomy') may provide a good reason why a contractual covenant not to work may be unenforceable. Post-employment covenants not to work (eg, employees promising not to compete with their former employer) may be wholly unenforceable because they are in restraint of trade. Not all such restrictive covenants are objectionable. If the promisee shows both that they have a legitimate interest to protect through the clause and that it is reasonable as between the parties to it, and the promisor does not show that it is unreasonable in relation to the public interest, it is enforceable.[59] Traditionally, a master craftsman would not train up an apprentice if the latter were going to set up business in the same town, and so the covenant not to compete was enforceable, so long as it was not too broadly expressed.

Less dramatically, a court may refuse an employer an injunction restraining an employee from working for someone else where this would compel the employee to continue to work for the employer. A classic example is *Page One Record Ltd v Britton*,[60] where the 'Troggs' pop group had employed the claimant as their sole manager for a period of five years but then entered into an agreement in breach of contract to be managed by someone else. The claimed injunction was refused on the basis that it would compel the Troggs to continue to employ the manager, but

[59] *Nordenfelt v Maxim Nordenfelt Guns and Ammunition Co Ltd* [1894] AC 535, 565 (Lord Macnaghten).

[60] *Page One Record Ltd v Britton* [1968] 1 WLR 157.

precisely the same result should follow if it had been the band that had sought to compel the manager not to work for another.

B. Third Parties

Attempts by contracting parties to prevent third parties from working or trading are more objectionable than the situation where a party has agreed to give up their own freedom and been provided with consideration in exchange for their promise. The best modern example of how the interests of third parties to the agreement may engage the restraint of trade doctrine, other than through the general interest we all have that the promisor not be restrained from working or trading, is the decision in *Eastham v Newcastle United Football Club*.[61] The decision arose from the 'retain and transfer' system, then in operation in the English football league. That system was a creation of the agreement between the clubs that made up the League. At that time, a club could put a player previously under contract with it on a 'retained' list, thereby preventing them from playing for another club. If, by contrast, the player was placed on the 'transfer' list, the player could apply to the League's management committee to have the fee reduced or eliminated and could transfer to a club outside of the League without any transfer fee. The 'retained' list was effectively a transfer list that removed these options from the player. Wilberforce J concluded that this 'retain' system was unenforceable as in restraint of trade: it unreasonably interfered with the liberty of players to work.[62] A declaration to that effect was made against Newcastle United, the League, and the Football Association. The transfer list system, under which a player, after the termination of his contract, could only move to another club if a fee were paid for his registration, was not formally ruled upon, although Wilberforce J indicated that it was unobjectionable.[63] It survived until the *Bosman* ruling when the European Court of Justice struck it down as incompatible with freedom of movement for workers under the Treaty of Rome.[64]

Similar, although more difficult, is the subsequent decision of the Court of Appeal in *Nagle v Feilden*.[65] Florence Nagle was a trainer and breeder of racehorses. The Jockey Club was in charge of flat race meetings in Great Britain. By its rules, no horse was entitled to run unless trained by a licensed trainer, and it had a monopoly in the granting of licences. She applied for, and was refused, a licence without reasons being given but, in fact, because she was a woman (she had previously bypassed this effective ban on women trainers by having her 'head lad' apply

[61] *Eastham v Newcastle United Football Club* [1964] Ch 413.

[62] ibid 427.

[63] ibid 427–438.

[64] Case 415/93 *Union Royale Belge des Sociétés de Football Association ASBL v Jean-Marc Bosman* ECLI:EU:C:1995:463, [1995] ECR I-4921.

[65] *Nagle v Feilden* [1966] 2 QB 633.

for and obtain a licence). She applied for a declaration that the practice of refusing a licence to women was void as against public policy, and an injunction ordering the stewards to grant her a licence. The court concluded that, although she had no contract with the Jockey Club, it was arguable that the practice was contrary to public policy, violating her 'right to work', and refused to strike out the action. (It would, however, have been very curious to conclude that the 'practice' was void. The practice may have been contrary to public policy, rendering any agreement to carry it out unenforceable, but the problem was that it existed, not that it did not.)

The unenforceability of the express contractual rules of the associations prejudicing the ability to work of third parties, as in *Eastham v Newcastle United*, and of the implicitly agreed rules in *Nagle v Feilden*, follows a fortiori from the more usual case of the unenforceability of restraints that limit the freedom of the promisor themselves to work and trade.

The declaration granted in *Eastham* seems readily justifiable. For standing purposes, a party may obtain a declaration even though they personally have no cause of action, or no right that is infringed. In *re F*,[66] a mother sought a declaration that it was permissible for invasive medical treatment to be carried out upon her mentally incapacitated adult daughter. Lord Goff confirmed that so long as a 'real question' arose and the party seeking the declaration had a 'real interest' in the outcome, a declaration of the rights of parties other than the claimant could be granted.[67]

Much more problematic, however, is why an injunction was thought arguably available in *Nagle v Feilden*. The doctrinal basis for this is obscure. It is one thing to conclude that an agreement to the prejudice of a third party is unenforceable; it is quite another to decide that the third party has a right to prevent its performance through an injunction. The traditional rule was restated in *North London Railway Co v Great Northern Railway* (refusing an injunction to restrain an arbitration hearing) as 'no Court would have issued an injunction in a case where if the thing went on there would be no legal injury'.[68]

In *The Siskina*,[69] Lord Diplock subsequently stated:

> A right to obtain an interlocutory injunction is not a cause of action. It cannot stand on its own. It is dependent upon there being a pre-existing cause of action against the defendant arising out of an invasion, actual or threatened by him, of a legal or equitable right of the plaintiff for the enforcement of which the defendant is amenable to the jurisdiction of the court. The right to obtain an interlocutory injunction is merely ancillary and incidental to the pre-existing cause of action.[70] It is granted to preserve the status quo pending the ascertainment by the court of the rights of the parties and the

[66] *Re F (Mental Patient: Sterilisation), F v West Berkshire Health Authority* [1990] 2 AC 1.

[67] See also *Guaranty Trust Co of New York v Hannay & Co* [1915] 2 KB 536.

[68] *North London Railway Co v Great Northern Railway* (1883) 11 QBD 30, 35.

[69] *Siskina (Owners of cargo lately laden on board) v Distos Cia Naviera SA (The Siskina)* [1979] AC 210, 256.

[70] 'Pre-existing' is too narrowly stated. 'Potential' would have been better: *Kazakhstan Kagazy Plc v Zhunus* [2016] 4 WLR 86, [57] (Leggatt J).

> grant to the plaintiff of the relief to which his cause of action entitles him, which may or may not include a final injunction.

A fortiori a final injunction must be based upon some pre-existing legal or equitable right. Regardless of whether the injunction is final or interim, it should not be granted unless based upon a right. This Florence Nagle did not have, unless the law is to recognise a general 'right to work', the very thing that had been rejected in *Allen v Flood*. In *R v Disciplinary Committee of the Jockey Club, ex parte Aga Khan*,[71] Hoffmann LJ stated that the order in *Nagle v Feilden* had an 'improvisatory air' and had probably not survived *The Siskina*. By contrast, Jacob J subsequently held that as the availability of a declaration was a 'cause of action',[72] this entailed that an injunction was available in its support, so that *Nagle v Feilden* could be justified. This reasoning must be incorrect. The more generous jurisdiction to grant declarations cannot legitimately be used to bootstrap a similar jurisdiction to grant injunctions.

More recently, however, Lord Diplock's statement of principle in *The Siskina* has been called into serious doubt by subsequent decisions of the Supreme Court.

The jurisdiction to grant injunctions is expressed extremely broadly in the Senior Courts Act 1981, section 37:

> The High Court may by order (whether interlocutory or final) grant an injunction or appoint a receiver in all cases in which it appears to the court to be just and convenient to do so.

Lord Mustill warned that these words 'are not to be taken at their face value and their application is subject to severe constraints'.[73] However, this warning does not seem to have been adhered to in recent years, and the courts have favoured invoking the equitable origin of the injunction as justifying a wide and flexible power to grant them, unfettered by any inconvenient principled categorisation.[74]

In principle, court orders compelling people to behave in particular ways can only be justified either to seek compliance with some underlying duty owed to the claimant, or in order to maintain the integrity of a litigation process (ie, in support of a cause of action). The latter is a relatively new development, but we are now familiar with *Mareva* or freezing injunctions,[75] and *Anton Piller* or search orders against parties to litigation.[76] Perhaps more boldly, where a third party has been an unwitting facilitator of wrongdoing, they can be ordered to provide information

[71] *R v Disciplinary Committee of the Jockey Club, ex parte Aga Khan* [1993] 1 WLR 909 holding that the private bodies, such as the Jockey Club, are not subject to judicial review as not exercising any public power.

[72] *Newport Association Football Club Ltd v Football Association of Wales Ltd* [1995] 2 All ER 87.

[73] *Channel Tunnel Group Ltd v Balfour Beatty Construction Ltd* [1993] AC 334, 360–361.

[74] *Castanho v Brown & Root (UK) Ltd* [1981] AC 557, 573 (Lord Scarman); *Wolverhampton City Council v London Gypsies and Travellers* [2023] UKSC 47, [22] (Lords Reed, Briggs and Kitchin (with whom Lords Hodge and Lloyd-Jones agreed)).

[75] *Mareva Compania Naviera SA v International Bulk Carriers SA* [1975] 2 Lloyd's Rep 509.

[76] *Anton Piller KG v Manufacturing Processes Ltd* [1976] Ch 55.

to facilitate the claim against the wrongdoer: *Norwich Pharmacal*,[77] and *Bankers Trust* orders.[78]

Startlingly for more conservative lawyers, the Court of Appeal upheld,[79] and the Supreme Court approved,[80] the granting of an injunction against an internet service provider whose services facilitated the infringement of a trademark but who were not themselves committing or threatening any wrong. The law has rules for determining when the actions of a wrongdoer are to be attributed to another, so that they are both to be treated as jointly committing the same wrong: authorisation, ratification, procurement, and (as we have seen) conspiracy. Facilitation does not, however, suffice.[81] So, the House of Lords had earlier concluded that the seller of twin-deck tape recorders could not be restrained from selling them, although it was known that one of the primary purposes for which the machines would be used was the infringement of copyright.[82] The assumption of the House of Lords had been that before an injunction could be awarded, the defendants must themselves have either committed or threatened an infringement of a right of the claimant, a view no longer shared by the Supreme Court. Courts should not be enjoining perfectly lawful activities that do not constitute the violation of any rights of the claimant merely because they may enable third parties, for whom the defendant is not responsible, to commit wrongs.

Equally bold was the decision in *Wolverhampton City Council v London Gypsies and Travellers* to grant injunctions against anyone who might commence an unauthorised encampment on land owned by the claimants.[83] The concern with an injunction of this form is not that the identity of the defendant is unknown: this is relatively commonplace and can be solved by the description of the party who is infringing, or is threatening to infringe, the claimant's right in the order sought. Rather, the issue was that no individuals were threatening to imminently commit the tort of trespass, so that the effect of the order was to transform a private wrong into the public wrong of contempt of court, with quite different sanctions for breach. The order was against the whole world, including you and me. It no longer seems to be required that the order is confined to those threatening to commit, imminently or otherwise, any right infringement.

As the order was given against the world, it inevitably did not give notice to those thereby bound, let alone the service of legal process upon them. The courts should be very wary before creating duties upon persons upon whom no process

[77] *Norwich Pharmacal Co v Customs and Excise Comrs* [1974] AC 133.

[78] *Bankers Trust Co v Shapira* [1980] 1 WLR 1274.

[79] *Cartier International AG v British Sky Broadcasting Ltd* [2016] EWCA Civ 658; [2017] Bus LR 1. The majority of the court justified this on the basis that it was necessary to ensure compliance with an applicable EU Directive. Briggs LJ did not so confine himself, and it is his view that has prevailed.

[80] *Cartier International AG v British Telecommunications Plc* [2018] UKSC 28; [2018] 1 WLR 3259.

[81] *Fish & Fish Ltd v Sea Shepherd* [2015] AC 1229.

[82] *CBS Songs Ltd v Amstrad Consumer Electronics Plc* [1988] AC 1013, recently cited with approval in *Lifestyle Equities CV v Ahmed* [2024] UKSC 17 [76].

[83] *Wolverhampton City Council v London Gypsies and Travellers* [2023] UKSC 47.

has been served, so that they can be given the opportunity to challenge, or at least be aware of, the new obligation of judicial creation. It hardly suffices that I will be given ex post notice of the new obligations created by the court order by either signage or officialdom and can then object. This result is further surprising given that the legislature has determined which forms of trespass are criminal and which are not.[84]

Despite these recent expansions in the availability of an injunction, *Nagle v Feilden* still appears incorrect. Although the granting of injunctions against third parties to right infringements, and against any person who may in the future infringe a right of the claimant, arguably go too far, they are at least based upon some pre-existing right of the claimant. *Nagle v Feilden* was not.

C. The Closed Shop

The result in *Nagle v Feilden*, in ending a ludicrous form of discrimination on the basis of sex, is not one that most of us would find objectionable today. However, at the time, the significance of *Nagle v Feilden* seemed to be that it meant that trade union closed shops were open to challenge at common law. Under a closed shop agreement, an employer agreed to hire union members only, and an employee was required to be a union member at all times employed. Could such arrangements be challenged on the basis that they infringed the 'right to work'? Trade union rules had, at one time, been unenforceable as being considered in restraint of trade,[85] but this had been reversed by legislation.[86] Could it be argued that the 'right to work' was distinct from the rules on restraint of trade and so unaffected by this statutory validation?[87]

There were (and are) policy arguments in favour of permitting closed shop arrangements. From the employer's side, it meant that agreements only needed to be made with one union, rather than several. During the 1970s, one cause of the levels of industrial disruption had been the weakness, not the strength, of trade unions, who had been unable to make deals stick, partly because they could not negotiate on behalf of all of a single employer's workers. From the unions' perspective, there were financial and collective bargaining advantages if all employees were members of the same union so that any industrial action would be effective. Such arrangements also avoided non-members, who did not pay membership subscriptions, free-riding on the advantages obtained by the union for all employees. In policy terms, the freedom *to* join a union is not the equivalent of the freedom *not* to join a union.

[84] Legal Aid, Sentencing and Punishment of Offenders Act 2012, s 144.

[85] *Hornby v Close* (1867) LR 2 QB 153.

[86] Trade Union Act 1871, s 3. See now Trade Union and Labour Relations (Consolidation) Act 1992, s 11.

[87] For this, implausible, argument being adopted, see *Greig v Insole* [1978] 1 WLR 302, 362 (Slade J).

Today, of course, such arguments seem to come as an echo from a different world. The first sign that closed shop arrangements would not survive came because of the expansive reading of Article 11 of the European Convention on Human Rights in *Young, James and Webster v UK*.[88] British Rail entered into a closed shop agreement with rail unions. Employees who were not members of a union were required to join one or be dismissed. A majority of the European Court of Human Rights had little hesitation in reading Article 11's freedom *to* associate as including a freedom *not* to associate. Somewhat insouciantly, it concluded that it did not need to consider the policy arguments in favour of the closed shop, as such arrangements, in general, were not in question, just their operation in relation to the applicants in the particular instance before the court.[89]

Soon thereafter, the Conservative Government enacted the Employment Act 1982, which made it unlawful to dismiss an employee for not being a member of a Union, unless a closed shop agreement had been approved in the last five years by either 80 per cent of workers or 85 per cent voting in a secret ballot. These thresholds were so high that they effectively banned the closed shop, and this formal step was then taken by the Employment Act 1990 (see now Trade Union and Labour Relations (Consolidation) Act 1992, section 137). Labour initially opposed this ban, but this policy was reversed in 1989, under then shadow employment minister, Tony Blair.

Today, therefore, the common law 'right to work' has little importance in the trade union context, which is now covered by statutory regulation. Rather, its significance is in the field of regulatory bodies that license people to work in particular fields, most commonly in relation to sport, as in *Nagle v Feilden* itself. Even there, the Jockey Club would today be committing a statutory wrong by discriminating on the basis of sex against Florence Nagle, reducing the significance of the common law position.[90] Despite Hoffmann LJ's entirely justifiable doubts as to the doctrinal basis at common law for the granting of injunctions against private bodies such as the Jockey Club that refuse to admit someone who has no contractual relationship with the association, the courts have continued to exercise a 'supervisory jurisdiction',[91] backed up with the award of injunctions, of dubious legitimacy.

If such private bodies seek to have the contracts that third parties enter into set aside on the basis that one party is unlicensed, they should be liable for procuring breach of contract, and capable of being enjoined from doing so, if their own rules are unenforceable. No defence of justification would apply. If they threaten to break contracts with others if the applicant is employed, they should be potentially

[88] *Young, James and Webster v UK* Series A no 44 (1982) 4 EHRR 38. Although nearly irrelevant today in the UK domestic law context, *Sorensen and Rasmussen v Denmark* no 52562/99 (2008) 46 EHRR 29 adopted an even wider reading of Art 11.

[89] *Young, James and Webster* [61].

[90] Equality Act 2010, ss 53 and 57.

[91] *Modahl v British Athletics Federation Ltd* [2002] 1 WLR 1192 [47] (Latham LJ); *Bradley v Jockey Club* [2004] EWHC 2164 (QB).

liable for the form of causing loss by unlawful means that is called intimidation. Absent a right to work, however, there is no basis for enjoining them from refusing to admit applicants as members, without more ado.

IV. Conclusion

This chapter has been a conservative one. Arguably it is reactionary. It has argued for the wisdom of those judges, at the end of the nineteenth century, who turned away from an expansive set of rights recognised by the common law. Such rights are necessarily minimalist, as judge created. Our rights to our persons, our reputations, and the clothes on our backs, form the basic set upon which a complex system of statutory regulation has been built. Court orders may only legitimately be granted where in support of the claimant's rights. The better judges know their place.

INDEX

www.ingramcontent.com/pod-product-compliance
Ingram Content Group UK Ltd.
Pitfield, Milton Keynes, MK11 3LW, UK
UKHW020802290926
15470UKWH00003B/903

9 781509 981588